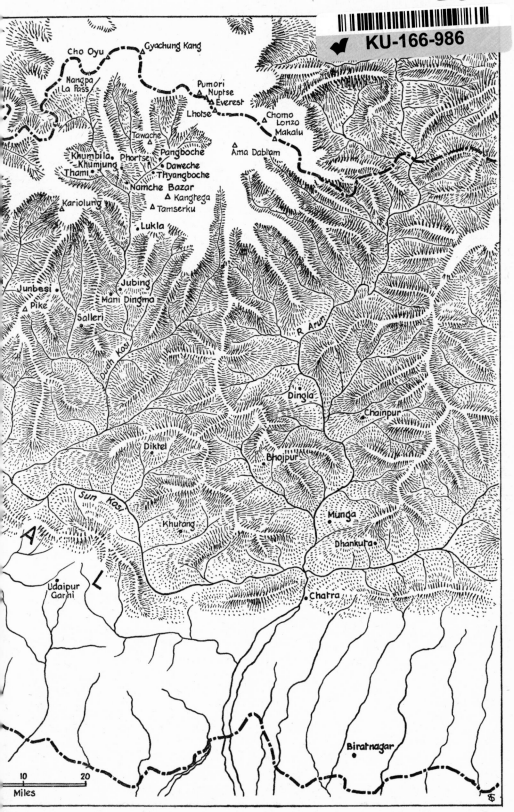

£3·00

Cho Oyu △ △ Gyachung Kang

Nangpa
La Pass

Pumori
△ Nuptse
△ △ Everest
Lhotse △

Chomo
Lonzo
Makalu

Tawache
△

Ama Dablam
△

Khumbila
Khumjung △ Phortse
Thami

Pangboche
△ Daweche
Thyangboche

Namche Bazar
△ Kangtega
△ Tamserku

Kariolung
△

Lukla

Junbesi
△ Pike

Jubing

Mani Dingma

Salleri

R. Arun

Dudh Kosi

Dingla

Chainpur

Diktel

Bhojpur

Sun Kosi

A

L

Khutang

Munga

Dhankuta

Udaipur
Garhi

Chatra

Biratnagar

10   20
Miles

HIGH TIME

By the same author:

KEEP CALM IF YOU CAN

A YAK FOR CHRISTMAS

HIGH TIME

by

Louise Hillary

HODDER AND STOUGHTON
LONDON AUCKLAND SYDNEY TORONTO

To Ed

Contents

Illustrations

CHAPTER I

Better Late Than Never!

"I COULD NOT RECOGNISE Sir Ed's children since their growth has given me completely different people," wrote Ang Rita, a Sherpa aged twenty, brilliant scholarship student of Khumjung village near Mount Everest in Nepal.

"Sir Ed's children," are Ed and Louise Hillary's children—Peter aged seventeen, Sarah fifteen and Belinda thirteen. It was not surprising that Ang Rita couldn't recognise them in December 1971 because five years had elapsed since he had seen them. Our family visited Nepal in 1965 and it proved such a wonderful experience that we were eager to return. It was only after much planning and quite a lot of unforeseen adventures that we finally succeeded in reaching Nepal again.

We had worked on our preparations for at least a year, made clothes, shipped equipment with long and detailed lists, learned Nepali, and sold the family piano to help pay for the fares. It was not going to be entirely a relaxing sightseeing holiday, as all of us wanted to help with the building of new schools in the Himalayas. Even just getting around the country would involve us in walking several hundred miles over steep mountainsides. We could hardly wait to get started.

Ed left for Nepal ahead of us to get on with the work, and six weeks later we planned to follow him. Our departure from New Zealand didn't turn out to be quite the happy occasion it should have been. Fighting had broken out between India and Pakistan, and was spreading fast—and in a couple of days we were booked to fly across those troubled lands.

One of my acquaintances had told me I was mad to go "to that part of the world—they (whoever they might be) would shoot civilian aircraft down like flies!" I was in such a state of school-examination jitters and so depressed by the tasks of packing and cleaning up that I quite believed him.

That departure morning I refused to look at the newspapers. I have often wondered in the past why it is that people travel to danger areas when they are just going for pleasure. Now I can understand. If you've planned and looked forward to something long enough you become completely obsessed with it all and refuse to accept any interference.

In the two and a half short hours that it takes to fly from New Zealand to Australia, it became tragically obvious that India and Pakistan were now engaged in a full-scale war—the newspaper stands screamed out the news in big black type. Our dreams of a gay week-end in Sydney soaking in sunshine and surf before continuing on our journey quickly vanished. What were we to do? Thai International's flights across East Pakistan to Kathmandu were cancelled indefinitely and no further bookings were being taken. Should we continue to Bangkok and wait in that expensive city until things improved? Or should we stay in Sydney, which would cost us just as much? Perhaps we should just hurry home? It was poor consolation to realise that there must be many other travellers in a similar position to ourselves. After establishing the fact that we could make no decisions about onward bookings that day I was faced with the task of keeping three very restless and disappointed young people occupied.

We agreed to take the hydrofoil across Sydney harbour for a swim at Manly beach. Our motel was less than a mile from the ferry wharf so we walked the quiet Saturday streets of the city and were soon skimming over the brilliant blue waters and zigzagging past the many gay pleasure-craft whilst our ears were being bombarded by loud and surprisingly classical symphonic music over the hydrofoil's loud-speaker system.

Manly was very crowded and the ocean beach was spread with salty, vociferous and suntanned humanity. There seemed no room for the dejected Hillarys to lay their white motel towels and their notice-ably unsunburnt bodies on the sand—if you could call it sand. It was made up of one part sand to two parts paper drinking cups and other trash. So I sat behind the beach in the shade of the fine old Norfolk Island pines being mesmerised by a long line of empty milk-shake cartons which were blown by a light sea breeze; backwards and forwards along the base of the sea wall in front of me. We soon agreed that the joys of Manly were not for us and retreated back towards our motel. The headlines on the afternoon papers stood out large and black, "Agra airport attacked by Pakistan Airforce". I became convinced that it would be a long time before we would be able to get to Nepal.

"That's the end of it for the time being," I said to my sad trio, "Let's go back home to New Zealand—it will be easier to wait there." I sent a cable to Ed in Nepal informing him of our change in plans and wondered if the message would have had more chance of finding him on the moon rather than somewhere in the depths of the Himalayan mountains.

Next day in the departure lounge at Sydney airport we were interviewed by a man doing a survey for the Australian Government Tourist Department. He tried very hard to be friendly to our silent little group.

"Have you enjoyed yourself in Australia?" he said brightly.

"No!" I replied.

Our interviewer smiled patiently with pencil poised.

"How long have you been here?" he asked.

"One night."

"For what reason have you been visiting Australia?"

"We have really come here by mistake," I said and didn't see much point in explaining any further.

"How much did you pay per night for your accommodation?"

"Far too much," I said, "and it was all such a waste."

He was starting to realise that we weren't helping his statistics very much but he was polite to the end.

"Well, that's all for now. Thank you very much for your co-operation."

In New Zealand the days went slowly by. Our main activity was booking flights to Singapore and then cancelling them. Our bulging luggage sat forlornly in the hall of our house. We refused to unpack so much as even our pyjamas as we were still determined to get to Nepal somehow. The war in Pakistan and India ground on with no sign of improvement. Finally a message came through from India that we should try and reach Nepal through Bombay and Delhi.

We had a family conference that night, and agreed that we were all thoroughly tired of hearing from our friends, "Oh hello! I thought you had gone away," to which we'd have to give the same monotonous explanation. It didn't help much either to see our much loved family dog mournfully eyeing our luggage in the hall, knowing only too well that any day we were going to abandon him once more.

Our decision was unanimous—we'd go to Singapore and wait for the world to settle down. We would then be in a good position to take the first flight available to Bombay or any other suitable port of call that would lead us to Nepal.

"You will be very lucky to find four seats to Singapore with the Christmas holidays so close," warned our booking officer "and as for onward flights to India, there may not be any." Despite his forebodings he somehow arranged seats for us on a Singapore plane, and soon the day arrived for our second attempt at reaching the Himalayas. It was easy to prepare ourselves for this departure as all our luggage was pre-packed but I was still having qualms of conscience about the trip—should I squander our precious air tickets on perhaps another abortive attempt? And was it right for me to take the three children into a country at war?

"You've got your passports and health certificates, I presume," said the man at the baggage counter at the airport.

"Oh yes, of course," I replied confidently. Then I heard a quiet strained voice behind me saying, "I haven't got mine." I looked round and there was Sarah pale and horrified as she slowly became aware of her predicament.

"*I* haven't got it," I said very firmly. "You know we all agreed to carry our own passports this time."

Being packed and ready to go for so many days had made us careless. This can't happen to us, I thought, as we squatted on the floor amongst the feet of busy travellers and burrowed through our airways bags. Within a minute or so it was quite clear that this *had* happened to us.

There was just time for Sarah to be taken home to hunt for the missing passport and as she disappeared out of the building I sat down and tried to appear calm. Phrases such as "You'll never get another booking before Christmas" came drifting into my mind, and I knew that if we didn't go now it would be too late and we would have to postpone our travels for another long year.

"You had better go down to the departure lounge," said an airline official. We said goodbye half-heartedly to our relations, not knowing if we would be back with them in half an hour or not.

Take-off time was nine o'clock and at nine o'clock there was no sign of Sarah. The Tarmac Co-ordinator with his two-way radio glanced at us as a shepherd would look at unruly sheep. He was in contact with the front of the airport and every now and then he would ask if Sarah had appeared. It was now five minutes past take-off time and we were told to board the plane. I walked slowly forward wondering what to do. Just as I put a reluctant foot on the bottom of the aircraft steps, the Tarmac Co-ordinator suddenly raised his voice.

"She's coming, she's coming! She's walking through the door! Now she's walking down the passage—" it sounded like a commentary at a race meeting and we listened breathlessly until at last Sarah was beside us. I stood limp and drained, and my children had to scoop me up and push me firmly into my seat on the aircraft. Such are the joys of travel!

It was good to be all together again. The long flight across Australia and up to Singapore passed quickly and it wasn't until we had to fill out our forms for landing in Singapore some time later that I realised we had no hotel bookings and no onward flight. But by this time we were filled with the excitement of our adventure and regarded such minor problems as part of the fun.

"We'll go straight to the Air India counter," I said, "and see if they can help us."

"And make sure you've got your passport this time," said everybody, turning on Sarah. We had hardly put our feet on Singapore soil when a smiling gentleman came up to us.

"If you are the Hillary family I have got some onward bookings for you."

I don't quite know what reaction he expected but he received a joyous and overwhelming one. This new friend turned out to be a representative of Air India. He must have been warned that our party was likely to lose things, for he led us through health and customs departments conscientiously counting and recounting us and our baggage until finally he put us very carefully into an airport bus.

"You have reservations at the Imperial Hotel," he said very firmly, "and you will depart from this airport at 2 a.m. the day after tomorrow. The bus will come and pick you up." It seemed that from now on we wouldn't have to think but just do exactly what we were told. What a delicious feeling! I had asked our Air India friend why our flight had to leave at such an unearthly hour and he told me something about blackouts and travelling at night due to the war. I couldn't quite follow his reasoning but none of us really cared as we were only too happy to enjoy our day in Singapore and fly onto Bombay the next night.

Our stay in Singapore was full of interest. We had a few things to buy and wrestled with the hard competitiveness of the shopkeepers and found the new shopping buildings with their set prices much more expensive than the older street shops where bargaining was the accepted method. As the day wore on we learned more about this amazing and industrious little country: about the action being taken to control the rising population; the legalising of abortion; the heavy fines for breaking the litter laws; the requirements for personal tidiness and behaviour. There was certainly a great deal to admire but I could feel the pressure of population and kept thinking longingly of the green spaces at home and the tall peaceful mountains of the Himalayas.

In the evening I rested in my room and idly picked up the Gideon Bible beside my bed. I glanced down the list of suggested readings for special occasions. I still couldn't shrug off my concern about taking the children to war-torn India, even though I knew we would be safe enough once we got to Nepal. I looked for the passages to be read by those about to go into danger. The first-suggested reading did not help me as it required the reader to have great faith. But the next reading was Psalm 121—"I will lift up mine eyes unto the hills from whence cometh my help." It was so appropriate and I read no more. The hills and mountains of Nepal were beckoning strongly and I felt full of confidence and enthusiasm again.

Although we couldn't understand why we should have to leave the hotel at 11 p.m. when the aircraft wasn't meant to be airborne until 2 a.m., we were so determined to catch our flight to Bombay that we moved our luggage and ourselves to the main lobby well before our bus was due. The minutes ticked slowly by and we realised that a dozen other people were waiting for the same flight and we were soon chatting together. As midnight approached our little group became quieter and quieter and still there was no sign of the promised bus.

At last, to our great relief, we heard the noise of slamming doors heralding our moment of departure. We squeezed into a small airless vehicle and sat passively, our minds devoid of all thought as we rattled through the dark Singapore streets.

The departure counter at the airport was like rush hour in Bombay or Delhi with rows of serious looking Indian travellers standing in resigned fashion beside their mountains of baggage. I couldn't see how we could possibly fight our way to the counter to check in for our flight, particularly when we discovered that the back door of our mini-bus had jammed shut and that we couldn't reach our belongings. Into this chaotic situation came our friendly Air India representative. He was determined to make sure that we finally left Singapore. With masterly thoroughness he organised our passports and tickets, and quickly extricated our baggage. I was about to congratulate myself on our efficiency when someone murmured "Airport tax".

I am a thrifty person and had made quite sure I had no spare Singapore money left when we departed from the hotel. "Would the bank still be open," I asked. Nobody seemed to know.

We hurried to the bank and were just able to stop two sleepy-eyed bank clerks from closing up for the night.

"Well, I think you'll be all right now," said our patient helper and he departed leaving us to manage the rest of our travels alone.

We followed the crowd and soon found ourselves divided into male and female queues where all our hand baggage was searched. An old blunt pen-knife was found in Sarah's bag and this was confiscated until she should arrive in Bombay. Then we all marched through a metal detector whose main function seemed to be to make the passengers look more tired and more jittery every minute.

At 3 a.m. we marched aboard the plane and squeezed into our seats —the amount of hand baggage of strange and assorted sizes in the cabin must have been a record. It seemed too good to be true when we roared off the runway and left the lights of Singapore behind. Belinda wanted to go to sleep immediately but when she put her seat back to the reclining position she found she was lying on a large collection of badminton rackets and bumpy-looking parcels belonging to the man behind. There was nothing that could be done as the owner of these parcels was wedged helplessly into place by his possessions.

We were a restless lot of passengers and many people kept their lights on all through the flight. I don't suppose anybody got any sleep—I certainly didn't. Just before landing at Madras a man seated at the front of the plane got up and started making signals to another passenger who was sitting in front of me. In my exhausted and bemused state I was quite sure that a hi-jacking was about to take place. But despite my fears we were soon safely on the ground in Madras. Many of the passengers disembarked here so the remainder of the journey was relatively comfortable.

It was dark and cold in Bombay. A blackout was in force and inside the airport building the lights were so dim that we found it almost impossible to navigate from the Customs area to the waiting room for internal flights. We were tired and apprehensive until we heard the good news—the previous evening, peace had been declared on the Indian sub-continent and immediately the whole atmosphere became enlivened and cheerful.

With scarcely a thought for the millions of refugees and the thousands of dead and dying we congratulated ourselves enthusiastically on the excellent timing of our arrival in India. Now we could continue on-to Nepal without any problems or qualms of conscience. Everything seemed right with the world and the few Indian Army personnel to be seen among the busy jostling crowd were looked upon with awe and admiration even though very likely they had never seen action on the war front.

The only complication created by this news was that all air services were suddenly fully booked, but by some lucky chance we managed to buy seats on the last morning flight to Delhi. Once again we were divided into male and female queues. We women were thoroughly frisked by two very serious tall ladies in saris and now that some of the tension had been lifted from our travels I found the temptation to giggle was too much for me. Everybody else seemed to control them-selves quite easily, much to my shame.

On the tarmac beside our plane there was a pile of untidy-looking luggage. I wondered why all the passengers stood about looking at it, and then realised that the baggage had been carefully searched and some of it hadn't been properly closed including two of our packs.

Delhi airport was gay and confused, and we were told there was no chance of continuing onto Nepal that day. More than anything we needed a good long sleep and we were very happy to spend the night in Delhi with friends in a very thoroughly blacked-out house. After a pleasant dinner I was just about ready to go to bed when the telephone rang. It was a telegram from Nepal. It read:

> Ed Hillary is now winding up his expedition and all his work is com-pleted. He will come back to Kathmandu as soon as possible without any intention of returning to the mountains. We are trying to get a message to Ed about Louise's probable arrival but it is unlikely to reach him before the middle of next week. Please inform Louise on arrival at Delhi that she and family will be most welcome here and can work out future Hillary plans over Christmas.

I listened disbelievingly to this message. It couldn't be true. I had tried so hard to keep Ed informed of our changing plans—perhaps my messages hadn't got through or hadn't been understood? Whatever had happened nothing was going to stop us now from having our holiday in the Himalayas, even if we had to forcibly abduct the father of the family and make him enjoy another six weeks in the mountains with us. I found it hard to believe that he could have finished all his aid projects. Well, if he had, then he'd just have to find some new projects for us.

"Right!" I said to the family, "We are getting on a plane to Kath-mandu first thing tomorrow and we'll organise ourselves a really good holiday no matter what happens." Much refreshed after a good night's sleep we were delighted to find that we had seats on the first flight in to Kathmandu. There was the usual baggage search and frisking but before long our plane was climbing up through the haze and speeding over the broad dusty plains of India. In the distance ahead of us we could see the snow-covered fangs of the Himalayan peaks. We landed in Kathmandu on a glorious sunny winter afternoon. It was impossible to believe there had been a war anywhere near Nepal. The wide valley of Kathmandu, encircled in its wall of high mountains, was saturated in an hypnotic atmosphere of deepest tranquillity.

This was the life—our holiday had started!

CHAPTER 2

First Find Father!

OUR FRIENDS TERENCE and Rita O'Brien, the British Ambassador and his wife in Kathmandu, had shouldered the awful task of having us to stay—a particularly brave gesture as they knew we had no definite date of departure. Waiting on the front steps of the British Embassy Residence was the O'Briens' eldest child, Roderick, aged seventeen. For some months he had been planning to spend three weeks of his school holidays with us in the mountains. Now that he was actually confronted with four members of the family, I couldn't help feeling that he might be having some second thoughts about the idea, and in return my children were examining him with critical eyes. Fortunately as the days went by, it became apparent that Roderick was the type who would fit in very pleasantly with any group—even a party of Hillarys.

The young members of the family quickly settled themselves into their new quarters and hurried off to enjoy the delights of Kathmandu and its bazaar. They rented Chinese bicycles for three rupees (approximately ten cents U.S. to a rupee) in preference to Indian bicycles at four rupees a day and from then on were only seen at meal times for the duration of our stay in the city. This left me time to concentrate on our future plans which were fast becoming an epic in the style of Stanley hunting for Livingstone. It had become clear that no one really knew Ed's whereabouts or even his future plans. Where should we go to find him?

It was in 1960 that Ed first talked to his Sherpa climbing friends about the possibility of helping them with their long-cherished wish to obtain modern education for their children. Most of the Sherpa people live in the remote north-east of Nepal and they have been isolated by the rugged terrain from the developments of the Nepalese Education Department. Like most people living on the northern border they are of Mongolian origin and their Lamaistic Buddhism is very much the same as that of Tibet. The Sherpas in fact originally came from Tibet and they are a tough, energetic, and industrious group with a great ability to mix with people of other cultures and races—

hence their success when employed by foreign climbing expeditions and foreign tourists. There are, of course, many other ethnic groups in Nepal, such as the Gurungs, the Rais and the Limbus who are predominately Hindu, and Hinduism is in fact the official religion of Nepal.

In 1961 Ed was able to grant the wishes of his Sherpa friends by providing them with a small two-roomed aluminium school in Khumjung village in the Khumbu, the mountainous region embracing the rivers and valleys on the south side of Mount Everest. Adjacent to the Khumbu in the west is another valley system called Solu inhabited mostly by Sherpas and a few Rai and Tamang tribesmen. During the next few years petitions for schools for the villages in Solu Khumbu were received by Ed in amazing numbers. By the end of 1970, eleven schools had been built and equipped with the help of a Sherpa construction group under the very able leadership of Ed's assistant Sirdar, (leader) Mingma Tsering of Kunde village. By the end of 1971, eleven elementary schools had been built and equipped and are staffed with Nepalese teachers, most of them Sherpas, who follow the Nepalese Education Department's curriculum. Khumjung school has a library, handicraft and carpentry department, a soccer field and many enthusiastic volley-ball players. Most of the other schools try to provide some of these luxuries.

There were many other ways in which we had been able to help the Sherpas—and I say "we" because Ed's family had been fully involved with his activities right from the start. There was great need to improve the standards of hygiene by providing more adequate supplies of fresh water. In some villages the water had to be carried more than half a mile, with a climb of a thousand feet. By using long lengths of alkathene pipe, fresh water was brought to the centre of the villages. A severe iodine deficiency in the region produced a high incidence of goitre and cretinism and this was counteracted by injections of iodised oil. The problem of isolation was tackled by the building of Lukla airfield on a terrace high above the wild Dudh Kosi river and about thirty direct miles south of Everest at an altitude of 9,000 feet and about a hundred and fifty walking miles from Kathmandu. Even many of the bridges over the mountain rivers were rebuilt or replaced. In 1966 our single biggest project, the hospital at Kunde village, a day's march north of Lukla, was completed and outpatient clinics were established at many of the new village schools. Public health education became part of the curriculum in the schools and a new lecture room was built at the hospital especially for this purpose.

It's hard to say how successful all these aid projects have been (or will be) but the local people support their schools with pride and enthusiasm. In 1971 Ang Rita, one of our first students at Khumjung school, topped the whole of Nepal in School Leaving Certificate examinations out of 19,000 students. Now Ang Rita is continuing his studies and hopes to become the first Sherpa doctor at Kunde Hospital. Ang Rita is one of a growing band of selected scholarship students from the village schools who have been given the opportunity to complete their secondary education at Nepalese high schools. We hope some of the other scholarship boys will become fully trained teachers and already some successful students have returned to teach in their village schools.

Where has the labour for the projects come from? Partly from a few western volunteers and largely from the people of the villages who donate their work most cheerfully. A few local craftsmen such as stone workers, pit-saw men and joiners are paid for their work and all this labour force is very efficiently controlled by Sirdar Mingma Tsering of Kunde and his staff.

Where does all the money come from? The first financial assistance came from Field Enterprises Educational Corporation, of Chicago, U.S.A., who publish World Book Encyclopedia. Since then, support has come from a variety of sources—from donations by individuals, service clubs, schools, and Church groups, and a great deal of help from the business community in the United States, New Zealand, Australia, England and Italy. Some years ago the Himalayan Trust was formed in New Zealand to organise our many projects and to continue the raising of money. The two hardest-working members of the Trust are Ed, who is Chairman, and Dr. Max Pearl of Auckland who is in charge of medical matters, but there are many others involved who give a great deal of voluntary assistance.

The Himalayan Trust has always tried to preserve the culture of the mountain people. That is why we have added a handicraft department at Khumjung school and put a new roof on the Khumjung *gompa* (temple) to preserve its old books and treasures. To prevent the Thami *gompa* sliding down the mountainside to destruction, we rebuilt the terrace in front and hope it will now survive for another hundred years.

I am an impatient person (a common weakness of the Hillary family) and I was determined to leave as soon as possible to search for Ed in the mountains. I consulted with two of our greatest helpers in Kathmandu—Reuter's representative, Elizabeth Hawley, a long-time resident in Kathmandu, also Himalayan Trust Executive Officer, and

(continued on page 24)

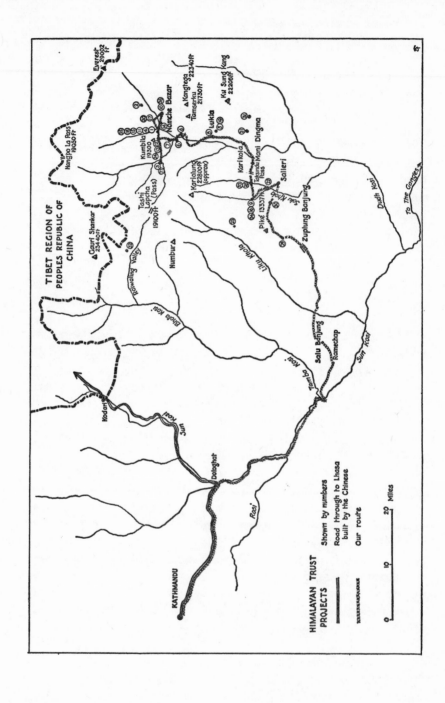

HIMALAYAN TRUST
PROJECTS

Shown by numbers

Road through to Lhasa
built by the Chinese

Our route

0   10   20 Miles

Himalayan Trust work to date, with a diagram opposite showing sites where the projects were carried out.

1961 1: Khumjung school (Khumbu)

1963 2: Pangboche school (Khumbu)
      3: Thami school (Khumbu)
      4: Khumjung water supply

1964 5: Lukla airstrip (Khumbu)
      6: Two bridges below Namche Hill
      7: Namche Bazar School (Khumbu)
      8: Chaunrikarka school (Khumbu)
      9: Junbesi school (Solu)

1965 10: Thyangboche school (Khumbu)
     11: Carpentry training shed, Khumjung school

1966 12: Kunde hospital
     13: Kunde water supply
     14: Bridge below Thyangboche
     15: Roof on Khumjung *gompa* (temple)

1967 16: Double size of Junbesi school
     17: Phortse school (Khumbu)

1968 18: Two new schoolrooms, Khumjung school
     19: Lengthening Lukla airstrip
     20: Phortse water supply

1970 21: Pangkoma school (Khumbu)
     22: Beni school (Solu)
     23: Bakange school (Solu)
     24: Addition to Kunde hospital (public health lecture room and store room)
     25: Handicrafts room at Khumjung school
     26: Thyangboche water supply
     27: Reconstruction of Thami *gompa* terrace
     28: New bridge at Ringmo

1971 29: Gypsoa school (Solu)
     30: Loding school (Solu)
     31: Yungu bridge (Khumbu)

1972 32: Rolwaling school
     33: Rebuilding of Ringmo bridge
     34: Junbesi middle school

(continued faom page 21)

John Clayden, who worked for the Nepal Department of Civil Aviation sponsored by the World Bank. We pored over maps and re-read letters from my lost husband hoping to discover some clue as to his whereabouts. We finally decided that we knew where Ed must be and that if we left in a couple of days' time we would meet him marching westward on his way back to Kathmandu and New Zealand from one of his biggest projects near Junbesi village. The only trouble was that there were two routes to the place where I hoped to locate him.

"Oh, that's all right," I said airily, "we'll just send a messenger on whichever route we *don't* take so as to make sure of finding him."

During the two weeks of the India–Pakistan war the tourist industry in Kathmandu had become almost non-existent so our little expedition was something of a rarity. Colonel Jimmy Roberts, Director of Mountain Travel, very kindly came to our aid. A Kunde Sherpa, Pemba Norbu, was appointed our guide and adviser and immediately started organising food and equipment for us. I knew that somewhere Ed had large quantities of camping equipment and clothes for us, but where was it all? We decided to hire tents and sleeping bags so we could get under way. I didn't even possess a padded jacket for the cold winter evenings of Kathmandu, but a Sherpa friend lent me one he had been issued when he was working for the International Everest Expedition the year before. With reluctance I purchased new flashlights and hot-water bottles—two of the most essential pieces of equipment for winter trekking in the Himalayas.

The two days of waiting before the "find Ed Hillary expedition" departed was a frustrating time for me. Normally I would have been frantically busy with a long list of housekeeping preparations. Such activities can be rather hectic but you start living your holiday in advance and on this particular occasion I could have enjoyed the delightful entertainment of shopping in Kathmandu bazaar for fresh vegetables, fruit and groceries. But now I had a professional Sirdar who had been told to do everything for me.

I have been coming to Nepal with Ed for twelve years now but we have never established a regular headquarters for our work. Across the road from the British Embassy is the home of Ang Tarkay, one of the most famous of the older generation of Sherpa mountain sirdars, and for some time he had generously let us use his garden as a place to sort our piles of gear. Then Mrs. Ang Tarkay offered us the use of her spare room for storing things during the year and we jokingly called this the "New Zealand Embassy", as there isn't one in Nepal. We were in very good company in this street—a sort of Embassy Row.

Up the road was the Indian Embassy and just two houses away was the residence of the Chief of Protocol for the Nepalese Government. We had no national flags fluttering over our headquarters but there was a fine array of Buddhist prayer flags strung from a tall fir tree on the border of the property, across the garden to the corner of the house. Ang Tarkay's house became the meeting place of all the people of Solu Khumbu, and his family, particularly his wife and his son Tenzing, were very long suffering and hospitable at all times.

One of my first tasks was to cross the road from the British Embassy and call on the Ang Tarkay family. I noticed a large crowd of visitors as I approached and then to my surprise and delight saw our dear friend Tenzing Norgay, Ed's Everest companion, and his daughter Pem Pem. Tenzing lives in Darjeeling but had been delayed in Kathmandu for several weeks by the war. Over cups of fine Darjeeling tea we had a marvellous reunion and Tenzing told me he had seen Ed in the Khumbu some weeks before.

It was fun to see many Sherpa friends. Ang Tarkay's niece, Passang Puti, was staying there with her six-month-old baby son, and three of the senior scholarship boys from Khumbu were also visitors. Ang Rita and Lhakpa Norbu were from Khumjung, Mingma Norbu was from Kunde, and they were all studying for public examinations to be held the following month in Kathmandu. When the boys saw me they immediately offered themselves as guides for my children during their stay in the city. Though English is their third language after Sherpa and Nepali, they all speak it very competently even if Ang Rita's style is delightfully poetic and not very idiomatic.

I searched through the store room and tried to find the possessions we had sent over from New Zealand earlier in the year, but all I could discover were a couple of sleeping bags, some air mattresses and four life jackets left over from a previous expedition when Ed had been exploring some Nepalese rivers with jet boats.

During our stay in Kathmandu most of us suffered from a mild dose of Kathmandu tummy bug. Many foreigners have trouble in combating the new set of germs in the valley. Ed and I have found that we are far less susceptible than our children and I think that age and experience have a lot to do with avoiding these minor discomforts. My safety rules are quite simple—make sure your hands are very clean before eating, and eat lightly if you are feeling at all queasy.

I decided to go and see a friend on the other side of town. I walked down to the main road and hailed a smart new Japanese-made taxi. I told the driver where I wanted to go and then sat back ready to enjoy a pleasant scenic drive. But when the driver pressed the self-starter, nothing happened.

"Wait a moment, I will push," he said. Luckily the car was on a downhill slope and he had very little trouble. He leapt back into the car and we juddered into motion and drove briskly on without having to stop at any intersections until we ended up on an unfamiliar lonely high plateau above the city with a narrow mud road ahead of us. Forgetting the flat battery, I asked the taxi man to stop so that I could enquire about our route. I received vague directions and returned to the taxi to discover that the engine had stalled.

"Will we start?" I asked rather unnecessarily. The driver grinned and shook his head. The road was muddy, rutted and covered with buffalo and cow dung. It was quite obvious that I would have to get out and push. I'm a strong and experienced pusher of cars, and had no trouble in getting us moving. I noticed that the driver was becoming a little nervous, I am sure he expected me to lose my temper at any moment, but now that my shoes were thoroughly dirty I was quite enjoying the unexpected pastime of pushing a vehicle through the mud. But we still seemed to be lost and a helpful passerby suggested that I should enquire at a rather dilapidated establishment across the next paddy field. I knocked at the door for some time until two beautiful black Tibetan Apso puppies came strutting out to greet me. Finally their owner appeared also and he gave me some clear and positive directions.

We had stopped this time in a wet narrow alley edged by high stone walls. We agreed it would be necessary for both the driver and me to push us out of this sticky spot. We laughed rather hysterically and then I shoved my weight firmly against the back of the car, very nearly squashing the driver against the alley wall. The motor grudgingly came to life and we leapt aboard and drove onto a disused field where a large bog barred our way. If we had turned back then, our instructions would have become useless. But the driver was now quite determined to go ahead. We roared forward like a Boeing 707 about to be airborne and swayed and lurched uncontrollably across the mud and out onto dry land where a well-formed road quickly brought me to my destination. I paid five rupees for my journey and considered it money well spent.

There were the usual busy rounds of pre-Christmas Embassy parties and I found myself sucked into the social whirl. At one such party I had a screaming match with a gentleman who kept saying, "I would like to spend Christmas at Betlam some day." I kept on saying, "Where's that?"

"Betlam," he said. "You know, Betlam." After about the tenth repetition I realised he meant Bethlehem and replied that, for my part, I was only too happy to forgo the spiritually uplifting experience of Christmas in Bethlehem for a peaceful Christmas in the high Himalayas.

As we drove back to the Embassy, Rita O'Brien told me about a disconcertingly realistic dream she'd had the previous night. She dreamt she was watching an exhausted Ed walking slowly up the driveway of the Residence at midday—only a few hours after we had departed into the mountains to look for him, and that she had the depressing task of breaking the news that he had just missed us.

Late on the afternoon before the departure of our small expedition I set off to find my Sirdar and check with him that all was ready for the morrow. Just as I was about to leave the house I received a message by phone that a mail runner had that moment arrived in Kathmandu with a letter for me from Ed.

"Oh, bother!" was my first reaction. "How could Ed be so thoughtless as to ruin all my plans."

Ed's letter was full of instructions.

> Junbesi
> December 17th

My dear Louise,

To-day I received a letter from Elizabeth Hawley by mail runner saying you are arriving in Kathmandu on 18th or 19th December. It was a great surprise but we really are delighted. We've made a rapid change in plans and will trek posthaste to Dologhat. Mingma, Siku and all are extremely excited. You've no idea how sad everyone was at the non-arrival of the family. My plans would be:

December 23rd: We arrive at Dologhat [a few hours' drive from Kathmandu] and you must meet us there, probably in the afternoon.

December 24th to 31st: For eight days we trek and float on air mattresses down the Sun Kosi river then climb up to Okeldunga. This should be a fabulous trip as it is the country that I have covered before during my jetboat expedition.

I will have sleeping bags, foam mats, pillows and the clothing you sent over from New Zealand including hot-water bottles, torches, etc. Please bring the life jackets and any food stored in Ang Tarkay's house. Bring the following food from Kathmandu to augment our needs and those of Kunde hospital.

Tinned Butter for all of us	2 4-gallon tins of sugar
30 lbs fresh onions	8 pkts candles
60 lbs potatoes	2 dozen pkts matches
6 cakes toilet soap	4 bars washing soap
12 tins Indian jam	60 lbs good quality flour
2 bottles dried yeast	12 packets tea
6 bottles orange cordial	2 large tins dried milk
6 rolls toilet paper	5 lbs chilli
20 lbs dhal [dried peas]	10 pkts cooking salt

Also, don't forget a few extra luxuries for Christmas

60 lbs good rice	10 bottles Nepalese cooking oil

1 large load assorted fresh vegetables

Our mail runner has received no money from us and will accompany you to Dologhat and give what help he can. I will pay him then. I only hope to goodness that you all really turn up. It will be a great trip after all and a big disappointment if it doesn't come off. (Ed still didn't know that the India–Pakistan war was over.)

You could perhaps enquire about the need for malaria pills down the Sun Kosi. Also we will have no medical officer with us so you'd better bring a collection of medical needs. Don't worry about anything. We are all O.K. here, although it will be a mad rush to meet you at Dologhat.

Love,
Ed.

Poor Pemba Norbu, we would no longer require his services, as Ed's energetic team of Sherpas would soon be taking over all his duties. I rushed off to see him and tell him my good news. He had everything ready and was obviously quite disappointed but took it very well, and as Jimmy Roberts said, "All his preparations could be used for somebody else."

These new arrangements gave us one more day in Kathmandu and I would need all the extra time to purchase the provisions listed in Ed's letter. I would have to find bamboo baskets for the porters to carry the loads of food and individual containers for the smaller items. For luxuries I bought only three large cheeses weighing five pounds each, personally selected from the warehouse behind the Kathmandu dairy by my friend Mr. Passang Tsering Sherpa, who is in charge of three cheese factories up in the mountains. Passang very kindly walked back to the Embassy with me to help carry the cheeses.

We met Rita in front of the Residence and were idly talking about cheeses and other matters when I suddenly noticed that she had become silent and was looking down the driveway. I followed her glance and thought for a moment I saw Peter walking up the drive accompanied by a Sherpa with a heavy pack. Then I realised it was Ed and Mingma, and the time was just midday. Rita's dream had nearly come true.

"Why are you here?" I asked rather inhospitably.

"I was scared you'd rush off and hunt for me," Ed announced, "and then we'd end up running after each other through the mountains of Nepal. Mingma and I decided we'd better change our plans a bit more and do a desperate dash to Kathmandu to stop you."

They had double-marched for five days and both looked tired and dusty—but I had to admit it was good to see them again.

The children returned from yet another sortie in the Kathmandu bazaars. They wobbled gaily down the neat driveway on their three-rupee-a-day bicycles accompanied by Ang Rita, Lhakpa and Mingma Norbu. "Hi, Dad," they said and then immediately embarked on an enthusiastic story of fierce bargaining with Kathmandu shopkeepers (with nothing to show for it except some glass bangles and incense), the exhilarating excitement of nearly colliding with a sacred cow, the skidding off a bike to avoid an oncoming truck, and the usual near misses with pedestrians. Life was back to normal. Their high spirits showed they were pleased to have the party leader back again. After all, mothers are O.K. but who would want them to organise an expedition?

CHAPTER 3

Sun Kosi Capers

THE DAY DAWNED clear and frosty. Much as we had enjoyed Kathmandu we were eager to be on our way. We had a feeling of joyous anticipation, for we were at the start of an adventure that would lead us south-east down the great, swift Sun Kosi river and then north up tall ridges and unknown paths to remote mountain communities. We expected to take ten days to reach the Solu district and be on familiar ground again, but as none of our Sherpas had visited this area before we could make no definite timetable. From then on there would be many people to visit on Himalayan Trust business and building activities for all.

Our final destination would be Kunde Hospital, and we would travel about 200 miles visiting many of the Trust's aid projects on the way including Gypsoa, Loding, Beni and Junbesi schools. Our journey would force us up and down many tens of thousands of feet over high ridges travelling from the fertile populated valleys, through forests and sparse scrubland to high mountain meadows and wind-blown ridges. Our route would go through many small villages and we would notice the racial variations between the Indo-Aryan Hindu people of the southern and central portion of Nepal and the more Mongolian mountain people of the north with their Buddhist religion and Tibetan culture.

Nepal is just a little smaller in area than New Zealand but it has a population of about ten million compared to New Zealand's three million. So it is not until you climb to the very high mountains or lonely ridges that you feel any sense of isolation. The steep stony paths that we were to follow were the main highways through the countryside and we could look forward to meeting many interesting local people as we journeyed on.

There was no time to waste. We gulped down some breakfast and loaded our belongings into the waiting vehicles—a hired Land-Rover and a Russian jeep. We had thirty-six winding miles to drive from Kathmandu to the bridge at Dologhat on the Sun Kosi river and then we would have to start walking. Sun Kosi means "Golden River" in

Nepali and this name added a touch of romance to an already exciting future.

The new Chinese-built road that links Kathmandu with Lhasa passes through Dologhat. It is well engineered but steep in places and many of its corkscrew corners hang above precipitous drops. We drove sedately enough through the wide Kathmandu valley and stopped in a town on the fringe of the valley. Our drivers disappeared and it took us quite a time to find them—eating a large meal in the local restaurant. Contrary to our usual practice they had been paid fully in advance and nothing that Ed or Mingma could say would hurry them up.

Finally we started off again along the narrow road winding down through the steep hills towards the river. Our driver in the Land-Rover proved to be very expert, driving slowly and carefully, and we felt no concern for our safety. Suddenly the Russian jeep with the children aboard gathered speed, overtook us and dashed crazily ahead weaving all over the road. It was horrible to watch our family lurch from corner to corner in what seemed an inevitable dash to death and destruction. We shouted at our driver to try and overtake the other vehicle and so check their reckless descent to the river, but it was hopeless, we just couldn't go fast enough.

Somehow we all arrived at Dologhat in one piece and the children crawled out of their vehicle looking decidedly shaken. Apparently they had two drivers in their jeep—one was experienced and the other one a learner. For some obscure reason the learner had taken the wheel over the most dangerous section and had become exhilarated with the speed, or possibly didn't know where the brake was. I am convinced that the motor vehicle brings out the worst in our characters and I was delighted that for the next six weeks we would have nothing to do with these fiendish machines.

Though it was winter time it was about eighty degrees Fahrenheit and humid down in the valley at an altitude of 2,000 feet, I had only brought cold-weather clothing with me for our high altitude holiday and I realised now that this would be most uncomfortable for walking down the Sun Kosi. As there was a small shop beside the road I bought five rupees' worth of maroon flowered cotton cloth to make up into a skirt for myself, and Mingma bought some blue cloth for covering sleeping mats. I could see we were going to have a busy evening sewing beside the camp fire.

During our two weeks of waiting and wondering we hadn't been able to get much exercise and I was afraid we might have lost the physical fitness we had achieved in our training programme. It was

with a certain amount of trepidation that we left the road and climbed
over the steep hill to where Ed's Sherpa staff and porters were waiting
at their camp. We were welcomed by many old friends. Siku from the
small village of Phortse was particularly glad to see us as he had cared
for our children during their first visit to Nepal five years before. He
is a slow and gentle but immensely powerful man and surprises everybody by very occasionally coming out with a wicked or ribald joke
which seems to surprise him about as much as it does his audience. He
is the proud father of two small daughters and is aged about thirty-five
years old. Aila, a sturdy Phortse farmer and an excellent builder in rock
was there to give us a warm and enthusiastic welcome also. He is quite
tall and craggy in build for a Sherpa, but like so many Nepalese people
he has the same gentleness and dignity as Siku. He is aged about
forty-eight and has four nearly grown-up children with a handsome
wife of great personality. Aila was a member of Ed's industrious and
elite building team.

It was good to see the fifteen Sherpa porters who were mostly
familiar to us from other trips. There were also two young men to
help in the kitchen department—a shy Sherpa called Passang whose
wife was one of our pretty girl porters, and a very lively young fellow
called Pemba Tenzing. As always in Sherpaland the kettle was boiling
on the fire and we were immediately handed mugs of tea. Before leaving Kathmandu we had been given packages of sandwiches and fruit
for our lunch. As I was contentedly munching my food I heard the
ominous cry of "Who would like my lunch, I don't feel like eating it"
which could be translated into "I feel a little sick". Perhaps it is only
the heat and the exciting drive, I thought hopefully.

Our camp had become the most popular sideshow for the populace
of Dologhat and as we were near the main trade route there were
clouds of hovering flies and a strong smell of human excrement.
Everyone was eager, despite the lateness of the hour, to shoulder their
loads and hunt for a more peaceful and salubrious place farther down
the river.

It wasn't long before Sarah succumbed to her turn with the Kathmandu tummy bug. It was unfortunate for her that when she began
to feel violently ill, we were walking across a steep bluff above the
river, and she had to stand against the side of the narrow track to let
all the porters go by before she could lie down on the path to rest.
When she recovered a little she said she would continue slowly onwards, but I think misery gave her wings and she went so fast that she
soon left me far behind.

By the time I arrived in camp a highly competitive and efficient

Going down a Sun Kosi rapid: left to right, Roderick and Peter.

Morning meal beside the Sun Kosi – Ed, Sarah, Belinda.

Sarah.

group consisting of Ed, Mingma, Aila, Siku, Peter, Belinda and Roderick had set up a very comfortable home away from home for our party. As it was such a fine night the porters, who have to find their own accommodation, were quite content to sleep under a group of tall trees nearby. For the rest of us there was a gay cluster of small colourful tents. Ed is adviser to Sears Roebuck and Company of Chicago, U.S.A., for the development of their camping gear and some of our tents were new models that we had never used before. Having a tent tester as a husband can have its drawbacks. I can remember very clearly one occasion when Ed hacked a weak corner out of a tent we were actually living in and sent it post-haste by airmail back to the manufacturers.

Our new camp site was on a dried-out paddy-field with the river and a sandy beach below. It was very peaceful, and sheltered by a hillside covered in terraced paddies that rose up behind us towards a small group of neat white and red plastered houses. Soon everybody was comfortably settled; Aila and I were busily sewing and Siku and Pemba Tenzing were cooking dinner to the accompaniment of a pleasant continuo of murmurings from Siku who always conducts a quiet conversation with himself when he is working. Sarah had disappeared into her tent and was sleeping soundly whilst everybody else was just sitting in a gloriously tired and dazed state.

The Sun Kosi river is the major river of east Nepal and its tributaries drain the highest mountains in the world. It rises in the highlands of Tibet and has carved a passage through the Himalayan range at Kodari and thence flows as a swift mountain torrent to Dologhat. The Chinese road also crosses the border at Kodari and follows the valley to Dologhat and then west to Kathmandu. The Sun Kosi changes at Dologhat into a swift-flowing expanse of water zigzagging over wide glistening sandy flats or gushing through narrow gorges. The mountains still rise steeply for five or six thousand feet on either side and high bluffs frequently block the way. You are left with the choice of clambering thousands of feet over them or of crossing the river in a dugout canoe to more hospitable terrain on the other side. The path beside the river is an important highway and small villages have grown up beside crossing places on the river where the locals operate ferry services in their unwieldy dug-outs—in the same manner as they must have been doing for centuries. The canoes are owned by the nearby village and the earnings from them must considerably augment the slim incomes of the farmers.

As the sun disappeared behind the ridges, the cool evening air drifted down from the high mountains and we pulled on our warm clothes and huddled closer to the fire. Roderick and Peter were impatient to get to grips with the problems and excitement of river travel. To the astonishment of our Sherpas they inflated two air mattresses and changed into brief bathing suits. Accompanied by an interested throng they approached the chilly dark green waters of the rushing river. With great bravado they jumped onto their air mattresses and flopped into the water. Yells of agony rent the air—the water was bitterly cold—and they paddled furiously to the other side, and paddled even more energetically back again, then scrambled wildly out of the water and stood shivering beside the fire. The local audience observed this all with the greatest of interest—they were obviously rather puzzled as to the purpose of the exercise.

We awoke to a beautiful morning and all felt greatly refreshed after a peaceful night under canvas. It was the day before Christmas. I sallied forth from my tent feeling comfortable and unrestricted in my new ensemble of maroon flowered peasant skirt which I had cobbled up the night before and a blouse made in New Zealand from mauve, green and white floral material. I was greeted by cries of "Hideous!— Frightful!—You can't!" but took no notice of these remarks as I knew how very much more cool I would feel than my detractors in their heavy cotton jeans. I resembled a colourful sack of potatoes and discovered at the end of the trip that there were no photographs taken of me in my Sun Kosi creation.

We had been advised to cross the river at this point to avoid some bad bluffs a mile or so down stream and there were two dugout canoes hauled up on the beach beside our camp. Our preparations didn't take long and we repacked our few possessions into a kitbag and a day pack. It was delightful to have so few material things to worry about. We each had a sleeping bag and small pillow, a change of clothes and a down jacket, a couple of books and writing material, camera and toilet gear, hot-water bottle and torch. Our very coldweather clothing, consisting of padded trousers, boots, caps and gloves, was stowed away in other loads. For trekking we wore light cotton clothing and gym shoes.

A traveller had joined our camp during the night and he commenced his early morning Hindu prayers and ablutions in the breathtakingly cold river. We watched with admiration as he repeatedly submerged himself without even a shudder. After he had finished he sat down on a rock and had his turn at enjoying the spectacle of our large party being ferried across the river.

There were twenty-six of us to be taken across—fifteen porters with bulging loads, two cook boys laden with bulky baskets of kitchen equipment, Mingma, Aila and Siku with small packs and the six of us with even smaller packs. The boatmen would make quite a few rupees from their morning's work. The fare was twenty-five *pice* (a quarter of a rupee) per person and there might well be some *bakshish* from the Burrah Sahib—as they called Ed. (Burrah means big in the sense of important or leader, and Sahib usually just means foreigner these days.)

Few of our Sherpas could swim and they entered the canoes with a great deal of trepidation. Sarah, Belinda, Peter and Roderick had all done some lifesaving at school so they stood at the water's edge ready to jump in the river in case of sudden disaster. Fortunately their services weren't needed as the rough dug-outs proved surprisingly stable. The boatmen, I suppose, have the same instinct for self-preservation as an airline pilot and they made sure that the passengers were safely spread along the canoe with their loads carefully placed on the floor. When the canoe was paddled out into the main current it shot down river at great speed for ten seconds until the boatmen skilfully guided it into the quieter water on the other side. Determined to take no chances the Sherpas, all good Buddhists, dipped their hands into the river and flicked drops of water skywards to placate the Gods and ensure a safe journey.

The road led across shimmering river flats towards the distant ridges that descended in endless folds as far as the eye could see. The porters left a great cloud of alluvial dust in their wake so we waited for it to settle and then followed across the hot sandy flats. The soft surface made it very hard work and we were glad to follow the track up out of the riverbed into a rich farming area with valleys of terraced fields sandwiched between steep bare ridges. There was an air of affluence and easy living in this fertile region. The village houses stood in snug clusters surrounded by papaya and banana groves, and the rice crops on the terraces were at all stages of development from the brilliant green of seedlings to golden heads ready for harvest.

A group of shady trees tempted us to rest in the cool for a while and we bought some sugarcane from a nearby grove. We cut off the hard outside covering and munched away at the inside that was particularly sweet and juicy. Then we noticed that the Sherpas managed to bite right through the cane with one chomp of the jaws. We were quite intrigued by this feat of strength and tried it ourselves. To our amazement we found that if you crunched suddenly enough it was quite easy to do. With every bite our faces became more and more covered in thick sweet syrup.

Mingma and his friends were not familiar with this area and had difficulty in understanding the local dialect. Our information on tracks was very confusing and later in the day I couldn't help feeling that we had followed the wrong advice—we'd been climbing up a very steep and dry mountainside while far away on the other side of the river was a much easier track. For hours we scrambled upwards and by 4.30 we were looking rather desperately for a camp site. We needed quite a large flat space for our group of twenty-six and the only fields we could see were narrow, rock strewn and nettle infested. We wearily approached the crest of a high ridge and hoped that the countryside might flatten out a little on the other side—but we saw the same inhospitable slopes with a few goats grazing amongst the rocks.

The daylight was fading as we entered a narrow gully with a sluggish stream and two small stubble-covered paddy fields. "We will camp here," said Mingma with his usual complete authority. Over the years we have grown quite used to obeying all his commands without question, for Mingma is a natural leader and though only small of stature what he lacks in height he certainly makes up for many times in personality. We were very happy to agree with his command, although it was hardly the beautiful location we had expected for our camps in the Sun Kosi valley. We were much higher here and it had become very cold. We searched hard for firewood but there wasn't a stick in sight. Pemba Tenzing and Passang, the two cook's assistants, were sent back up the track to a lonely farm house to buy expensive bundles of wood. They arrived back with heavy loads plus the owner of the house who appeared quite distressed that we weren't staying with him.

"Please come," he said, "strangers seldom pass through here." That was not difficult to believe, but we politely declined his kind invitation. There were so many of us and our tents were now up and we were comfortably established. We sat around a small spluttering fire on the prickly rice stalks and surveyed the day's damage done to our feet during the very hot hours of walking. Nearly all of us had blisters, particularly Sarah who seemed to have more blisters than whole feet. We patched up the more tender places with some of our small stock of precious sticking plaster. Even Ed, who had been walking in the cold high parts of the Himalayas for a month, had a couple of large blisters. Our feet were going to have to toughen up very quickly.

The valley was so cramped that it was almost impossible to find secluded spots for toilet purposes—round every bed we would find another cosy little encampment of Sherpa porters or the impossible discomfort of a large patch of nettles.

"Well, I give up," I said to Belinda who was searching with me.

"Well, you can't do that," she said.

"No, I don't mean that," I replied impatiently, "I mean I give up being modest."

The porters sat crosslegged in chattering groups around minute fires of dried rice stalks and stirred their evening meals of rice or *tsampa* (barley meal) with thin soup flavoured strongly with chilli. The difference between their possessions and ours was quite ludicrous. They had an old blanket of some kind, a cooking pot and mug, a bag of grain plus some salt and chilli, and perhaps an onion. With this they quickly and easily made themselves cosy and contented in about five minutes. We had tents, sleeping mats, sleeping bags, changes of clothing and a vast collection of kitchen implements and food, all of which we deemed absolutely necessary.

That evening we established our routine for setting up camp and it became very clear from the outset that the Sherpas planned to do most of the work. The boys were allowed to put up their own tents and Ed, who loves playing around with tents, usually put ours up with the help of Mingma. The only jobs left to me and the girls were such things as hunting for the torch, candle and toothbrush that would be needed later in the evening and then having to make the very difficult decision about a dinner menu—would we have a chicken and vegetable stew with rice, or would we have a chicken and vegetable stew with potatoes?

During the night my sleep was disturbed by two porters camped nearby who coughed incessantly and by another group who talked and laughed for hours. At the nearby farmhouse the dogs howled at the moon and I started worrying about all sorts of unnecessary details. How would Sarah walk on her blistered feet? How could we ensure that all our drinking water was boiled? What would we do if anyone became seriously ill or badly injured? My responsibilities as Medical Officer pressed heavily on my shoulders. While I suffered Ed slept peacefully on.

By 2 a.m. I had succeeded in persuading myself that it was unlikely my family would survive the journey; and to add to my miseries every muscle in my body was aching from the unaccustomed exercise. And then, quite suddenly, I dropped off to sleep and was woken at 5 a.m. by the jingling of the glass bangles that Sarah and Belinda had bought in Kathmandu. It was still pitch dark.

"Why on earth are you getting up so early?" I enquired rather petulantly.

"We have to," came back their vague reply.

"Well, wait a bit longer and stop jingling those bangles."

"We've got to be ready when the Sherpas come to pull down our tent," they said in worried voices, "and it takes us so many ages to pack up."

By the time we had finished discussing the need for new sticking plaster on blistered feet the whole camp was stirring. I had to steel myself to face the dreaded transition from the warmth of my sleeping bag to the chilly morning air but then I quickly dressed and packed the day's necessities—camera, soap, towel, toothbrush, diary, pen, and dirty clothes. It was amazing how much mental effort was needed to accomplish such simple tasks—I suppose the strange environment and the excitement made it difficult to concentrate.

I crawled outside the tent to find a glorious morning and my worries of the night were quickly forgotten. Even the dreary campsite of the night before seemed to have taken on new life and colour. The sky was glowing in the early morning light and speckled with fine-weather clouds; the stream rippled over shining rocks; and the young corn plants on the stony fields above looked green and succulent. The few houses on the ridge overlooking us stood neat and white against a background of green mango trees, and far across the valley the steep eroded mountainsides climbed up to the heavens.

"Happy Christmas!" we called out—and "Happy Christmas!" replied our Buddhist Sherpas with deep-throated laughter. The camp was alive with activity. Pemba Tenzing and Passang rushed around serving tea and biscuits while our tents were collapsed and disappeared into porter loads, and next moment, or so it seemed, we were under way across the stream and up the steep hillside.

The path soon lost itself amongst newly dug fields and we darted hither and yon. When you are unfit you appreciate a wide open track to swing along in rhythm without the need to watch too closely where you are going. But here we were climbing over little walls and threading our way between newly planted potatoes, wheat and corn while we sought an easier gradient for our puffing selves. We reached the crest of the ridge and expected the track to plunge down to the river but it stretched endlessly upwards.

At every house and village the locals came out to stare and they greeted us shyly. They were tough, attractive people of the Tamang tribe. Despite the steep eroded land on which they lived they had made an adequate life for themselves and their solid little houses with neat thatched roofs and whitewashed walls reflected this. The Tamangs are Buddhist although like most Buddhism in Nepal it is strongly flavoured with Hinduism. Certainly their lives revolve around their religious beliefs and their festivities are enlivened by colourful singing and dancing. In many parts of Nepal the local people are used to foreign trekkers passing by but here it was quite different.

"What is your business?" we were constantly being asked, and "Are you American?" It seemed that anyone large and pale-skinned in this part of Nepal must automatically be an American. They always seemed rather disappointed with our answers: they had high hopes, we were told, that we were the forerunners of a big work party that was supposed to build a new hydro-electric scheme on the river. Such a project would bring work and wages to these subsistence-living people.

Several hours of brisk walking brought us to a little stream and beside it was one of those pleasant wayside stopping places you find all over Nepal—a grove of tall trees whose foliage rustled invitingly in the cool wind and the parched earth underneath was dotted with the remains of many fires. We were ready to stop here for our morning meal. We had already settled down into our trekking routine—a long walk in the early morning followed by a mid-morning break for the first meal of the day. There was time then to wash clothes, write diaries or have a good rest before travelling on until late in the afternoon.

The girls and I wanted to do our laundry and we were conducted by one of the local people to a man-made water hole complete with a bamboo spout and flowing water and here we were soon joined by some of the porters. We worked away industriously for some time until Pemba Tenzing arrived with a very dirty cooking pot from the previous night's dinner and he started scraping this with such energy that he made our efforts seem very half-hearted.

Back at the resting place we joined a large and talkative group of the local people. One of them offered to sell us some small bony chickens for dinner that night but we were horrified to discover he wanted nearly a dollar each for them—inflation seemed to have reached even this quiet corner of Nepal. Some vociferous arguing brought no difference to his price and in the end we bought the chickens for Christmas dinner. We spread out our washing on thorn bushes to dry and then came the most important announcement of the day.

"Porridgee ready, Memsahib!" And what a meal it was—a huge plate of porridge covered with milk and sugar; fried potato chips and eggs; Kathmandu bread and jam; all washed down with a large cup of tea. How pleasant it was to eat all you wanted and not have to be strong-minded in the interests of retaining a slim figure. Most of the Sherpas had vigorous appetites but Pemba Tenzing astonished us with the vast amounts of food he could consume—no wonder he had so much energy.

After breakfast the Tamang villagers gave us some good news—our path would now return us to the river again. We plunged knee-shatteringly downwards for 3,000 feet through straggling pine forest, past eroded scrub-covered slopes, and finally to the fertile terraces in the valley bottom. The climate changed, too, from crisp freshness to warmth and humidity, and perspiration soaked through our shirts. It was worth it, though. Now we were making horizontal distance instead of just battling our way up and down.

In the warmer air our thoughts returned to our plans of making a raft for floating down the river. We had four air mattresses available but, "We'll have to get some bamboo poles" announced Ed. To our surprise we discovered that bamboo wasn't easy to find in this fertile region. We entered a pleasant village where the houses were tucked away behind mud walls and fruit trees and commented that nobody seemed to be doing much work that day. Perhaps they had declared it a holiday to watch the foreigners trooping past their gates?

"I'm sure we'll find bamboo here," said Ed walking up to a tiny thatched roof structure and examining its bamboo framework with interest—much to the consternation of its owners. The party scattered in different directions to search for bamboo, and I sat down to wait for them.

Soon a friendly head popped up from behind a stone wall on the other side of an irrigation ditch. "Where are you going?" I was asked. "What is your business? Where do you come from? How many days have you taken from Kathmandu?" The questions were never-ending and they strained my Nepali vocabulary to the utmost. "Goodbye," I said hastily when there was a gap in the conversation, "I must join my children," and I hurried off. I was passing the house at the edge of the village when a huge black dog leapt out at me, barking viciously. As usual I quaked with fear, I had nothing I could use for my protection. Then I remembered the well tried and traditional method of dealing with dogs. I quickly raised my arm as though to throw a stone and the dog immediately stopped barking and slunk away. Most Nepalese dogs are kept only as watchdogs and they are usually broken spirited and hungry so it doesn't take much to frighten them. But with rabies fairly common it doesn't pay to take any chances.

I climbed over a dozen terrace walls and splashed my way through irrigation channels until the path twisted down to the riverside where the young members of the party were waiting. Before long we were joined by Ed and the Sherpas who were carrying two large bamboo poles. The valley floor was now wide and flat with no dangerous rapids in sight—it was an ideal place to try out the raft. Soon there was a vast amount of puffing and blowing as the four air mattresses were firmly inflated. Then Ed lashed them tightly onto the bamboo poles. By the time it was finished it looked like a comfortable double bed.

Meanwhile Peter and Roderick donned bathing suits and life jackets and made quite plain that they were the rafting experts. Ed and Mingma carried the raft down to the water and launched it in the chilly water. Accompanied by shrill whoops of delight from the onlookers the boys scrambled aboard and were soon bumping down the centre of the first rapid in a most controlled manner. The local populace plus most of our party hurried off after the raft in an excited, chattering group.

Sarah, Belinda, Siku and I didn't go with them, we had some shopping to do. Sarah badly needed some new gym shoes—she had cut up her old ones to relieve the pressure on her blisters—and across the river a small village slumbered peacefully in the afternoon sun and we planned to visit the village shop. We stepped aboard a canoe and were expertly paddled to the other side, then walked up a broad path bordered with banana palms to the centre of the village and the one shop. As we approached, the place came to life, the elders abandoned their gambling to watch us, and the rest of the inhabitants came pouring out of their homes.

Inside the shop were well-fingered bolts of bright coloured cotton, bags of grain, tins of sugar and flour, and a good selection of kitchen utensils. The footwear department was well stocked but the sizes appeared to be very small. As Hillarys have big feet and Nepalese people don't we were fortunate to find one large pair of rubber-soled sandals for Sarah. Siku had been looking a little worried, and we learned why when he bought the next largest pair of shoes for himself. The friendly crowd talked incessantly with us and gave us their company all the way back to the waiting boat. They waved us a cheerful good-bye as we paddled back to the other side.

We hurried on to catch up with the others and for five miles clambered across sand banks, over paddy walls and boulders, and around a steep bluff covered in a tangle of pampas grass and spindly tendrils of bougainvilia weighed down with orange blossoms. By the time we rejoined Ed we were ahead of the raft as the river gave a great swing to the other side of the valley. There was an exciting rapid just ahead of us so we clambered up onto a headland to watch the boys go through.

They came bobbing down the river and as they entered the rapid we expected the raft to be thrown about on the surging waves but it was amazing how easily the air mattresses negotiated this section of turbulent river. "Get out as soon as you can!" Ed called as they went skimming by. "We'll be camping soon."

Mingma selected a perfect camping site on a grass-covered flat. There was plenty of driftwood lying about and by the time the shivering raft men arrived we had a magnificent fire going. As they warmed themselves they related their exciting adventures. Then Sarah and Belinda announced that they intended to go rafting next day.

"What clothes will you wear?" I enquired.

"My bathing suit, of course," said Belinda.

"You can't do that," said Sarah, "There's not enough of it." And she was certainly right. The minute bikinis used by the girls would have been most unsuitable in this country of modest Hindu women.

We busied ourselves with preparations for Christmas dinner. The boys disappeared to hunt for a Christmas tree and the girls attempted to make a sauce for the large pudding donated by Roderick's family. The ingredients were very coarse-grained sugar, rancid canned butter, and whisky ... and it wasn't very successful. Ed with great pride unpacked his special portable shower box which was really a small square tent with a canvas bag and shower rose which you hung from the centre of the roof. To his great disappointment no-one seemed very keen to face the cool valley wind until Sarah agreed to make the sacrifice. The shower didn't prove a great success either.

The Christmas tree turned out to be a very untraditional branch of worm-eaten broadleaf shrub. It was set up beside the fire and decorated with silver bells and stars specially brought for the occasion. As darkness fell the fire leapt higher and the scene became more and more colourful. Excited shouts and screams of laughter showed that everybody was thoroughly enjoying their unorthodox Christmas. Even the tough stringy chicken with stew and vegetables was greeted with pleasure and the Christmas pudding was declared delicious.

There was only one regret, four important members of Ed's Sherpa staff were missing. A message had been sent asking them to come and join us but still they hadn't turned up.

"If they don't come this evening," said Ed, "it will probably mean they've gone back to Khumbu to wait for us there."

We had just finished eating when there was a call from Mingma, "Look! Torch coming." Across the river flats we saw a swinging light and then we heard the faint sound of voices. "Is it them, Mingma?"

"Coming!" he said with obvious pleasure. In a few minutes we were rushing out to welcome four old friends, Ang Tsering, Ang Passang, Passang Tendi and Nawang—looking very cheerful but a little tired. To catch us up they had crammed three of our days into one.

The leader of the group, Ang Tsering, works for the Himalayan Trust as Mingma's assistant. He and his brother, Passang Tendi, live in Khumjung village; they are both handsome lively men who enjoy hard work and adventure. Ang Tsering is aged about thirty-seven and Passang Tendi is in his early thirties, and until three years ago they were greatly sought after as high-altitude climbers for expeditions. But they have young families and after the many climbing tragedies in recent years their wives had persuaded them to withdraw from high climbing. Ang Passang is one of the finest cooks in Nepal as well as being a tough man in the mountains, he is neat and tidy and always on the go, with just the trace of a smile on his face. He started his career as a shy junior cook boy on one of Ed's expeditions twelve years before. Over the years he gained more and more experience with trekkers and climbers and was well known as being a fine organiser. From this he graduated to cook at the house of Major Dudley Spain of the British Embassy. Here he quickly learnt all the finer points of Western cooking embassy-style and the English language, but after three years of working in the quiet British Embassy compound he decided he needed a more active and challenging life, and so he accepted the job of hospital cook up in Kunde. There his jobs consist of interpreter, medical assistant, cultural adviser and friend as well as cook for the doctors. The fourth member of the party was Nawang who comes from the village of Solung in the Solu district. Nawang is a kindly learned man who spent some years as a *tawa* (monk) in a Sherpa monastery. Aged about forty, strongly built and very tough he has been a faithful helper whenever there has been a school building project in the Solu district.

The new arrivals were soon drinking large mugs of tea and eating enormous helpings of rich Christmas pudding. Sarah tuned her guitar while we settled ourselves in a big circle around the fire. Then we started singing, song after song—the most popular was "Kumbaya" and soon the Sherpas were singing it too. A debonair and handsome porter who I had particularly noticed as always carrying his shoes in his hand when he was on the march, took the guitar from Sarah and started playing music in Tibetan style. A game of quoits was started on sloping ground near the fire and the competition was very fierce indeed. I was amazed we didn't lose one of the quoits in the flames—or a member of the party. The sky was deep black velvet studded with stars and we were tiring now and thinking of our warm sleeping bags. It had been a very happy Christmas—one of the happiest I could remember.

The soft jingling of Kathmandu bangles once more heralded the new day, which also happened to be Peter's seventeenth birthday.

"You don't need to get up yet," I called.

"Yes we do! There are four extra Sherpas this morning and they may come any moment and pull down the tents." The frenzied jingling continued as they stowed their gear in their kitbags and put plaster on their blisters. Ed and I, with our years of experience behind us, had another half-hour of comfort in our sleeping bags, then dressed and packed everything in a few minutes, and put our heads out the tent just in time to receive a cup of tea from Passang and Pemba Tenzing.

"What will the path be like today?" we asked Mingma who had been enquiring from the local inhabitants.

"Some little up going, and some little down going," he replied with a shrug. We all laughed, for that meant some little ups and downs of a few thousand feet each. Whenever Mingma told us there were big ups and downs we could confidently expect a six- or seven-thousand-foot mountainside at the very least.

The porters were eager to leave camp early to avoid the heat of the day so we departed when the valley was still shaded and misty. As we walked briskly in the cool morning air, Ed told us about the perfect camp site we could expect that night. It was a grassy river flat sheltered by a grove of beautiful trees and they had camped there during his 1968 jet-boat expedition. The mental picture of this haven of refuge spurred us on during the hottest part of the day.

The steep sides of the valley closed in to force the river into another gorge—not at all suitable for rafting—but to compensate we passed through a number of prosperous and interesting villages. Each village followed a similar pattern. On either side of the main path were two- and three-storeyed houses with small shops in the front of them. Wide-eyed children shivered in their thin cotton shawls and rushed about trying to see all of us. Their parents stared down from the safety of their upstairs windows. In the centre of each village there was always an old gnarled tree with stone walls for resting heavy loads. Here Mingma would inspect the village chickens and bargain enthusiastically for them. Later in the morning we passed some schoolhouses filled with chanting children.

As we were inspecting one of the schoolhouses we were joined by a well-dressed traveller with whom we chatted for some time. During a gap in the conversation he noticed that Roderick had a packet of English ciagrettes.

"What kind are they?" he asked Roderick and then continued, "I am very interested in cigarettes, I would like to do some testing for you." This was a surprisingly resourceful method of asking for a cigarette and a somewhat overwhelmed Roderick duly gave him one.

The valley had widened considerably and the sun was now beating down from a clear sky. Ed chose a lonely beach to reassemble the raft and as if by magic another excited crowd gathered. Just below the launching place was some rough water that looked ideal for photographs. I scrambled along the rocky shore to find a good vantage point and stumbled over the skeleton of a small child, half buried in the sand. It was a grim reminder of the dangers to be found on a great river. I turned my back very firmly on the sad sight and tried to concentrate on preparing the camera for my pictures. Yells of joy from the river heralded the approach of the raft which swept drunkenly into view. I clicked furiously as the boys bumped from wave to wave. Months later the results of my photography proved very out of focus and I shall never know if it was the skeleton behind me or the thought of my first-born being swept relentlessly down the torrent that put me off my aim.

Our track and the Sun Kosi parted for a while after this and it grew uncomfortably hot as we toiled up a dry side valley. We thought enviously of the two floaters reclining on their raft. Ed and some of the Sherpas rushed ahead to get a view of the boys as they rounded the next corner, but Sarah, Belinda and I walked more slowly. We were interested in a field of sugarcane which the owners were busy cutting and processing. They had a simple sugar press turned by a water buffalo and next to it were great cauldrons of syrup boiling over hot fires. It was fascinating to watch, and I was just wondering if we could buy a little hunk of the brown sugar when—bang!—there was a most terrifying explosion close at hand. We nearly collapsed with fright and our reaction made the people roar with laughter as though it was the funniest happening they had seen for years.

"What was it?" I said in bewilderment to Siku who had suddenly appeared just as he was needed.

"I don't know," he said, "but not a gun."

We noticed a group of people bent intently over something which I thought must have been associated with the bang. To escape yet another explosion we climbed rapidly up the hill with the laughter of our tormentors ringing in our ears. We were safely out of range before the next resounding bang filled the valley. We never did find out what had made the noise.

The land became poorer and more eroded. We were surrounded by hot, red, bleached-out earth and there were great mounds of eroded red gravel with a few miserable patches of scrub clinging to them. The land was so cut up by the action of water that it was like crossing a glacier with huge crevasses and séracs. This strange red serrated world made the temperature soar and we felt unbearably hot. The Sherpas wear their heavy mountain clothing at all times and they were particularly uncomfortable. I decided to share out the last two small oranges that I had hidden in the depths of my pack. The cool sweetness of the oranges was like nectar on our parched throats and even Mingma, a strong man, was only too happy to be offered a small portion. The countryside seemed quite dead as if no amount of scientific knowledge could bring it back to life again. In the past there had been small terraced fields, but now only the vague outlines of these remained like bleached skeletons on a sandy desert.

We reached a high promontory with a good view of the river and waited to see the raft when it came around the next corner. It was half an hour before it slowly floated into view and stopped beside a crowd of people who must have come from the small settlements along the river flats. We discovered later that the boys had decided to stop and get advice about the next portion of the river. It seemed a long time before the raft set off again and we wondered if they would ever reach camp that night. The next rapids were fenced in by a line of fish traps and as the raft approached them a man rushed wildly into the river to try and make them change direction, but the current pulled them strongly into a narrow side channel so averting disaster—no doubt much to the relief of the fish-trap owner.

The next obstacle was a steep and violent rapid, almost a small waterfall. Ed muttered that they shouldn't try and ride down that, and great was our relief when they beached their craft and portaged it around the shore.

We moved on after our long rest and bumped and thudded our way down a steep track to the slippery boulder-strewn edge of the river. It was difficult going, made more difficult by a herd of a hundred goats and two horses making their way up it in the opposite direction. The goats were no respecters of persons and pushed us onto precarious footholds unpleasantly close to the cold river.

We could now see Ed's favourite camp site across the river.

"It looks a bit brown and bleak to me," I remarked. His response was very grumpy and gave me to understand that things had changed a lot since he was there last. There was quite a queue of travellers waiting for the local dugout ferry so we had to sit down and wait our turn.

"Where are Sarah and Belinda?" I asked, "I haven't seen them for quite some time." Apparently they had gone on ahead, I was told, with Nawang and Ang Passang so I didn't worry about them any more. It always amazed me how all members of our party found their way to camp despite the many and confusing paths along the way.

The canoe was unusually long and narrow, and it was impossible for big westerners like us to sit down inside the boat or for the porters to cram their awkward loads into a safe position. As a result the canoe lurched terrifyingly as it was caught in the grip of the current. I was glad to reach the other side although our boat-men seemed very calm and confident. The missing members of our party had now appeared and were waiting their turn to cross. We sadly surveyed the camp site which was a scene of sandy desolation after severe flooding during the previous monsoon.

"Couldn't we go somewhere else?" I asked Ed.

"Where?" he enquired, and I had to agree there was nowhere else to go—we were cut off by a wide side river and there were steep cliffs behind us. We took advantage of the heaps of dead thorn bushes and made a great bonfire and soon we felt warm and comfortable in our rather draughty new home.

I watched in admiration as Ang Passang set to work over his small cooking fire and made a stew of potatoes, onions and two pounds of canned beef—enough for fifteen of us. Next on the menu was a large fruit cake as a birthday present for Peter. He creamed the shortening and sugar in the normal way and added flour, eggs, baking powder and some of our precious dried fruit that I had brought from home. The mixture was then put in a small greased *decchi* (cooking pot). While this was being done his largest *decchi* with an inch-deep layer of sand in the bottom was being heated over the fire. When the sand was very hot he put the small *decchi* inside the big one, put on the lid, and heaped a pile of coals on top of it all. In less than an hour the cake was baked to perfection.

Ang Passang also started making fresh bread for us nearly every night. He used dried yeast which he activated by adding it to warm water, sugar and flour and then mixed it into the dough which was kneaded by one of the kitchen boys with such energy that this mild domestic chore turned into something closely resembling a boxing match. There can never have been such a well-cared-for group of trekkers in the Himalayas before.

The trekking life is a very healthy one and consists mostly of hard exercise, sleep, and wonderful scenery. Usually at some stage of the day you wonder if you have the power to take another breath or the energy to make one more tottering step. To compensate for this there is the absolute relaxation when your day's walk is finished. There are no telephones, no appointments to be kept, no social life, no television —nothing to do but fix the blisters on your feet, mend a sock, sit and talk and dream, and eventually struggle into the warmth of a soft sleeping bag. After about a week of this type of life you learn the new and priceless art of being able to sit and do nothing—just looking at the view or watching the sparks flying out of an evening fire.

Within an hour and a half of our arrival at Ed's "favourite" camp site we were sitting down to a delicious dinner with a dessert of hot fruit cake decorated with slightly melted birthday candles which, because of the wind, were quite impossible to light. The long hot day had made us all tired and everyone disappeared early into their tents. I decided to finish my coffee beside the few remaining coals of our thorn bush fire. I had no sooner made myself comfortable than Pember Tenzing appeared with a large *decchi* lid and proceeded to scoop up all the coals.

"What are you doing?" I asked horrified.

"Ang Passang is making bread."

There was nothing left for me to do but to crawl into my tent and go to sleep.

The village of Salu Banjung.

An old Gypsoa house.

Ed at work on Gypsoa school.

CHAPTER 4

High and Dry

THERE WAS A new air of feverish activity and gaiety next morning as the camp was dismantled. Ed had been poring over maps and he and Mingma had decided that we should leave the hot river valley a little ahead of schedule and turn north towards the mountains. For some time now, we would be travelling through country that none of us (not even the Sherpas) had visited before. The Sherpas were all relieved to be exchanging the uncomfortable and unfamiliar humidity of the Sun Kosi for the fresh cool air of higher altitudes. For our part, air-mattress travel had lost its thrills and we were eager to climb up higher on the great ridges and get much closer to the distant snow peaks.

Ang Passang's culinary efforts surpassed our wildest dreams. For our 6 a.m. departure snack we were handed rich golden slices of lemon cake. It took two hours to move our large party across to the other side of the river and then down valley another quarter of a mile to recross it once again below the entrance of the side river.

"Very expensive," muttered Mingma, "very bad." But the rest of us forgot about the money and enjoyed our extra river crossings with their moments of panic, their giggles of alarm and the marvellous feeling of relief each time the canoe swung safely into the sandy bank.

We headed up a long steep ridge that would eventually lead us to the district centre of Ramechap. The land was harsh and eroded but was being cultivated by the farmers and it was hard to believe that the dispirited corn seedlings could ever mature into tall grain-producing plants. As we climbed higher the barren land became a little more fertile.

The day sped swiftly by as it always does when trekking. We peeped through thick cactus hedges at the tidily swept mud courtyards of farmers' houses, where families were sitting in the warm winter sun drying out household grain or doing some other domestic task. Life was undoubtedly precarious here, the small pockets of arable land were being preserved by the use of contour terracing, but the greatest problem was shortage of water in the winter months and shortage of firewood.

Every so often we found small shops beside the path and were intrigued with their stocks of cigarettes, packets of biscuits, candy, thread, decorated hair clips and other small items. Their interior walls were covered with pages out of glossy Chinese magazines and we found ourselves surrounded by the smiling faces of Mao Tse-Tung and friendly cadres addressing groups of young people. We noticed that the local schools were similarly decorated and that the schoolchildren carried the magazines amongst their schoolbooks.

"Perhaps we'd better do the same thing with some of our magazines in Solu Khumbu," someone suggested. My mind immediately flashed to scenes of gorgeous mannequins modelling hot pants, or mouth-watering pictures of the latest weight-reducing diet. No, that wouldn't be very good propaganda.

As we approached the town of Ramechap the weather became cold and cloudy. For a district centre and market place, Ramechap was situated in an unusual place. Its main street straggled along the top of a narrow, dry and draughty ridge at an altitude of 7,000 feet. It must have been a miserable town to live in at any time of the year and the pinched faces of the cold inhabitants confirmed this. The street was littered with an array of faded paper and plastic rubbish which served as a reminder that market day was held here every Saturday, as it is in most parts of Nepal.

The only bright scene on this chilly ridge was the Army headquarters, manned by a dozen handsomely uniformed soldiers who were standing to attention beside a magnificent and highly polished brass cannon. We couldn't imagine what duties the soldiers could have in this quiet distant outpost.

We noticed a steel water pipe and taps in the middle of the street but Mingma was told the water was very scarce and the village supply was only turned on for one hour at three o'clock in the afternoon. It must have been nearly three o'clock then and we noticed that the two taps were surrounded by a collection of empty buckets and old cans.

"Well, that's no good for us with our large party," said Ed.

"There must be water somewhere else along the ridge," Mingma stated with confidence. Our eyes wandered up the long dry slopes and then down 4,000 feet to a wild mountain stream—it was the only visible water and quite unobtainable. It was hard to believe that Mingma's forecast would be right this time.

Ed looked with distaste at the Army headquarters, and the post office.

"Let's hurry out of here," he said, "we don't want to get mixed up with officialdom. We'll have to find a camp site with water before it gets dark." We had just left the town behind and were congratulating ourselves on escaping from the clutches of civilisation when a smiling gentleman approached us around the corner of the track. He greeted us with much enthusiasm and told us that he was an agricultural inspector from Kathmandu who had been sent to the area to advise the people on water conservation, erosion and the selection of more suitable crops for the steep leached-out land. He told us there had been a severe shortage of water here for a number of years. We felt most cheered to think that the people of the Ramechap district hadn't been forgotten in their struggle to survive.

Quite a few farmhouses lined the path, but some had been abandoned by owners who must have lost their battle against nature and the elements. Although it was clear that the ordinary grain crops were having the greatest difficulty in surviving, we noticed that beside each little white plastered home were magnificent citrus trees covered in heavy crops of golden fruit that brought bright patches of colour to the otherwise sombre scenery. No scientific pruning or fertilising had encouraged these trees to bear so prolifically; the climate and soil must have been perfect for them. We wondered if the farms could be turned into orchards specialising in such fruits as citrus, passionfruit, grapes, and guavas, but how would the products be carried to the centres of population? We bought a number of the lemons for our own use, they were big, smooth-skinned and juicy.

For an hour we walked on beyond Ramechap and we were starting to feel rather tired. Mingma had been searching on ahead and he finally appeared and announced he had discovered a camping place complete with water supply.

"What's the water like, Mingma?" said Ed.

"It's a well, not far away. Come and have a look." So we all marched over for an inspection. It looked an unhealthy place to me, with a small amount of dark cloudy water surrounded by slime-covered bricks. The fact was there was nowhere else to go, so this would have to do.

We pitched our tents beside an old derelict schoolhouse and in no time Ang Passang and Ang Tsering had tossed out the rubbish from previous travellers, built a cooking fire and handed us a cup of hot lemon tea and another slice of lemon cake. We were soon feeling most contented with our lot. During the rest of the afternoon the inhabitants of the area filed past our tents in a long line.

"Perhaps we could charge them ten *paisa* a look and give the proceeds to Kunde hospital," suggested Roderick.

We were early out of bed into a cold damp morning. A mug of tea

gave us the strength to continue up the path and for five minutes we
floated effortlessly along. Then the higher altitude started to have its
effect and a lethargic feeling crept into our limbs to be banished only
after half an hour's firm rhythmic walking.

"We should find good oranges to-day," announced Mingma. "I will
buy a big basketful for the children."

"What about me?" I enquired.

"Oh yes, for you too," he replied rather disapprovingly. Mingma is
well aware that pampered sea-level people need plenty of fruit, eggs
and chicken to keep them walking happily. But he had long ago decided
that Ed and I were quite old and tough enough to manage without
them.

We stopped for our morning meal in a saddle on the crest of a ridge.
Many of the valleys below us were filled with mist and we seemed to
be floating on top of the world. After the lack of water the night
before, Sarah was feeling the need for a wash and she hurried over
towards a small nearby stream—and slid flat on her back into an irrigation ditch, covering herself and all her spare clothes and towel with
mud. Luckily it was a fine sunny day, so she was able to wash herself
and her clothes and get everything dry again.

While we were waiting for Sarah, a woman brought two bottles of
black liquid to show to the Sherpas.

"What is it?" I asked Ang Passang.

"It's a sort of Nepalese vinegar," he said. "It's lemon juice that has
been boiled so that it will keep. We use it for pickles and with shredded
turnip salad." I tried a little of the liquid and found it excessively bitter,
but it definitely had a fresh taste that would have possibilities when
mixed with a raw vegetable and eaten with hot curry.

"Wait till we get to Kunde and I will show you," he said. The
Sherpas thought it a fine brew and bought many bottles to take home
to their families.

One of the joys of Himalayan trekking is the variety of new and
interesting things you find around every corner. During the day the
countryside became a little richer and we passed a handsome old farmhouse with neat stone-paved courtyard encircled by high whitewashed
walls and a magnificent orchard of yellow and gold citrus fruit. Our
mouths started to water with anticipation as we were sure we would
be able to buy some. The owner was standing at the gate but before
we had time to speak he was offering to give us some of his oranges and
lemons. We sat down on his steps and started to cut up some of the
oranges but he didn't approve of our amateurish efforts. He got out his
own little knife and peeled an orange very skilfully by splitting the

skin down the sides like petals from a flower, and then very graciously presented it to us.

"May we buy some more of your fruit?" I asked.

"No," he said. "Please take these." And offered us a generous pile. "I don't sell my fruit. I just give it away." We talked to him a little longer and discovered that he was a prosperous Brahman farmer who enjoyed talking to travellers and giving them fruit.

Soon after this we came to the small town of Salu Banjung where Sarah and Belinda were waiting for us. They were full of embarrassment about their recent adventures for they had passed the Brahman's house and he had come out to welcome them. "*Basnus, Basnus,*" (Please sit down, please sit down,) he had said. But as they couldn't understand him they had tried to say in Nepali "We speak no Nepali," but instead of that they had said, "Nepali *kukur chaina*." (I have no Nepalese dog.) After this hopeless lack of communication, they decided to concentrate a little harder on learning their Nepali vocabulary.

Salu Banjung was a very pretty village with a group of thirty beautifully kept houses decorated with bright window-boxes of colourful flowers. The houses were quite large and freshly whitewashed with clean pavements and shops full of interesting merchandise. The porters had a wonderful time stocking up on food and clothing here. They said the prices were very good and many of them bought cloth and presents to take home with them. We watched over their shoulders as they haggled and gossiped with the shopkeepers amidst much laughter. After about an hour Mingma became a little restless and told Aila to make them move on.

"*Loh, loh,*" (Let's go, let's go,) said the gentle but formidable Aila, the Phortse farmer, and soon we were marching out of the town.

We were still short of oranges and we noticed a heavily laden tree about five hundred feet below the track. In true Sherpa style Mingma called in reverberating tones that he wanted to buy some and enquired about the price.

"Come down and find out if you want them," came back the cheeky reply. I assured Mingma that the oranges weren't important enough to warrant a trip that far down the hill, but he just smiled and departed with Siku. It was two hours before they caught up to us again, for their packs were so heavily laden with oranges that it dampened even their tremendous vigour. We never actually saw all the oranges in one pile, they were issued out to us meticulously each morning before we started walking, two each per person. No wonder we called Mingma the "boss"—Ed was just the "leader".

Like ants moving along the limb of a tree we toiled over the high ridges enjoying our bird's-eye view of Nepal—terraced fields, bare and brown, but patched here and there with the pale green of winter growth; clusters of white and terracotta houses; heavily laden citrus trees making a splash of gold across the landscape; dark pine forests in the steep side-valleys; and far below the wild stony riverbeds. To the north another series of ridges stretched up into the hazy dust-laden air of winter. The haze was caused by the very dry winter climate and would last until the first rains of spring. The paths become rivers of fine choking dust and it never pays to travel downhill behind a large group of people. I've tried everything from putting a scarf over my face to "zigging" when other people are "zagging"—but all to no avail. As a constant background to our travel there were the sounds of a Himalayan community at work—the chattering of women, the laughter and cries of children and the harsh instructions of a farmer driving his cattle-drawn plough.

We climbed up and over for many hours and to entertain us on our way we practised Nepali numbers with the help of a horde of different teachers, all with varying pronunciations. Finally the younger pupils decided they had received more than enough education from their many teachers. "Aila, how do you say 'Shut up' in Nepali?" they asked.

"*Chupa lagnus*," he told them.

"O.K.—*Chupa lagnus! Chupa lagnus!*" they said to their grinning instructors who roared with laughter.

Passang, the cook's assistant, was a gentle soul and it had been his task all through the day to carry a clucking chicken that was destined for the pot that night. It was very hot and Passang's basketful of kitchen pots and pans must have been very heavy. He had been holding the squawking bird in his hands for some hours but finally even his patience failed. When he thought no one was looking he took his load off his back and started to stuff the complaining bird into the kettle. The poor thing looked like some new type of Easter egg with its head sticking out the top, but in the interests of good housekeeping the meticulous Ang Tsering very firmly told him to remove it from the kettle.

We were starting to tire now. We had been descending a long and dusty hill for quite a long time and came to a small meadow shaded by a huge spreading tree. Just beside it was a shop and teahouse with bunches of ripe bananas hanging outside. We decided to stop and buy ourselves a glass of tea, and stretched out on the grass and stared peacefully up through the whispering leaves. While we drank our sweet milky tea, a very irate lady was trying to control her stubborn buffaloes just in front of us. When a young man appeared on the scene she hurled a torrent of curses at him in her strident voice. He was understandably cowed and immediately started to help her with the animals. All our Sherpas laughed loudly.

"What did she say?" I asked Passang Tendi.

"Oh, she's just angry," was the guarded reply, for in the hill country the phrases used in anger are frequently earthy in the extreme.

A thousand dusty feet below the teahouse was a pleasant stream with two small dry paddy fields for the tents. It was an ideal place to camp. There were irrigation channels flowing with water on either side of us and we hoped that no one would carelessly switch the water onto our terraces during the night. It was still only half-past two and we had a glorious free afternoon ahead of us. What joy! With miraculous speed Ang Passang produced a cup of tea and a slice of his latest culinary masterpiece, a Madeira cake. We unpacked our kitbags and sorted out our gear. I wandered down to the stream where a busy washing session was taking place. It was quite difficult to find a washing place that wasn't directly below somebody else's sock-water. Some of the girl porters were washing their hair until they were ambushed by the men and soon a wild water fight commenced with much noise and enjoyment. I hastily retreated to the safety of our paddy field.

I relaxed on the terrace and watched the world go by. This was the main road and a wide variety of people were going up and down. Pember Tenzing and Passang were collecting dead wood from a tall tree beside the camp, swinging through the branches in Tarzan style. Woe betide anyone who walked below when the dead branches came down. The girls did some sketching and the boys went off to explore while Ed slept blissfully inside the tent. I offered to teach Ang Passang a new recipe for a simple dessert that he couldn't possibly have learnt at the British Embassy. It was dumplings cooked in a sauce of lemon, sugar, golden syrup and water. This new dish, I thought, would be a welcome addition to the menus of Himalayan trekking parties. I'm not clever at explaining recipes and the dumplings turned out like yellow bullets in a sticky paste. Everyone complained of stomach ache after dinner and I tried very hard to cheer up the crestfallen Ang Passang by assuring him that it was all my fault.

That night the still mountain air of our remote valley was not conducive to a good night's sleep. The sounds of the camp were magnified to a maddening degree and the moon spread a weird and brilliant light over the countryside. The girls awoke every half-hour or so to look at their watches and reassure themselves that it wasn't yet time to get up. Every time they moved I could hear the hated glass bangles. Then at

2.30 a.m. there were sounds of a fire being made and a pot going on. I was not at all ready for a new day and I hoped it was all a bad dream. Then there were a few gruff remarks from Mingma and all the kitchen noises subsided at once.

When morning genuinely came no one felt very strong and it took a while before sluggish limbs and uneasy stomachs were forgotten. We tramped briskly over a small pass and down to the swift Liku Khola river and the large town of Sangutar. The townspeople were hardly awake on this cold morning but it was amazing how quickly the fronts of the shops opened in readiness for our invasion. It was quite a thriving town complete with large police station, post office, hospital and a high school built of brick in a rather opulent Victorian style. Most of the people here were of the Newari tribe who are well known for being good businessmen and fine craftsmen. The only people to be seen on the streets were a few children on their way to fetch their family's daily supply of milk. To protect themselves from the bitingly cold air they were wrapped so thoroughly in their large cotton shawls that only their eyes and one hand holding the can of milk were visible. Our porters commenced haggling over *pattis* (1 *patti* is equal to 8 lbs.) of rice, bottles of oil and a few spices, and the rest of us admired the local Nepali cloth available in all the shops. The off-white coarse cotton weave was hand-printed in simple floral designs, usually in a maroon colour. At the end of an entertaining hour our large party straggled out of the town well satisfied with our purchases. We had bought two four-yard lengths of cloth for eleven rupees each and our porters were now supplied with enough food for three more days. The iron chain suspension bridge over the Liku Khola was labelled "Made in Scotland 1936" and still looked solid and reliable after all these years.

A thousand feet later and high above the river was the popular resting place "Kuwa Pani" (Nepali for water hole). We joined quite a number of other travellers beside the clear bubbling spring to have our morning meal. Four of our new companions turned out to be a family of young students aged between ten and sixteen years who were walking back from their boarding school in Kathmandu to their home in Solu for the winter vacation. I couldn't help comparing their simple mode of travel with the complicated transport procedures of pupils in more developed countries. They carried their few possessions on their backs and were revelling in the freedom of the mountains after their months of school life.

For hours we continued on upwards winding our way across steep, terraced hillsides. It wasn't an ideal place for an attack of dysentery but now Peter was well and truly in its grip. Our path was cruelly steep and we experienced the sort of physical tiredness that makes you feel as if your body is a lump of lead and every footstep a conscious effort. Peter propelled himself upward by munching on a large stick of sugarcane and we copied him because it helped alleviate the unpleasant rough dryness of our mouths caused by so much puffing. Periodically Peter would make a desperate dash for the nearest clump of trees.

All the while we were accompanied by a garrulous porter who teased us about our bad Nepali language. Despite his heavy load he was never short of breath for talking and he was clearly amused by our use of the words "*ramro*" (good) and "*naramro*" (bad) which we repeated far too often to cover our lack of vocabulary.

"*Khana ramro cha* (the food is good), Nepali *bato ramro cha* (Nepalese paths are good)," he chanted over and over again, very successfully mimicking our awful conversation. Every now and then he would roar with laughter at his wit and bound even more energetically up the mountainside. We decided to name him "Ramro Bato".

Towards the end of the day we came to the foot of a great bare rock ridge bathed in the hot afternoon sunshine. "We can't be going up there," we chorused incredulously, for high up the ridge narrowed alarmingly and behind was the rocky face of a mountain peak.

"Up going, Sherpa village finding," said Mingma with obvious pleasure. So up we went, in many places scrambling along a very narrow trail. During one of our spasmodic rests a great Lammergeyer floated across the ridge only twenty feet above us. We felt small and land-bound in the presence of such a supreme master of his environment. With his wing span of at least eight feet he hovered motionlessly on an air current and surveyed us poor gasping mortals below.

Camp was at 8,000 feet on a flat ledge of land covered in thick scrub. We were 6,000 feet above the town of Sangutar and the Liku Khola river—and a mighty climb it had proved to be. It was decidedly chilly in our mountain eyrie but the air was fresh and clear. A ceiling of clouds hung over the ridge like a great canopy and the setting sun sent shafts of gold and red light onto our camp and its surroundings as if some weird spotlight was beaming down onto us from out of space. We sipped hot lemon drinks beside a glowing fire and listened contentedly to the busy camping noises of our companions.

Suddenly there was a commotion near the kitchen department. One of our chickens with its legs firmly tied together had somehow or other escaped and was now rolling noisily down the mountainside.

"We'll have to change the menu a bit," said Ed lugubriously. But no worthwhile Sherpa was prepared to lose a chicken as easily as that, and before long half-a-dozen men were hurtling downwards after it.

An hour later they returned, triumphant, with the now lifeless bundle of feathers that was soon despatched into our cooking pot.

Our porters were completely at home in this environment. They made themselves very comfortable by cutting small nest-like clearings in the scrub. They sat on soft mattresses of springy brush and cooked their evening meals over generous fires—gossiping and laughing most jovially. At "Ramro Bato's" camp fire the laughter was quite uproarious as he entertained his friends with never-ending renditions of foreigners' Nepali. Yes, all of us were very content and life was good.

CHAPTER 5

"Full many a glorious morning have I seen
Flatter the mountain tops with sovereign eye."
                    Shakespeare, Sonnet XXXIII

THERE WAS A definite change in our senior Sherpas next morning for
they had returned to their familiar environment of cold high mountains, and there was a new twinkle in their eyes and a new sense of
purpose in their actions. Ang Tsering and Passang Tendi had put on
smart woollen climbing clothes and looked extra determined as they
advanced towards the girls' tent to pack it up for the day's march.
Passang Tendi and Siku were both carrying ice-axes in anticipation of
ice on the track which could be very treacherous for heavily laden
porters. The terraced hillsides still sleeping far below us seemed now to
be a different world.

We climbed up the narrow track above the camp and traversed
around the side of our steep rocky spur to find an endless forested
ridge stretching out ahead of us with many subsidiary ridges leading
down from it. The weather had been brilliantly clear but now we
entered cold damp cloud as we made our way through tall rhododendrons and pine trees. It was incredibly quiet and still and the air was
scented with starry pink daphne blossoms. There was a rugged wild-
ness about the scenery and we scrambled for half a mile across huge
piles of rock and rubble that had slid off the face of the mountain above
us. The Sherpas warned us that this area had a bad reputation for
attacks by the Himalayan black bear so we kept close together.

Quite suddenly we reached an open glade with a Buddhist *chorten*
standing in the middle of it—we were on the outskirts of one of the
remote Sherpa communities that we knew must be here. The *chorten* (or
stupa) was a tall conical stone structure and beside it there was a long
mani wall (prayer wall) made of large flat slabs of rock inscribed with
Buddhist prayers. It is the custom in this area to keep all religious struc-
tures on your right, and this we did most conscientiously. After a while
we came to large areas of alpine meadowland and could see scattered
groups of whitewashed and slate-roofed Sherpa houses. The high
meadows provided good grazing for herds of zums which are a cross
between the tough hairy Himalayan female yak and the Indian cow.

They have the good milk-producing qualities of the cow and have retained the toughness of the high-altitude yak. In place of narrow terraced fields of grain there were wide tracts of arable land on which the people grew potatoes—the staple food of the Sherpas.

We must have walked sixteen miles that day at altitudes between eight and nine thousand feet and I don't think I would have reached our camp if Siku hadn't walked stubbornly behind me—thud—thud—thud—so that I was compelled to keep going. We crossed high passes; zigzagged through dense forest; and grimly plodded along narrow ridges. In the end we reached the isolated Sherpa village of Zuplung Banjung and I was vastly relieved when Ed gave the word to stop.

The inhabitants of Zuplung Banjung were very surprised to have visitors, for we were now more than a day's journey from any well-used mountain route—and I don't think they'd ever had Europeans there before. The village was made up of a scattered group of houses on a windy pass (Banjung means pass) at an altitude of 9,000 feet, and although the people spoke the Sherpa language it was a slightly different dialect from that of the Solu Khumbu Sherpas.

Our porters were noticing the effects of two long hard days and were very late to arrive with our camping gear. We inspected the shaky wooden travellers' shelter which Ang Passang had commandeered for the cook's headquarters hoping we could warm ourselves at his fire. He was still methodically preparing the fireplace. First he dug three small holes in the ground with his *kukri* and then placed in them some evenly sized stones to make a firm pot stand. After much work he completed a three-burner fireplace and then started his fire and put on the water for tea. Such cooking fires are amazingly efficient and use very little firewood. Most foreigners soon realise that the Sherpas are very expert at cooking on an open fire and wisely leave the work to them. There was no need to conserve firewood at Zuplung Banjung but there was a considerable shortage of water, and it took the energetic Pemba Tenzing half an hour to fetch one small bucketful. To conserve this precious commodity the six of us shared a small basin of warm water for our end of the day washing and by the time we had bathed our dust-streaked faces the water resembled strong tea. To mask the sweaty smell of our clothes we decked ourselves and our tents with sprigs of daphne blossom.

The entire population of Zuplung Banjung had gathered by this time to look us over. Clad in their traditional working clothes they seemed quite oblivious to the strong cold wind. The women wore the usual Sherpa dress of a long black tunic (*ingi*) over a blouse, while around their waists they had work-stained striped woollen aprons tied back and front for extra warmth. Some of the men wore long Sherpa coats tied at the waist and with one sleeve hanging free, but many of them were dressed in a collection of Western-style clothes. The children were not as shy as their parents and were soon sitting amongst us close beside the fire. They told us they spent the day looking after the village sheep and cattle and to our question about school facilities in the area they showed a complete lack of interest—probably they didn't know what a school was? They were very talented at controlling their animals with fiercely thrown rocks, and they all took great pride in the large *kukris* they had in their belts. Quite a few of the adults had large goitres due to lack of iodine in the diet and there were some cretinous-looking people with stunted growth, heavy features and vacant looks. But altogether they were a very friendly crowd and clearly enjoyed our presence.

The porters raced off to find the most sheltered camping places and then with a hearty disregard of fire risk built flaring conflagrations to warm themselves. Our friend "Ramro Bato" had cunningly taken the most-protected camp site for himself and his gay friends. He pulled on his shoes and squatted contentedly beside his fire. Just before dark a large herd of about sixty cattle were driven towards the village, returning to the safety of their various owners' houses for the night. Their normal pathway must have been directly across the clearing where we had our tents and fire. They stopped abruptly when they noticed us and nervously tossed their heads and stamped their feet. With their great spread of horns they were an awe-inspiring sight. We retired hastily to the far side of our fire hoping that we wouldn't be noticed. Finally a large black zum plucked up courage to charge wildly past us and the villagers cheered enthusiastically to encourage it on. With much hesitation the other animals followed, and I became quite adjusted to this nerve-racking routine. Finally only two gigantic, hairy, black yaks remained, standing on a bank above us like shadowy-horned devils about to pounce on our defenceless group. Then, with a violent snort and a toss of their horns, they plunged past us making the ground shake and the dust fly.

A sort of wind-swept peace descended on our camp. It was impossible to sit comfortably in front of our fire as the flame chased us relentlessly from place to place. We were hungry and tired and not a little scratchy so it was a great relief when our evening meal finally appeared. Most of the family went very early to bed but I warmed myself over the bed of hot coals. When Pemba Tenzing appeared with a large pot and scooped most of the fire away I knew it was my time to go to bed too.

When we woke next morning a cold mist had us in an icy grip.

Always thoughtful, Ang Tsering lit a fire so we could warm our hands and feet as we drank our tea. Some of the villagers joined us too. They told us the track continued up the ridge behind their houses and ultimately went over the top of quite a high mountain. There was even some talk of us helping with a school, but nobody seemed quite clear on what they wanted. The fire was so pleasant that we let the porters get well ahead but once we were on our way we soon caught up to them. Weighed down by their heavy loads their pace was just too slow for us and yet it was often difficult to pass them on the narrow path or find enough space and energy to make a quick acceleration into the lead.

The children were going very well up the hill and succeeded in over-taking all the porters. Even Ed and I became competitive and with com-plaining lungs and straining muscles we made our attempt to reach the head of the line. We only succeeded with a certain amount of danger to ourselves. On one occasion I was nearly pinioned by a tentpole when a Sherpa suddenly turned around to talk to a companion. We left the tree line far behind and followed a stone staircase that zigzagged up the steep slopes. Clouds drifted away and we could see a maze of valleys far below while above us the golden grass-covered summit, now frosted white, beckoned to us tantalisingly.

It was still very early and the distant mountain peaks glowed softly red against a pale pink backdrop of clouds. The world under our feet was clothed in sparkling hoar-frost that turned every blade of grass, every shrub and rock into a treasure-chest of diamonds. Our spirits soared with the beauty of it all. We rushed on upwards forgetting tired muscles and labouring lungs. We just wanted to get there as quickly as possible and see what glories lay ahead.

And what a reward we received for our labours! The other side of the mountain was bathed in warm glowing morning light. Trails of delicate white mist wreathed the distant and sombre valley walls and the horizon was lined with scores of brilliant white Himalayan moun-tains. No conqueror of those glistening peaks could have felt any more exhilaration than we did on our humble grass-covered mountain.

For a moment everything was silent except for the faint sounds of singing from our toiling porters far below. Then the mountaineering instincts of the party came to the surface and the spell was broken.

"That's Gauri Shankar," said Ed. "I'll get out the binoculars and we can have a good look at it."

"I'm sure there's a route on the left," he said after a long and care-ful scrutiny. Gauri Shankar, 23,400 feet, is one of the highest unclimbed peaks and possibly the most challenging ascent remaining in the

Himalayas. It is thirty-six miles west of Everest and stands alone amongst lesser peaks on the border between Nepal and Tibet.

"Surely you don't want to climb that!" I said, rather weakly. The summit looked like an ugly spike and I had the feeling that any foolish mortal who tried to climb it would be crushed to death by its cruel leaning precipices. Mingma and Ed carried on quite unconcerned and spent a very happy half-hour discussing all the possible routes on Gauri Shankar. All mountaineers love these discussions, it doesn't really matter whether the mountain is climbable or not, it's just a pleasant pastime, like talking about catching the biggest fish or about scoring a winning goal.

We were loath to leave the top of our mountain but it was cold up there at 11,000 feet and Ang Passang and his helpers had been long gone to find a breakfast place. We followed down the frozen mountain pastures and 1,500 feet below we found Ang Passang in a sheltered alpine valley dotted with abandoned summer grazing huts. What a sight this place must be in the spring—there were the shrivelled remains of thousands of alpine flowers, mostly primulas and poppies, and the dark pine forest close by was bordered by azaleas and rhodo-dendron bushes. We could hear a rushing stream tumbling through the boulders out of sight amongst the trees. Some day, I resolved, we would come back when the people were in residence with their animals. Just imagine the flowers, and all that delicious cottage cheese and curds and sweet zum milk—my Western mind painted enticing pictures of gastronomic delights.

The colder and more energetic our travelling became the more we thought about food, talked about food, and organised more food to eat. I noticed on the other hand that the Sherpas' eating habits didn't change at all. They always had their two large meals a day for which they were thankful and they certainly never mentioned food at anytime. It was shamefully true that we lived to eat, while the Sherpas ate to live.

"Stop talking about food. What must the Sherpas think?" I would sometimes say to my family. But I didn't really need to worry for the Sherpas quietly accepted us for what we were and never seemed to question our strange ways.

We lay in the sun on sleeping mats, ate a large breakfast, did some washing and hung it on a briar rose bush, and wished that we could stay there for ever. We started talking about our plans for the next few weeks and then we remembered it was New Year's Eve and that it would be pleasant to have some special food to celebrate the occasion. Ed had been absent from home for about three months by now and had a strong desire to eat a large meal of meat.

"Mingma, in our country this is the day before New Year. It is a big festival at home and we must celebrate it properly. Do you think you could buy us a sheep for dinner?" Mingma frowned. He was far too thrifty and careful with Ed's money to approve of buying a tough and expensive sheep that would only be big enough to last us all one meal.

"I will see what I can find," he said non-committally.

"Also, how about a little *arak* or *chung*?" Ed continued. *Arak* is the local spirit made from distilled fermented potatoes or Jerusalem arti-choke tubers, and *chung* is a national beer drink made from fermented grain and generally fairly innocuous. For the rest of the day Ed was so busy searching the countryside for these luxuries that every goat looked to him like a sheep and every traveller's load seemed to be crammed with bottles of *arak*. Mingma gamely followed up all these sightings without success and it seemed a singularly protein-lacking and abstemious community. Late in the afternoon we heard the cluck-ing of captive chickens and Pemba Tenzing passed us on the path with several of them tucked under his arms.

"Oh well," said Ed, "it was worth a try. At least Mingma has been a little more generous and bought us three chickens instead of the usual two."

We had lost a lot of height by now and were coming into a valley inhabited by Rais—industrious Hindu mountain farmers. The valley was quite heavily forested in places and, we were informed, was famous for its paper-making. We were told that many of the scattered houses had flourishing cottage industries and we were most interested to see how the paper was made. Unfortunately the paper-making had ceased during the cold winter months but Ang Tsering explained to us the procedure that was used.

The main ingredient was bark off the yellow daphne bush which grows in great profusion in many parts of Nepal. The bark is cut up and boiled for quite a long time until most of the fibres and flesh are broken down into a thin soupy mixture. This is then poured onto flat cloth trays and placed in the hot sunshine to dry out into paper. The finished paper is a very attractive oatmeal shade, and is a little bit coarser than rice paper and very strong indeed. I use it as gift wrapping paper, and for wallpaper and lampshades.

Our New Year's Eve celebrations took place at the low and warm altitude of 6,000 feet in a deep gorge beside a very noisy mountain river. It was a dusty and stony corner with nettles growing in profusion and a few small pockets of arable land farmed by rather miserable-looking people. Their houses were in disrepair and it was definitely

From our camp at Nourr on the way up Mt. Pike. Two *chortens* in the foreground.

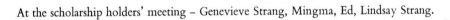

At the scholarship holders' meeting – Genevieve Strang, Mingma, Ed, Lindsay Strang.

Kunde hospital.

Building a new courtyard for Thami *gompa*.

one of the most dejected areas that we had seen so far. When I had asked why this should be, I was told that the people were mainly tenant farmers who worked for the more prosperous Sherpas living on the ridges above. To me it seemed decidedly feudal and the tenant farmers were clearly underprivileged. Later I had the chance to talk to the Sherpa owners and they commented that their tenants were "lazy"—a common reaction by the "haves" in our own communities towards the "have-nots". However that night there was nothing we could do to raise the standard of living of these depressed people. We could only hope that some of their children might be able to attend the new Gypsoa school up on the hill.

"Let's have roast chicken and roast potatoes tonight," I suggested to Ang Passang. Two hours later he arrived beside our fire, proudly bearing a *decchi* containing two golden chickens surrounded by roast potatoes in a sea of rich brown gravy. It looked delicious.

"What about the *arak* and *chung*?" I asked him.

"We haven't found anything yet," he replied. But a little later Pemba Tenzing appeared with a tray of empty mugs.

"Ah, that's more like it," said Ed with pleasure. Ang Passang handed me a well-filled teapot and I started to pour. It was water, and everybody had a good laugh.

We all felt a little tired after our eight days of energetic and continuous trekking and Sarah and Belinda were unusually quiet and restrained. Mingma noticed this and told them that next morning they must on no account get up and start packing until the tea had been brought around. Ed assured them that Ang Tsering and Passang Tendi had been ordered not to pull the tent down until they were sure there was no one inside it—and only then would they agree to rest a bit longer.

Our preparations for bed were punctuated by cries of pain as we stumbled amongst the rocks and nettles. Our flashlight batteries seemed to have gone flat all at once, just on the night when we really needed them. Most mornings we would take the precaution of reversing the batteries of our torches so they wouldn't switch on inside our packs, but sometimes in the confusion of an early departure it was very easy to forget to do this.

Finally we were all safely in bed, determined to have a good rest for we had a very steep climb ahead of us in the morning. The tumultuous roar of the river filled our ears and we were sure we would never sleep—but gradually the talking quietened and all of us dropped off to sleep.

E

CHAPTER 6

Gypsoa School

THE CLIMB OUT of the precipitous gorge was certainly exciting enough for anyone. The first few hundred feet was easy enough until we reached a small level area with a lonely house and a number of cows tied up outside. As we walked past, two huge mastiffs hurled themselves towards us. We stood helpless not knowing where to turn until the Sherpas averted disaster with some well-aimed stones. After this encounter we kept in a tight little group. For the next thousand feet our way was along a very narrow exposed stone stairway clinging to the cliffs and with many difficult, and indeed dangerous, corners. I was very glad not to be a porter with a cumbersome load on my back to push my body away from the comforts of the few handholds available. Ed later told me that he had considered getting out a climbing rope for this particular section.

The track then levelled out and became less of a rock-climbing adventure and we slogged up through a wide grazing area which must have been, long ago, a fine forest. The few remaining trees were being regularly harvested for their crops of leaves and they looked like dreary skeletons, their mis-shapen limbs silhouetted against the blue sky. We reached the lowest terraces of the village of Gypsoa and for five hundred or more feet we climbed up through them—first past simple houses covered by bamboo mats and finally up to the substantial establishments of the well-to-do. It was an exciting moment when the new Gypsoa school came into view with its shining aluminium roof and handsome rock walls. I had been involved in the initial stages of the Gypsoa school when a petition was brought to Ed by the hand of Pooli, a Gypsoa girl who had married a Kunde man. In response to this petition Mingma, Ed and I had visited the village in 1970.

That first visit had been in the spring. We had approached the village from the north-east on our way back to Kathmandu from the Khumbu. This had entailed a high traverse across the side of Mount Piké (13,337 feet) which is claimed by the few people to have been on top to be one of the finest viewpoints in the Himalayas. For most of our journey we had been enveloped in thick cloud and we saw little of the mountains but at least our path was edged with a fairyland of rhododendron trees draped in delicate mauve and yellow flowers, and at our feet amongst the damp stones and the moss were starry patches of pale yellow and pink primula. The complete isolation and stillness of the area was rather terrifying and I, for one, was most relieved to meet another traveller on the path who was more familiar with the route. We discovered he was from Gypsoa and we told him that in Kunde, Pooli had told us to contact her brother Tendi. Our new acquaintance most kindly offered to go ahead and warn Tendi of our approach.

The rhododendron forest changed to tall shadowy fir trees and we hurried on through the mysterious gloom, winding amongst the great tree trunks. Suddenly there was a violent thunder clap followed by torrential rain. Our umbrellas were almost useless protection against such a downpour.

"There's a *gompa* (temple) somewhere on this route," Mingma called. "Let's hurry." We scattered down the hill in disarray and to our relief found a small group of buildings with a dilapidated *gompa* in its centre. Mingma led us inside a small house where we found a room crowded with other fugitives from the storm. There was a small fire in the centre of the floor but as we were the last to arrive we had to sit shivering and wet against the wall. The first two travellers to reach shelter were already making some tea. They were tax collectors, rather thin and miserable-looking men with expressionless faces most suitable to their calling. When they had finished with the fire we cooked some rice and thin soup which helped to warm us up while the rain continued to drum on the rickety wooden roof. Another fellow traveller was eating popcorn which she kept inside the front of her tunic and she smilingly offered the corn to all of us in her grimy work-worn hands, and very good it tasted, too. All the time we were continually dodging drips of water from the roof and chickens and puppies were scurrying amongst our feet. The owners of the house were squeezed into the far corner of the room, from where they quietly observed their unexpected visitors with resigned patience. The name of this isolated place, we discovered, was Nourr and as soon as the rain stopped we were only too happy to depart from it.

Our track was now a rushing stream and we ran hectically down the mountain between trees whose trunks were garlanded with exquisite pink and white orchids. I collected some of the plants and carried them all the way back home where they are still surviving in my garden.

The storm had cleared the air and now below us through the trees we could see sunbathed terraced ridges and the twin villages of Gola and Gypsoa. We hoped that Tendi would have us to stay and went straight to his house which we discovered to our dismay was the newest and smartest residence in the village with bright windowboxes and verandahs. We felt rough and dirty and very much the country cousins, but Tendi and his wife and two children were most welcoming and led us to a fine sunny room covered in bright woollen Sherpa carpets. Soon we were drinking glasses of tea and finding out more about our hosts. Tendi had been manager of the Piké cheese factory for about four years. This had been established as part of a Swiss aid programme and the vast areas of good grazing land on Piké and its subsidiary ridges had proved ideal for a dairy industry. It was now an entirely Nepalese venture and most successful.

Tendi told us that he was keenly interested in education for his children and had already sent his elder child to school at Khumjung where she lived with his sister, Pooli.

"We are hoping very much that you will help us with a new school here," said Tendi to Ed. "Our existing school is in very bad condition and we have great trouble in keeping suitable teachers as a result. We have no teacher at present."

"Let's have a look at it," said Ed.

So off we went through the village to a lonely terrace above a deep yawning valley where we found the old school building. It had a rough shingle roof, small windows and an uneven mud floor. The sparse and ramshackle school furniture sat drunkenly on the bumpy ground.

"The school is damp and dark and the children don't like coming in the monsoon," said one of the school committee who had joined us.

"There are about three hundred families in the area who need a school for their children. The Sherpa families of this village and many Rai and Chetri (the Hindu warrior caste) families living below here will be very happy to help build a new school," said the head man.

Without realising it the head man helped his cause a great deal by mentioning co-operation between Sherpa and other tribes. Many of the mountain tribes of Nepal are separated by topography, religion, and local customs and it was good to hear that at Gypsoa the different groups were quite happy to work together. While we waited for Ed to make a decision our eyes were drawn to the dramatic contrast in the great canyon below us. At the bottom of the canyon night had virtually come, but up here on the ridge the light was only just

fading as the sun sank farther and farther behind the opposite mountain ridge.

"Well ... yes," said Ed after he had pondered for an unbearably
long time. "I think I might be able to find some money to help you
with your school but I think you'll have to abandon this present
building." He explained that it would be easier and cheaper to con-
struct a new school, that it would certainly be better in the centre of
the village so it could be a focal point for the people's lives, and then
they could look after it properly and be proud of it. We all agreed
that there was a need to improve the educational facilities in Gypsoa
and although the village received a standard Government grant towards its education, it wasn't enough even to pay half a teacher's
salary, let alone cover the cost of a new school. Given time, no doubt,
the Nepal Government will be able to make much more generous
education grants, but the people of Gypsoa wanted their new school
NOW. They were delighted at Ed's decision and to show their appreciation for this timely aid marched us all triumphantly back to the
village to receive generous and long drawn-out hospitality from the
senior families of the community.

The heart of Gypsoa is a row of eight dignified old homes just above
the main path. The rest of the village is scattered over a large area of
mountainside. These eight old houses were the stately homes of the
area and were owned by descendents of the original land owners. Most
of them had been built about a hundred years before and had been
decorated with beautifully carved door and window frames. In front
of each home was a paved courtyard protected by high stone walls and
against these grew gorgeous old-fashioned pink roses and clumps of
bright dahlias. There were also small orchards of healthy young peach
and apple trees which are part of the Government's new programme to
upgrade the standard of fruit-growing in this region.

We entered the front door of the head man's house and groped our
way up gloomy solid timber stairways to the living room which was a
handsome smoke-darkened room built of giant slabs of timber. All
the household copper and brass utensils glowed mellow in the firelight.
We, the honoured guests, sat in very formal style on a row of chairs
while the locals sat comfortably crosslegged on low benches.

After this description of gracious living you may well ask why
such a village should need to receive help with its school. The answer
is that only a few of the families in the village are wealthy and they
are not wealthy in money but in possessions like yaks and potato and
grain fields—and money is needed to buy roofing and glass and nails,
and to pay the salary of a school teacher. Many of the schools built in

the Solu area have been unsuitable in design and both teachers and children have become disheartened with the uncomfortable conditions. We have found that by providing a dry, clean, wooden floor instead of the old mud floor, a good waterproof roof instead of leaking shingles, and enough windows and skylights to make the place cheerful and bright, education becomes very much more attractive and exciting to the village children and to their parents. The parents take a pride in their school and make some effort to keep it in operation.

While we talked about plans for the school we were offered *arak* which was strong and of good flavour, followed by onion omelets and *soljar*—Tibetan tea made with salt and butter. *Soljar* always tastes like mouldy soup to me no matter how hard I try to like it.

After a while we were invited to another house where the treatment was exactly the same except that I broke ranks and went and sat on the floor beside the fire. Our host at first looked startled by my strange behaviour but then expressed pleasure that I should want to be comfortable in his home. The discussions went on and on and it was decided that a new petition must be written out immediately with as many signatures as possible in the short time available.

When we returned to Tendi's house a wonderful meal was ready for us. We summoned what little appetite we had remaining and enjoyed pieces of fried chicken with pickled beans and pickled lemons as a side dish, and then for our main course consumed bowl after bowl of *tukpa*, a noodles, vegetable and meat mixture which we had to eat with chopsticks. We realised with much pleasure that such a meal in a protein-hungry land is a sure way to let you know you are appreciated. During the meal the petition was being finished in the next room and when our dishes had been cleared away it was presented to Ed with great ceremony by about a dozen people representing the three tribal groups.

We had lost our hearts to Gypsoa—both to the people and to the village itself. But next morning we had to move on towards Kathmandu. With Tendi's father to guide us we dropped 3,000 feet to the next valley, stopping now and then to pick wild strawberries and admire the groves of scarlet rhododendron.

During the next two years a great deal of work had to be carried out before Ed could fulfil his promise to the people of Gypsoa. First of all permission had to be granted for a new school by the Nepalese government. Corrugated aluminium roofing and plastic skylights plus nails and tools were shipped all the way from New Zealand; timber was sawn in the forests above Lukla and carried to the village; great quantities of rock were broken and carried to the site of the school. One of the landowners had donated a terrace for the new school in the centre of the village in a sheltered and sunny position. This meant that even in winter at an altitude of over 9,000 feet the classrooms would be warm and comfortable.

In November 1971 Ed arrived back at Gypsoa to carry out the construction programme. Unlike the previous quiet arrival he was given a great welcome by crowds of villagers who garlanded him with flowers and *katas* (white cotton scarves that are presented in the Buddhist Himalayas rather like a *lei* in Hawaii). By the time they had finished he could hardly see over the top. As soon as the construction team could escape from the very pleasant welcoming ceremonies they set to work on the foundations of the school, laying out a building forty feet long and twenty feet wide. Traditional Sherpa methods of building were used, with no cement or mortar—basically dry rock walls with a little bit of clay for filling. Once progress was well under way Ed and his party departed for another project leaving Aila in charge to carry on and complete the walls of the building.

I enjoyed my visit to Gypsoa so much that we had planned the building of the school would be a Hillary family affair. But the war between India and Pakistan and the resulting confusion over our travel arrangements, persuaded Ed regretfully to finish the Gypsoa school without us. His diary describes the activities:

An enjoyable day with everyone working very well together. We completed the floor, put up the *kars* (upright beams) and *dungmas* (horizontal beams) and then got to work on the rafters. A lot of progress made.

Next day. At an early hour the purloins started going on and were completed by breakfast. Then the roofing commenced. I took time off to go over my finances and then built two partitions to make a three-roomed school.

5 p.m. We went down to Tendi's house for an official village dinner with much formal pouring of *chung* and *arak* by the pretty village maidens. We had *mormors* to eat (meat balls covered with dough and steamed). Then we moved *en masse* to the schoolhouse and dancing commenced. It was a very happy party. By 10 p.m. I went off to bed, and I was awakened by some of the others returning noisily at 12.30 a.m.—and still the dancing went on. Passang Tendi got to bed at 5 a.m.—quite a night.

Next day. At 11 a.m. there was the official opening of the school.

There were many speeches and I cut the red tape with much clapping and laughter—then it was all over. We had a quick lunch and said goodbye to everyone. I felt quite sad as I set off up the hill with Mingma. Our time at Gypsoa has been most happy despite the war news we hear each evening on a borrowed radio. We have been very busy and it's a glorious spot here. The only thing missing is the family. There is immense disappointment that Louise and the children aren't here.

But now the Hillary family had arrived—and quite without warning. At first no one noticed us and we managed to have a quiet look at the school on our own. It was situated in a commanding position on the edge of the deep valley and already showed signs of being an important part of the village life, with a welcome arch festooned with greenery and a well-trampled playground complete with a seesaw.

Then a group of children appeared accompanied by Tendi's father, looking dignified and handsome with his white pigtail dangling down his back. Soon Tendi and Kusang, the chairman of the school committee, came to greet us with a large wooden bottle of *chung*. After our energetic walk we were more than ready for a cool drink.

"Be careful, don't drink too much," I cautioned Belinda. "You never know how potent these brews will be, or how much they will affect you at high altitude." It was delicious Ningoo *chung*, clear and slightly fizzy. Ningoo is the first pouring off of *chung* from the fermented rice and it is always the clearest and the strongest.

"We are very pleased to drink your *chung* to-day as it is our New Year's day," I told Kusang and Tendi.

"Oh, Losah, that's very good," they replied. Losah is the Sherpa New Year which is celebrated for a week starting on the 16th January in some places, and on 16th February in others depending on the weather and the amount of work that has to be done in the fields. Everyone seemed very happy that we should have come to Gypsoa on our Losah day and they were obviously making a mental note to entertain us accordingly.

"Eat plenty of breakfast," I said to our party, "it will act as blotting paper." Sherpa hospitality is renowned for being very liquid and usually fairly alcoholic.

At Kusang's house we had a second breakfast of *arak*, tea with zum milk and *sheru* (rice cakes). "We must go soon," whispered Ed, "if we ever hope to reach our camp tonight." At the first propitious moment we stood up, said our thanks and made for the door. As we stumbled down the dark stair I asked Mingma if we would be leaving any of our porters in Gypsoa and was told that "Ramro Bato" and two of his friends would be remaining here as they lived nearby. It was probably too late to say goodbye to them and we felt very disappointed. Outside in the bright sunshine I turned to have a last glance at Kusang's lovely old house and there peeping from a high window was the grinning face of "Ramro Bato". He waved and we gave him a vociferous farewell. He looked almost sad as we walked away but I imagine his stories and mimicking are still producing gales of laughter around his camp fire.

Our grand tour of Gypsoa continued. Next stop was Tendi's father's house where we were presented with *katas* as well as the usual liquid refreshment. My *kata* was different from the others, it was an *ashi kata* made of fine silk with a traditional geometrical pattern woven into the cloth.

"Why?" I asked in great surprise for it was always Ed who got these honours. It was Kusang who answered me.

"We hope that you will be able to help your husband find a way to improve the water supply of this village." Everybody thought this was a great joke and laughed uproariously.

As we left Gypsoa, Kusang thrust into Ed's hand a big bottle of *arak* which was fresh and warm from the still. "For New Zealand Losah," he said.

Tendi and his son, Kulsang, aged six, had decided to accompany us for the remainder of the day. To fortify us he had brought a large wedge of his best Piké cheese wrapped in daphne paper. As soon as we left the houses behind the children rushed ahead with terrific speed.

"What's the hurry?" said Ed. "We have plenty of time to get to Nourr."

"Perhaps the *arak* has given them new strength," I replied. Around the next bend we found them all emerging from various bushes beside the track.

"Those bushes came just in time," we were told. "We've never had to drink such an assortment before."

We drifted up the ridge in a delightful daze feasting our eyes on the cold white snow peaks we could see to the north through a curtain of fir trees. It was hot and enervating in the afternoon sun and we felt so lethargic that at every comfortable viewpoint we collapsed on the ground, grateful for any excuse to rest. We had completely lost the will to move and we just didn't care.

"You go ahead," said Ed to Mingma, Ang Tsering and Tendi, "we're just too lazy to-day." But they were in no hurry either, so we all had another rest and Tendi brought out his cheese, and I found some oranges, and we sat and ate contentedly as the afternoon wore on.

It was only a thousand feet above us to Nourr *gompa* and our camp. Ed kept describing the beauties of the place but I found it hard to believe him. I had vivid memories of two years before when I was drenched in a heavy thunderstorm.

Mount Piké and the Falling Porter

NOURR WAS INDEED a glorious camping place. From my tent high on the ridge at 11,000 feet I looked south over two tall white conical *chortens*, a long Buddhist prayer flag, and the black outlines of fir trees, to row after row of distant hazy foothills almost down to the plains of India. To the west, long mountain ridges swept away like ocean waves until they reached the barrier of the Himalayan mountains in the far distance. More great ice-clad mountains filled the horizon to the north of us, and curved gently from west to east until the ridges of Piké blocked them from our view. Soon the golden light of afternoon changed to a pink sunset and then gradually faded into an exquisite ethereal colourlessness. The stars came out very brightly like crystals in a giant chandelier. We felt isolated and at peace with the world. No wonder the monks chose this place for their meditation and devotions.

But it was New Year's day and time for more worldly pursuits. We opened our bottle of *arak* and gathered around the fire with the Sherpas to drink a few sips from large enamel mugs. I had saved some precious cashew nuts from Kathmandu and we stood around in the freezing wind and drank to 1972. I think the combined feeling of excitement at being in such a beautiful place, plus the high altitude, made us all rather hysterically cheerful. We started singing to keep ourselves warm, and clapped and stamped in the frosty air while the porters and local inhabitants crowded round to enjoy the spectacle.

I always find that when we are in high places our spirits seem to rise accordingly. Trekking in Nepal is like a long musical composition which crescendoes to an exciting fortissimo and then fades to a soft slow interlude before the next high summit. The sense of freedom that you feel on a high ridge is also found in the rich sounds of a symphony and a composer of music would have found plenty to inspire him on the slopes of Piké.

We had only been in bed a short time and were just dropping off to sleep when Belinda appeared at the entrance to our tent.

"Mum and Dad, come out and see the view. It's fantastic!" With extreme reluctance we crawled out into the frosty air but it was worth every moment of it. The moon was shining brightly, bathing the whole

scene in its soft kindly light. We could see little patches of fog in the
valleys and on the summits we could distinguish every glacier, ridge and
peak. It was incredibly beautiful and unbelievably peaceful.

We dropped off into the sleep of healthy exhaustion and woke to a
bright frozen morning feeling brim full of energy. From our camp the
summit of Piké looked a short easy stroll and we had to keep reminding
ourselves that the view was very foreshortened. The porters, with
Siku and Aila to guide them, were going to take the lower route across
the cold, sunless traverse on the northern slopes of the mountain. Siku
would take an ice axe for cutting steps across the frozen streams in the
steep gullies.

Normally there would have been deep snow on the upper slopes of
Piké, but this year the winter had been slow in coming. Temperatures
were very cold but as yet there had been no great falls of snow. The
summit party needed their woollen caps and gloves for the icy temperatures we could expect at 13,000 feet. We almost looked like
serious mountaineers except that our light gym shoes and thin socks
spoilt the effect. We set off, full of excitement, and at first our path
was covered with hard ice and crunchy frost, which was very slippery.
We stopped for a short while to cut strong stakes as walking sticks and
then we managed very well. Tendi had decided to come with us but
left his little boy with some people at Nourr. Our guides were Mingma,
Ang Tsering and Passang Tendi—a formidable trio. They were all unusually quiet at first, probably due to an overdose of good Sherpa
hospitality at Gypsoa the day before.

The rest of us were a cheerful and garrulous crowd, but as the
altitude slowly increased the conversation became less and less. The
young members of the party walked straight up the grass slopes
towards the summit but I noticed that the more experienced men of the
party zigzagged slowly and steadily with very little waste of energy. I
decided to follow them. The higher we got, the harder the wind blew
until at the top, it was almost impossible to stand upright. We took a
few hasty photographs and then retreated to a more sheltered position
from which to enjoy the view.

Piké is the central pivot of a great ridge system which stretches away
in all directions like the giant tentacles of a starfish. The winter frosts
had tinged the grass with gold and this rich colour contrasted drama-
tically with the vibrant blue of the sky. As the ridges dropped towards
the valleys they became clothed in a dark green mantle of forest and
finally disappeared into the unseen depths far below. The wide view
of the Himalayas was the best I have ever seen and Ed and Mingma
were reeling off name after name of the great peaks—Gauri Shankar,

Cho Oyu, Lhotse, Tamserku, and of course dominating everything the great triangle of Everest. Far to the east we could see the regal Kanchenjunga floating ethereally on a sea of cloud in far-off Sikkim.

Ed wanted to take some colour pictures of one of our small tents with a backdrop of Himalayan mountains, for Sears Roebuck and Company, the American makers. The top of Piké was the perfect place except that it was difficult to find a flat area that was reasonably out of the wind. In the end Passang Tendi very kindly offered to crawl inside the tent so that it didn't blow away. He proved to be an exceptionally good anchor and lay there with his grinning face poked through the door enjoying the confused scene of tottering figures battling against the wind whilst they peered unsteadily through the various lenses of their cameras. It certainly wasn't an ideal day for such photography.

Despite all our warm clothing the bitter cold was being driven into our bones by the force of the icy blasts and it wasn't long before we started hurrying down towards our meeting place with the porters 2,000 feet below. We couldn't even see the rendezvous col—it was almost underneath us—and it looked a mighty difficult descent. The grass-covered slopes were so steep that it was almost like walking on slippery ice and we used our long walking sticks to balance us like ice axes. We started down a ridge which looked rather terrifying as it was a series of rocky bluffs but the grassy slopes linked up quite easily and we didn't have too much trouble. Soon we were amongst the steep rhododendron forest and small patches of snow and ice made the descent exciting as we flung ourselves from tree to tree.

In a pleasant sunny corner down on the col the rest of our party were waiting for us. Siku and Aila stood leaning against their ice axes looking thoroughly pleased with themselves after the responsibilities of the morning. At first glance everything looked quite normal but then we were told that one of the porters had narrowly escaped death on the traverse despite all the precautions.

"What happened?" said Ed to Mingma. "Was the man hurt? Where did he fall?"

"He's all right, Burrah Sahib, but he slipped on one of the frozen streams."

"Good Lord! Probably jolly lucky to be alive," said Ed. "Where is he now?"

"Some of his friends went back to help him carry his load. He should be arriving soon." So we waited with nervous anticipation for the arrival of the poor victim.

"Falling Porter! Falling Porter coming!" called Siku, rather disdainfully I thought. I looked up quickly and was relieved to see that the "Falling Porter" was walking on his own two feet, though rather stiffly and painfully.

"You know more about first aid than anybody else here," said Ed to me. "You'd better examine him and make sure that he is quite all right."

"I wouldn't know where to begin."

"Oh, there's nothing to it," said Ed. "Just feel him all over for broken bones."

The falling porter was led to a comfortable place where he sat down rather gingerly. Perhaps a cup of tea would help him, I thought. Ang Passang had just made tea, so at my suggestion he poured a big mugful and carried it over to the patient. I followed rather nervously wondering if I was going to be a success as a medical officer, but before I had time to ask the poor man how he felt, Ang Passang had started a forceful but efficient examination of all the bones in his body.

"He's all right," he said to me when he had finished. "Nothing to worry about, just some ice grazes and bruises."

"I'll go and get some dressings for those," I said very humbly. While I handed out large strips of dressing Ang Passang very competently covered the grazes.

"I think two aspirins would be a good idea with his cup of tea," said Ang Passang with authority so I hurried away to get those too.

Now that the porter was comfortable we tried to find out exactly what had happened to him. Evidently the shaded gullies of the traverse had been completely covered with wide sheets of hard slippery ice. To make a safe path across these, Siku had gone ahead and cut big steps while Aila stood guard in the middle of the icy slopes to help the porters across. On the very last stretch of ice the poor "Falling Porter's" nerves could no longer stand the strain. Rigid with fear he became deaf to Aila's instructions and finally just let himself fall. He slid quite a long way on the ice screaming desperately as he shot downwards, with the horrified onlookers watching helplessly from above. The situation looked quite hopeless as he was fast approaching a sheer forty-foot drop over a frozen waterfall. He started tumbling head over heels and this is really what saved him. A tentpole on his back became caught under the root of a tree and he came to an abrupt halt—right on the edge of the drop. He had been as near to death as it is possible to be and we were horrified to think that one member of our cheerful gang had been so close to disaster. The "Falling Porter" meanwhile rested quietly looking terribly shocked and downcast, for the accident had hurt his pride as well as his body. No mountain man likes to appear weak, especially when the older men and the young Sherpa women shod in slippery Indian gym shoes had negotiated the ice with ease.

We watched Aila give a blow-by-blow account of the accident to an admiring group of friends. His rendition of the story became most realistic when he mimicked the blood-curdling screams of the falling man as he disappeared down the icy slopes. There were loud roars of laughter from everybody around but I don't think the poor victim even noticed. He was too lost in his own troubles.

Three thousand feet below us in a wide sun-bathed valley was the scattered village of Loding and we could see the shining aluminium roof of yet another one of our new schools. We raced downward, along the ridge, through the forest and past the high potato fields. An hour and a half later we were approaching the school site. It had been a bone-shaking experience, jolting down 5,000 feet from the top of Piké, and our senses were numbed and our knee joints battered. But now there was plenty of time to rest and enjoy the pleasant feeling of being utterly lazy.

The old school at Loding had been destroyed in a landslide—fortunately when all the children were at home having dinner. After many petitions Ed had agreed to rebuild the school in a much safer location. We inspected the building with a connoisseur's eye and agreed that it looked a good job. There was still a floor to be put in and windows to be installed but that was planned for a few months' time. As we came away from the school mugs of tea were thrust into our hands.

"You made that fire very quickly, Ang Tsering," I commented.

"Oh, no trouble," he replied, "we are using the roofing shingles from the old school for firewood. There is a great pile of them inside the new school."

I noticed that Pember Tenzing was carrying an enormous load of the shingles to the cooking fire and that the porters were helping themselves also.

"Those shingles look quite good," I said to Ed. "Couldn't they have been used again?"

"No," said Ed, "they're ours. When we demolished the old schoolhouse it was agreed that we should have them." Though the timber was old and cracked it was still quite strong so we used some of it to make benches to sit on. What a pleasant change it was not to have to sit on the hard ground. Most trekkers, particularly the ones over the age of forty, feel the lack of a comfortable chair more than anything else and those who are lucky enough to be able to sit comfortably cross-legged are fortunate indeed.

The peace and comfort of early evening was soon shattered by a strident angry voice screaming at us from the path above. It was hard to understand all that was said, but there were many mentions of firewood. The owner of the voice eventually appeared and strode to our fire giving us withering glances of fury, and then marched to the cooking fire and the many porters' fires, gesticulating furiously. She was a handsome Rai woman who was clearly enjoying her one-sided battle with our party.

"We are burning all her firewood," said Mingma. "She says she bought the shingles from the Loding school committee, but had left them in the schoolhouse until she had time to move them to her house."

"Well, I'll be blowed," said Ed. "I had a suspicion this wasn't a particularly strong school committee, now I can see I was right." Ed asked the woman how much money we should pay her for the loss of her firewood and she said fifteen rupees. She was given five rupees which she accepted most happily, tossing her head back to laugh in high glee. She had probably paid the school committee about five rupees for the whole pile of timber, so the incident had proved highly beneficial. As she patrolled the camp picking up our seats and other spare bits of wood she talked to us all in very friendly fashion. When not a splinter of her timber remained in the camp she disappeared for a short time. She soon returned with a troop of friends and relations who helped her remove the rest of her property to a safer place. Women's liberation was never needed here, for the mountain women have always done their share of the hard physical work and shared the right to property too. They are excellent bargainers and very good businesswomen.

Not all education projects go smoothly and at Loding Ed and his helpers had experienced a number of problems. The villagers had been very slow in carrying the cut timber from the forests to the school site, and the headmaster had proved rather unreliable and lazy. After the firewood episode it became very clear that Loding school would need a strong headmaster who could manage both the pupils and the school committee.

During the evening we were visited by the ex-assistant teacher. The last time Ed had seen him he was being chased around the village by the headmaster who had a large stick in his hand. Apparently there was a difference of opinion on academic matters. The assistant teacher arrived in our camp clasping a bottle of *arak* and some fine silver cups. His aim was clearly to soften up the Burrah Sahib and Mingma so that he could either have his job back or be given some help with further training as a teacher. He presented us all with *katas* and then with due

All home comforts for the porters on the march.

On the march, above Junbesi. Sarah in the lead.

Junbesi camp and *chorten*.

On top of Zuplung Banjung. Ang Tsering, Mingma, Siku, Sarah and Belinda.

ceremony we drank the necessary few drops of *arak*, and then waited for the expected appeal for help.

"Why can't I have a scholarship like some of your other young teachers?" he asked. "Then I can get far better qualifications."

"Yes, but all the other people on scholarships have already proved themselves as fine teachers," said Ed. "If you can prove yourself, then perhaps in two or three years I will consider helping you." When the interview was over our silver cups of *arak* were still standing beside us brimming over with their heady liquid.

"We can't possibly finish it," we said to Mingma.

"That's all right," he said, "no trouble!"

He turned around and his voice increased in volume. "Oh Siku, oh Passang Tendi, come here and drink some *arak*." They soon arrived beside the fire and obediently tossed down the spirit as if it was water.

There are three important requirements for all people working for Mingma—they must be able to work very hard, they must be scrupulously honest, and they must have a strong head for liquor. In Sherpa country it is not good manners to leave your drink, but it is quite acceptable for you to say "*Upsah*", and pass your drink to someone else. As Mingma and Ed are always being offered liquid refreshments it is reassuring for them to know that they can resort to this custom without hurting anyone's feelings. However, this custom has its disadvantages—in a region where tuberculosis is rife, *Upsah* helps to spread the infection.

CHAPTER 8

Official Circles

LODING SCHOOL IS only a brisk two-hour walk from Salleri, the administrative centre for Solu Khumbu. While the school was being built, Ed received an invitation from the District Government or Dilla Panchayat to come and discuss education facilities in the area. He and Mingma and the other members of the party were very pleased to have this opportunity to talk with the committee.

The simple Panchayat form of rural government used in Nepal was first introduced by the late King Mahendra, following the pattern of the Indian Panchayat system. It is based on the Hindi and Nepali word for five—panch. To start with each small village elects its own council of elders who manage the affairs of the village. Originally these elected elders would number only five but nowadays the number of elected people to any one council seems to vary a great deal. The leader or head man of the village council is called the Pradhan Panch. The villagers are then grouped into districts and each Panchayat elects one member who is sent to the district Panchayat or Dilla Panchayat. In Salleri the Dilla Panchayat represented the whole of the Solu Khumbu area and had about fifty members, the leader of whom was Mr. Lama Passang, whose title was Sabati Pati. From the Dilla Panchayat a representative from each district of Nepal is sent to the Rastriya Panchayat (National Panchayat) which is the same as a central government or parliament. However, in Nepal the final authority on all matters still rests with the King.

Relations between Ed's organisation and the Dilla Panchayat at Salleri had until now been almost non-existent. This had not been anyone's fault in particular for the Himalayan Trust schools carefully follow the Education Department's school curriculum and they are inspected regularly by the inspector from Salleri. But despite all this there was never much personal contact. Perhaps it was because Ed, in typical Western fashion, was always in such a hurry when he visited his schools that no one could ever catch up with him. It probably wasn't helped by the fact that Mingma, the capable executive of the aid projects, had never been educated and felt ill at ease amongst sophisticated officialdom. But one of Mingma's greatest strengths is that he is a man of the people and has a great ability to understand and motivate them. He has been most valuable in counteracting Ed's impatience with his philosophy that projects that are undertaken "slowly, slowly" give a much greater chance for the village to become involved and interested. But in November 1971 occurred the big breakthrough in the relationships between Ed and the Salleri District Education Committee when Mr. Lama Passang invited Ed to visit Salleri and have discussions with them.

Ed and his party marched down the Loding side valley to the main river and then up the hill to the small village of Paphlu where they met Mr. Lama Passang's entourage. The following extract from Ed's diary describes how the Himalayan Trust became involved in yet another school project.

After scarf presentations and some excellent tea drunk on the roadside we were handed the day's programme. It was very extensive indeed and I was amazed at such unexpected and precise organisation.

JAN JAGRITI HIGH SCHOOL
Solu—Salleri
Sagarmatha Zone

Ref No......   *Date......*

Subject:

PROGRAMME
DURING THE VISIT OF
SIR EDMUND HILLARY
ON 16TH MARGASISH—2028

9 a.m. .... *Reception at Paplu*
(By School Committee)
11.00 a.m. to 11. 30 a.m. .... *Tea Party at District*
Panchayat Office, Sallery
11.30 a.m. to 12 noon .... *Jana Jagriti High School, Salleri visit*
12 noon to 1 p.m. .... *Lunch (at Ananda Restaurant*
given by J. J. High School)
1 p.m. to 3 p.m. .... *Presentation and*
discussion on school matters
4 p.m. to 5 p.m. .... *Tiffin (at Bhimprasad*
Shrestha, Head Master's quarter)
5 p.m. to 6 p.m. .... *Entertainment*
6 p.m. to 8 p.m. .... *Dinner*
(at Yungzi's father Mr. Ganva's residence)

We set off from Paphlu and moved *en masse* to Salleri—marching four abreast in very formal fashion along the wide path with its superb views of the Numbur and Kariolung mountains to the north. I felt a little like a prisoner being marched off to the gallows and noticed the considerable difference in the formal dress of the committee and of our scruffy selves. I surreptitiously tried to pull my long socks up to cover the bare leg below my climbing pants.

We duly arrived at Salleri and were taken to the Dilla Panchayat building for formal introductions to the Commissioner and the Panchayat's staff. We drank more tea and then moved onto the high school to greet the new headmaster. He took us to see his sixty-odd pupils who were all crammed into one room and sitting their annual examinations. One of the older boys gave a brief welcome speech in English and then presented me with a *kata*. Then we moved onto a local restaurant, owned by one of the committee members, for lunch. Lunch took a long time coming, so discussions with the committee commenced.

The situation now became clearer. Salleri high school had in the past been supported by the rich Lama families from Paphlu. Now these families spent most of their time in Kathmandu and their support of Salleri institutions had waned. The Salleri school committee received some Government support, and had been maintaining itself by selling off pieces of excess school land. Now all the land had been sold and in a couple of months they would be broke. What they needed was help—now—and wanted me to give it. They explained that they had received a large grant of 50,000 rupees towards a high school hostel, but this could not be devoted to teachers' salaries or a new school building which was desperately needed. I told them that a good high school at Salleri was most important as it was the only high school in the Solu Khumbu area and explained that at present the reputation of Salleri high school was not good and that I was getting many requests from families to help send their children to schools farther afield. With some reluctance they agreed with me and said the school must improve.

I was informed that some land had been donated for the site for a new school and I said I would like to see this. So off we marched once more. The site for the new school was superb—above the market place on a level grassy bench with a fantastic view of mountains and a good fresh-water stream. We were all most enthusiastic. Then we walked back into the town again where we were summoned to another meeting where the committee asked me to state precisely in what way I was prepared to help them. I said I would like to see a good high school at Salleri but that I had problems of my own that they could perhaps help me with. I needed permission to start middle or intermediate schools at our already well-established Junbesi and Khumjung elementary schools. The new Inspector of Schools was in the room and after he had asked a few questions said he could see nothing to stop Khumjung and Junbesi becoming middle schools. I thereupon said that I appreciated this support and as this had taken a burden off me, I felt that I could now help Salleri build a five-roomed high school on the new site and also assist in the paying of the headmaster. The meeting finished on a high note of bonhomie and we arranged to meet again in Kathmandu on 20th January to see the various Government departments and get the whole matter approved.

We all swigged down our *chung* and were generally very cheerful. The evening concluded with dinner taken with the parents of one of our hospital nurse trainees, Yungen—very pleasant too, and we were able to depart by 7.15 p.m. Using our torches we dropped down to the river and then took advantage of bright moonlight to trudge the long walk up to Loding getting in about 9.30 p.m. A mighty full day! All we have to do now is raise the necessary money.

As a result of Ed's official visit to the Solu Khumbu Panchayat our family was very interested to visit Salleri and see the new high school site. We planned to carry on the same day up to the village of Junbesi where we now had permission to build a new middle school. Even though we were a little tired by our walk over the top of Piké we made an early start next morning and were led by Ang Passang at a relentless speed towards Salleri. By the time we arrived, the weather had become cloudy and bitterly cold and the market place, which only functioned once a week, was dismal in the extreme in its deserted condition. There wasn't a soul in sight and it was disturbed only by whirlwinds of dust and scraps of paper. Still we weren't completely disappointed, for it was fun to see the big circular market area and I could remember how different it had looked during a previous visit in the summer when the place had been a mass of laughing, jostling, brightly-clad humanity, all wrestling good-humouredly for the best bargain in delicious fresh dairy products, gory lumps of meat, grain and fruit. Now it was too cold to linger and even the restaurants built on the outer perimeter of the market that usually served tea, *tukpa* (noodles) and *mormors* looked abandoned.

We started up the hill towards the new Salleri school site. Just as we were leaving the main path we met four very well equipped Nepalese trekkers.

"Good morning," we greeted each other.

"Where are you going?" Ed enquired.

"We are returning to Kathmandu after visiting Namche Bazar in the Everest region," replied their leader who turned out to be a Professor of Economics from Tribhuyan College in Kathmandu. His companions were three of his senior students.

"What are you planning to do?" asked the professor, clearly worried by our unprofessional garb consisting of light cotton clothes, gym shoes, and day packs.

"We're going to Namche Bazar too."

"I don't think I would advise you to go there now, it's getting too cold," said the professor. "There'll be much ice on the path and the route may be impossible."

"We'll be careful," we promised.

As we reached the new high school site the clouds parted and we could see a wonderful view of white snow peaks at the head of the valley—certainly a fine outlook for a new school. We gleaned a few twigs for a fire from the much-frequented hillside and sat near its comforting warmth making toast for breakfast. When our fire collapsed into a pile of grey ashes we poured water over it and then continued on towards Salleri town. On the track we met a herd of small attractive-looking ponies which Mingma told us had been brought down from Tibet by one of the local businessmen and he planned to sell them at a good profit either in Nepal or India. Just then the owner of the ponies cantered up the path behind us. He was a big, handsome and prosperous-looking gentleman, very formally dressed. He nodded to us in rather scornful fashion and once again I had the feeling that we were inadequately clad and bordering on the disreputable.

Salleri was very quiet as the senior Government officials had moved to Kathmandu for the cold winter months. Most of the remainder of the population were valley Nepalese who looked cold and miserable in the bitter temperatures of this high country. The streets were lined with attractive houses, shops and offices, but there was very little business being done that day.

We had a few purchases to make and so visited the shop belonging to the father of our trainee nurse at Kunde hospital. Here we received a very cheery welcome from the smiling, rotund proprietor who called out to his wife to bring tea for us all. He sat cross-legged on a huge bearskin whose head yawned hungrily with sightless eyes from behind his left shoulder. On a low table in front of him were account books and a collection of empty tea glasses. He smiled cheerfully at us as we sipped our hot and very sweet tea and selected some cloth for patching our tattered clothes. There was an interesting selection of merchandise to examine but Mingma was looking impatient, so we made our apologies and departed.

The slog up the Solu Kola valley seemed endless. We were undoubtedly tired from the previous day and Ed set a racking pace, telling me (out of the hearing of the children) that unless we got cracking we probably would never make it that night. We walked limply but thankfully into the exquisitely beautiful village of Junbesi where a pleasant camp was already set up ready for us on the school playground. Our porters (including a very stiff "Falling Porter") and most of our Sherpa staff had taken the direct route from Loding and looked even fresher than usual after their easy day.

CHAPTER 9

"Good Junbesi Men"

JUNBESI SCHOOL WAS built eight years before, and one of its first teachers was an elderly retired army officer who is also a well-known poet. He very kindly translated some of his poems for us and the following is in praise of the school builder written in old-fashioned Nepalese traditional flowery style. As the teacher's English wasn't very strong, the translation is delightfully ungrammatical.

Verse I
Sir Edmund like the bright full moon on this village is very
  pleasant.
The school in Junbesi is so charming like the golden peak
  glittering in the sun,
Your heart is filled with joy in the Himalayan pagodas,
And the young Sherpas thank you much all together.

Verse II
Sir Edmund, like the bright full moon on the valley of Junbesi
  is very pleasant.
The smile on the face of Sir Edmund is like the dances of
  majestic peacock,
In the solitude which looks like the divine cherry on earth,
We express our heartfelt gratitude but don't have anything
  to present, and accumulate knowledge which will help us in
  future.

Verse III
Sir Edmund, like the bright full moon on the valley of Junbesi
  is very pleasant.
We were confined to this region to carve on stones,
Surviving our meagre lives on potatoes and vegetables
We were anxious to greet you face to face,
And to-day we are blessed with this opportunity but in future
  when shall we again see your glamorous figure.
Sir Edmund is really like pleasant bright full moon in this
  valley of Junbesi.

None of us felt like a "bright full moon" after our long walk from Salleri, but the children and I had enough energy left to appreciate the changes that had taken place in the village since we had been there five years before (Ed is there once or twice every year). The school was twice the size—whitewashed and with red window frames and shutters. In front was a large playground enclosed by a handsome stone wall and on one side was the pupils' vegetable garden with the remains of good crops of cabbages, cauliflowers and lettuces. There was even a flower garden with a row of healthy rose bushes. At the far end of the playground was the new village Panchayat building—a rather draughty place but nevertheless an important status symbol. We were using it as a temporary storehouse and cookhouse and with the usual Sherpa disregard for fire hazards, the cooking fire had been placed right up against the wall of the verandah.

Behind our tents the tall white village *chorten* stood like a sentry guarding our camp, its wide-spaced painted eyes watching us benignly. Long lines of prayer flags stretched from its top in all directions like an umbrella and flapped soothingly in the late afternoon breeze. There seemed to have been quite a lot of recent building in the village. I noticed at least three new whitewashed houses, and a small wooden hotel right in the centre of town.

"The place is looking very prosperous," I commented to Mingma.

"Yes, many people are making money from tourists here," he said. "Also they are carving wooden *mani* (prayer) printing blocks and selling them to the tourists in Kathmandu." The printing blocks were traditionally used by the monks for making prayer flags, books and daphne paper prints which were sold to the faithful.

We had already observed as we travelled through the higher and colder country how many of the families had temporarily left the area to spend a couple of months in warmer climates either working, having a holiday, or going on a pilgrimage. This year the exodus was larger than usual as the last season's potato crop had been a failure after heavy rains followed by severe blight. As a result many families were going to be hungry before the next season's crop. If the blight became any worse it could cause a famine as serious for the Sherpas as the one in Ireland in 1845 and 1846. The average farmer doesn't have enough money to buy sprays to control the blight and cannot afford to purchase disease-free seed potatoes. If only we could do something—but where would the vast sums of money be found?

Our first day at Junbesi was a pleasant change from walking. First we did two weeks' washing of clothes while Ed and Mingma started to measure up the site for the new middle school. Over the next few days we planned to lay the rock foundations for the building and every hand would be needed to carry stones from the quarry some distance away. When the children departed with their bamboo baskets and rope headbands to carry rocks in company with most of the villagers, I remained behind to help Nawang move the school rose garden to a safe refuge, far away from the advancing army of foundation diggers. I carefully pruned the roses with my nail scissors and then as the wind was now blasting fiercely down the valley, I fastened our washing onto the climbing rope clothes line with safety pins.

As I did this a tall thin monk arrived with incense and *chung* to perform a *puja* (sanskrit word for prayer) for the success of the new building. For some strange reason he chose to set up his religious equipment directly below the family pyjamas. He was a strange and wild-looking man and looked even more extraordinary as the smoke from the incense swirled about his head and the flapping pyjama legs almost engulfed him.

There was a good turnout of village people for our work day and the headmaster arrived to make a record of every worker's name. He brought out his desk and chair from the schoolhouse and sat in state in the middle of the playground. As the villagers arrived he would write their names down and give them a carrying basket. Our names were also included on the list with the letter "P" beside them.

"What's that for?" I asked.

"It stands for 'present'," he giggled. Just then the first group of rock carriers returned to the school site and amongst them were the children. They looked incredibly uncomfortable with their loads on their backs but they were smiling hard to reassure their workmates who were greatly enjoying the novelty of having four strangers to work with them.

"Ooh, my neck muscles! My head's going to fall off," I was told.

"Cheer up," I replied. "Unless you've been using a basket with a headband since you were five, you can't expect to have the right muscles. I suggest you cheat and carry most of the weight of the basket with your hands over the back of your shoulders."

"We've already tried that!" I was informed rather sharply—really, mothers don't expect their children to have any intelligence.

I found a basket and went off to join them. Mingma had said that the source of rocks was very close at hand, but that was in Himalayan terms; it took me about a quarter of an hour of puffing steadily up hill to reach the quarry. Here I was greeted by two stalwart and cheerful village men whose principal task was to loosen rocks and pile them on people's backs. I turned so that my basket was facing one of the loading men, and the next moment two large hunks of rock were dropped unceremoniously into it. I desperately grabbed the basket to ease my neck muscles and tried to look unconcerned.

"Enough?" asked the loading man.

"One more," I called with great bravado.

"You are all good Junbesi men," called one of the admiring audience.

"*Tuche, tuche,*" (thank you, thank you,) we said, very pleased with the compliment. As I walked back to the school I felt as if I had torn at least two muscles in the back of my neck. "If I get there alive," I said to the children, "I don't think I'll carry with that basket again."

When I arrived at the building site I tried to get rid of my load in the traditional manner by flicking it out of the basket onto the ground in front of me. With a wild lunge to one side, the stones tumbled to the ground alarmingly close to my feet, and all the onlookers let out a gasp of appreciation. "Anybody like my basket?" I asked and a small schoolgirl of about nine leapt forward and took it.

There is quite a lot of skill required to carry rocks on your back and hold them in place by hand. First you must select a reasonably flat piece and put it on a ledge two or three feet above where you are standing. Then you bend down so that the small of your back is level with the rock, put your hands underneath it and scoop it onto your back. With your leg muscles straining as you straighten up from this awkward position you hurry as quickly as possible to your destination. Alternatively, one of the men in charge of loading would place a good-sized rock on your back for you and this is a much less tiring method. It is amazing how much weight you can carry in this way with very little lasting strain on the muscles. We noticed the more experienced basket carriers doing their own loading—they bent down and picked up smaller rocks and threw them with unerring aim into the basket behind them.

Later in the day when the foundation ditches were completed, Ed joined us in our work. The locals were overjoyed by his participation and there was quite a party atmosphere amongst us. He surpassed himself with his first load which happened to be a colossal slab of thin stone which looked a lot heavier than it actually was. Such an example inspired us all to work even harder. By four o'clock when the villagers would normally have gone home to attend to their domestic chores, they all decided to continue for another hour and a half.

As we rested from our labours that evening, Danu the Junbesi carpenter called on us. He had made all the windows, doors and furniture for the Solu schools and we have known him for many years. He brought oranges, spinach and a large Thermos of tea which he served us in little plastic teacups decorated with rosebuds. He spent the evening with us and kept our fire going by throwing on it liberal doses of wood shavings that he had brought specially for this purpose.

I was lulled to sleep that night by the gentle flapping of the prayer flags behind the camp and by the pleasant thought that I would be staying another day in Junbesi and that in the morning I could sleep in for as long as I liked. But by 6 a.m. it was very clear to me that I would have to get out of bed in a hurry and find a secluded spot before the entire population of Junbesi, in particular the young zum herders, were dotted all over the hillsides. I walked down the hard, frosty main path of the village towards a scrub-covered area near the river—only to be met by two desperate daughters rushing with bare feet and flimsy pyjamas in great disarray towards our camp.

"What happened?" I said.

"We're too cold, we can't tell you now but Belinda fell in the river."

"Wait a moment. Where are your shoes?"

"Belinda's are in the river," said Sarah.

"And Sarah's are in the bog," said Belinda.

"Go quickly and get warm and I'll see if I can find them," I told the girls.

"You never will!"

Down at the river I hunted around for the sandals and to my amazement saw one floating sedately down towards the bridge. I hurried across to a likely spot a little farther down and found both sandals floating in a small whirlpool. Thank goodness for that—I was constantly worried about our footwear as it was so difficult to replace. We found the sandals most useful as "après-walking" shoes with a pair of warm woollen socks inside and they were ideal as a replacement for sweaty gym shoes after a hard day's walking.

"How did you get yourself into such a mess?" I asked the girls when I returned.

"It was the frost, it made the swamp near the river look like hard ground, and we rushed into it," said Sarah. "Of course we sank into the mud and then both lost our sandals, but Belinda found hers again."

"And then I went to the river to wash my sandals," continued Belinda, "and slipped on the ice-covered rocks and fell into the water." By this time Ang Tsering with the help of Danu's wood shavings had lit a fire and the girls quickly thawed themselves out.

Before the stone carriers arrived that morning a strong and bitter wind started to blow down the valley. It blew clouds of dust and leaves over everything and we could find nowhere to escape from it. It seemed a good opportunity to go and visit the Tibetan monastery of Tuten Choling that could be seen at the head of the Junbesi valley. Leaving Ed happily admiring the foundations of his new school we prepared for our walk.

"Siku will come with you," announced Mingma.

"We don't need Siku, thank you, Mingma," I said. "Look, you can see the monastery from here. We can't get lost."

"Siku will go with you," said Mingma—and Siku did.

Tuten Choling had been built by a group of Tibetan refugee monks about five years before. Their head Lama was a Rimpoche or reincarnate. He was famous as a good leader and a great teacher, and the new community prospered both spiritually and materially with the help of generous donations from the local people. The monks also brought with them from Tibet many fine religious artifacts, silken draperies and clothing, and the Gompa was well known for its beauty and its preservation of the Lamaistic Buddhist traditions of Tibet. The *gompa* was about an hour and a half's journey from Junbesi and about a thousand feet higher up the valley. We enjoyed the walk up the valley but sat down to regain our breath half-way up the hill—then noticed that the sun was now behind a great pall of smoke caused by a huge fire raging high up in the forests above Junbesi. Siku told us that the fire was probably started by hunters or children minding the sheep and cattle.

Fire is still the worst enemy of the Nepalese scenery. In the winter the young cattle herders light fires to keep themselves warm, and these often spread out of control in the dry windy conditions. The hunters are more to blame because they deliberately set fires and burn off the forests to drive out the musk deer and other game. They will go to any ends to make money from the musk which sells at astronomical prices in the markets.

The closer we came to Tuten Choling the more difficult it was to see the Gompa as it disappeared behind the high protective walls. But we could see the small white houses of the many monks and nuns, scattered around the main buildings. The place was bathed in soft sunlight and there was a wonderful atmosphere of tranquillity and timelessness. Below us was a perfect pastoral scene, the sparkling river twisting down through sunny fields, and dark strands of forest with here and there a small farmhouse nestling in some sheltered corner. At the valley's end, vague, distant mountain ridges melted into nothingness in the midday glare of the sun.

Suddenly our dreamlike admiration of the landscape was rudely disturbed by four large mastiffs who leapt out at us from the *gompa* courtyard and stood bristling with murderous intent on some rocks close above. We hastily picked up large stones ready to defend ourselves to the last.

"The people here don't seem very fond of visitors," said Peter.

"I hope someone comes and saves us," muttered Belinda.

"Eh *Tawa!* (monk) Eh *Tawa!*" called Siku urgently. After a fairly long wait in which no amount of stones heaved in their direction would persuade the dogs to go away, a monk came to our rescue.

"May we come in and have a look?" I asked.

"Yes, of course," the monk replied. "Follow me. I am sorry that the Rimpoche is away in Dharamsala (the Dalai Lama's retreat in India) but you are very welcome."

We entered through a narrow entrance in the high stone walls and found ourselves in a sunny central courtyard. On the ground was a golden patch of corn laid out to dry in the sun and nearby four elderly and toothless women worked busily at their spindles while they protected the grain from any hungry birds. Nestling close beside one of the old women were some small rotund mastiff puppies. It was hard to believe that their parents were such terrifying beasts. We stopped and loudly admired them.

Across the courtyard was the red-plastered *gompa* and over its front door was hung a heavy black yak's wool blanket topped by a traditional white pleated curtain to protect the precious wall-paintings beside the door. We peeped hesitantly through the heavy blanket and caught a glimpse of a strange scene from an ancient world. Seated in long rows in their magenta robes were about eighty monks and nuns in the midst of their morning prayers. They were surrounded by a priceless treasure house of art—the walls and the ceiling were decorated with intricate and intensely colourful religious paintings, embossed with gold; and rich silk hangings and *tunkas* (scroll paintings) hung from the central beams. The wall behind the Rimpoche's throne houses a complete Buddhist library and the floors were made of honey-coloured timber which reflected the shafts of sunlight that filtered through the incense-laden air. We were so filled with awe that we dared not enter.

"It's all right, come on" said our guide.

"What about our shoes?"

"Don't worry. Please come."

Feeling as if in a dream we tiptoed inside and listened to the low-pitched chanting that rose and fell like sweet music.

"Please look at everything—go where you like," we were told. So we poked and pried uninhibitedly to the mesmerising accompaniment of the chanting, while a young novice went the rounds of the chanters and refilled their silver-lidded tea bowls with Tibetan tea. The great collection of religious books was particularly interesting—each book was wrapped in a scarf of silk and stored in its own decorated and labelled niche.

Our inspection of the *gompa* was interrupted by a Sherpa visitor who came and prostrated himself in front of the main altar. He then placed a large sum of money on the table just beside me. Very stupidly I hadn't thought to bring any money. What was I to do?

"Siku, should I give some money?" I whispered.

"Yes," he replied very firmly.

"I've only got one rupee!" We formed ourselves into a little huddle and counted up our combined funds. It came to five rupees.

"Oh, Siku, can I borrow some from you?"

"Here's ten rupees," he said. "It's all I've got."

"Thank you, thank you, Siku, you've saved the day."

Back outside in the sun once more, one of the old ladies in the court-yard signalled to us to go down a passage behind the *gompa*.

"*Mani, mani,*" (prayer) she called. We walked down a stone passage-way to a room completely filled with a huge prayer wheel. Here also the walls of the room and the gigantic wheel were completely covered in colourful embossed religious paintings, and seated beside the wheel was a monk whose task was to turn it and so manufacture prayers for the monastery. He was sitting comfortably on a thick mat with his bowl of tea beside him. He smiled at us and pulled the wheel round faster for our entertainment. As it twirled round and round, a sweet-sounding bell rang at the end of each complete circuit, and the bold Tibetan lettering on the wheel blurred into a band of gold as the sacred words were converted into beneficial prayers.

Waiting for us outside the prayer-wheel room were five young monks with schoolbooks under their arms. They were bright-faced and mischievous and one of them I recognised as the Rimpoche from the monastery at Thami in Khumbu. In good Buddhist fashion we con-tinued round the main *gompa* building in clockwise direction and ended up in a small visitors' room beside the central courtyard. Here we were served Tibetan tea from an ornate copper teapot, and also rice cakes, Indian biscuits and oranges. This was followed by Indian tea in case we hadn't enjoyed the unusual flavoured Tibetan variety.

As our guide led us towards the monastery gate we glanced at the small mastiff puppies.

"You can have one, if you like," he said. Everyone was most enthu-siastic except me.

"No, thank you," I said flatly.

"Oh come on! We could give it to Kunde hospital."

"No, definitely not," I said remembering the previous mastiff which had been at the Kunde hospital. In its cheerful boisterous fashion it had started nipping many of the patients—and even a friendly nip from a mastiff is not to be disregarded.

We said our thanks for all the hospitality and walked out of the courtyard into the twentieth century—and back to an energetic rock-carrying afternoon with our Junbesi friends.

By the end of the day the walls of Junbesi middle school were starting to grow out of the foundations and everyone was very satisfied with their labours. A large pile of rocks had been accumulated and Mingma and his men would return to complete the walls at a later date. We were very thrilled at the number of new friends we had made during our rock-carrying efforts and many of them sat resting with us on the playground after work.

"How I wish there was a common language for all the world," said Sarah.

"We don't need a common language for deck tennis," said Peter. "I saw a quoit inside the school this morning—let's all play."

Very quickly a few of the less shy Sherpas joined us in an energetic game.

"Come and play," I said to the headman's pretty fifteen-year-old daughter.

"Oh, no," she giggled.

"Belinda, you come and pull her onto the court," I said as a last resort. There was really very little pulling necessary and it was soon quite apparent that she was by far the most cunning player in the village. Ang Tsering and Passang Tendi joined in and Aila and Nawang stood laughing at them from the sideline. It wasn't long before a gay village free-for-all had developed.

Darkness put an end to our sport and now we could see high up on the ridge above Junbesi a great wall of fire as the pinetree forests continued to burn in the strong winds. It flared and receded in ghostly and menacing fashion like a fiery tidal wave that was determined to overwhelm us. Belinda and Sarah were very concerned both about the damage that was being done and the possible danger to our village and ourselves. We tried to convince them that it would be impossible for the fire to jump over the many dry terraced fields separating us from the forest. But they didn't go to bed in a happy frame of mind. It isn't pleasant to have a forest fire on your doorstep when there's wind blowing.

On top of the pass above Zuplung Banjung. Sarah and Belinda. Mounts Numbur and Karyolung in the centre background.

Peter, Sarah and Belinda with
Sears Roebuck camping gear and Everest be►

Monks parading at the Mani Rimdu
Festival at Thami *gompa*.

Kappa Kalden at work in his studio in Khumjung.

'The Four Harmonious Brothers' by Kappa Kalden.

On the path above Junbesi with Hadley.

Yeti by Kappa Passang.

Buddhist temple painting by Kappa Passang.

Eight lucky Buddhist signs.

One of the 'the Girls' who worked on Ringmo bridge.

CHAPTER 10

Wandering with Hadlemina the Zum

"*LO! LO!*" (LET'S GO, LET'S GO) called Aila the benign slave driver, shattering the peace of the quiet pale dawn. There was a heavy frost on the ground and the only sign of yesterday's fire were a few tendrils of grey smoke on the hillside far above us. Not even the young zum herders were up at that early hour to farewell us—but Danu the carpenter came to say goodbye and decided to accompany us for the first mile or so and carry my pack. Just then Ang Passang appeared from behind one of the houses in the village leading a big fat black zum.

"I've just bought it," he said with great pride, "very cheap."

"How much?" asked Ed.

"Two hundred rupees and they say it gives very good milk."

"Are you taking it back to Kunde?" asked Belinda.

"Yes," replied Ang Passang hitting it none too gently with a bamboo switch. "*Lo, lo,*" he said without any success. "*Ut Dericah,*" he cursed and gave the animal a hard pull with the lead rope. The zum tossed its head in anger and very unwillingly started on its way. It was going to be a long slow trip.

"What should we call it?" said Sarah. "It must have a name if it's coming along with us."

"How about Wilhemina?" suggested Roderick.

"Or Daphne," I said, inspired by all the sweet-smelling shrubs in the forest.

"No! . . . Something more ridiculous. I know—Hadley!" announced Peter.

"But that's a boy's name," we complained.

"Well Hadlemina—and Hadley for short," said Ed. So Hadley it became. With the six chickens that Mingma had bought recently for our dinners and this unco-operative zum we had become the owners of a small travelling farmyard.

We climbed up through tall and graceful pine forests to a high traverse and we seemed to be floating along, for the valley below us was filled with fog. Danu had been unusually quiet for some time but now he plucked up courage to ask Ed a well-rehearsed question.

"Please, Burrah Sahib," he said, "could you find a job for my son,

Lhakpa Gyalzen? He wants very much to teach." Lhakpa Gyalzen had just finished his schooling at Salleri high school where he had proved himself hard-working and a good student.

"We might be able to give him a job at Bakanje school. What do you think, Mingma?"

"Lhakpa Gyalzen is very good boy," said Mingma giving his blessing. Danu was very happy and I had high hopes of his carrying my pack for the rest of the day. But, no—his main task concluded, he explained he had some timber to buy and duly departed. The path became even steeper leading across the broad mountainside. We were making good progress until we came around a corner and found our way barred by Hadley who was having a sit-down strike—and nothing that Ang Passang could do would move her.

"We'll never get breakfast this morning," I worried. Normally by this time Ang Passang would be well ahead of the main party so as to start cooking the morning meal. Aila generously took over the task of leading Hadley and managed to get her under way again. Ang Passang disappeared off into the distance. Our path was now bathed in golden sunlight and we gambolled on exclaiming with delight at the distant white snow peaks, the frost-covered valleys and the dark outline of trees against sunlit ridges.

Half-way across the high traverse we came to a cluster of houses surrounding a spring. This was Salung, where Nawang lived and we were invited into his home for a round of traditional Sherpa hospitality—first tea, then *chung*, followed by presentation of *katas*. Finally a plate of oranges and bananas was handed round with great ceremony and we all felt duty bound to eat some of the fruit as it must have been specially bought for us at considerable cost.

Like all Sherpa houses, the room temperature was exceedingly low—almost as cold as the frosty air outside. The best way to keep warm was to sit close to the small fire or you could do as we did and put on all your thick cold-weather clothing. We noticed that Nawang was the proud owner of a water pipe and tap, but he told us that the water only flowed for about six months of the year and that for the rest of the time it was frozen.

Mingma glanced at his watch.

"Is it time to go, Mingma?" asked Ed as he always does on these social occasions.

"Yes," replied Mingma.

Far below was the Ringmo river where Ang Passang would now be waiting for us. Although it was normally a very pleasant descent it now became a hazardous journey, for many zums were grazing along the path and they snorted and tossed their heads as we approached them. Perhaps they were frightened by our smell but it was all rather alarming. Farther down we passed a deserted shanty and with horrifying suddenness a savage mastiff leapt out at us with madness in his eyes. He was only held by a thin bending stake driven into the ground and Ed picked up a huge piece of pine tree and stood ready to flatten the dog until we passed safely by. Closer to the river we walked in peace through a forest of fir trees, whose delicate foliage filtered the sun's bright rays and transformed the glade into a jade-green temple.

The Ringmo bridge was a sorry sight. Only part of the rock foundations remained, all the rest of it had been washed down the river in the floods of the previous monsoon. This was the first of Ed's Himalayan projects that had actually failed.

For many years the people of Ringmo village had asked Ed to help build a strong bridge over the river. It was an important link for them with the outside world as it was on the main route to Kathmandu and Salleri. In the past, the bridge had been re-built many times only to be washed out again by the flood waters of the monsoon. Every time Ed passed this way he would be stopped by a deputation of villagers asking for help in building a higher and more long-lasting structure. Finally he agreed to come to their aid, but only in return for their promise to provide the timber and a large work-force to carry the timber to the bridge site and to collect rocks for the bridge foundations.

Ed and I arrived at Ringmo in April 1970 with a band of workers ready to commence the project, but the place was deserted and there was no sign of timber or rocks.

"Where is everybody, Mingma?" Ed asked.

"I'll go and find out," he replied. Mingma returned quite soon with an explanation from the local people. We had come at the wrong time of the year, they told him. It was potato-planting time and everybody was needed in the fields. "We will work for you next week," they said.

"A whole week! We can't wait a week," we chorused. "We want to do it now."

"We'll either have to wait, or do a lot of the extra work ourselves," said Ed. And so for the next five days we worked very hard indeed carrying rocks and pulling the large tree trunks down to the bridge site. In many ways it was an exhilarating life. We were up at 5.30 in the morning and finished work at about 6 o'clock at night. I felt rather like a middle-aged Red Guard having a period of re-education in the countryside. I worked at carrying stones with a group of elderly

women who weren't needed in the fields. After a while they paid me
the great honour of calling me *Arni* (woman in Sherpa) instead of
Memsahib, and I really felt one of them. They would share their cold
potato lunches with me and every so often they would draw me over
to where they kept a large wooden bottle of *chung* and force me to
have a good swig. Soon our little team of ladies was being called
"the girls" by the rest of the party.

The new bridge foundations were built very strong and high, and
reinforced with fencing wire and wire-netting. Surely they were
high enough for the main span to be well above flood level. At the
end of five days the villagers had finished most of their potato planting
and came to help us. Large pine trunks were cantilevered out from
either side of the river from the top of the new foundations, and
weighed down with many tons of rock. Then another set of fir-tree
poles were placed in position on top and eased out another ten feet
over the river. By the time they were weighted down with more
rocks there was a gap of only twenty feet remaining to be bridged
with beams and a simple timber decking. The "girls" were allotted
the job of carrying the wooden decking from where it had been pit-
sawn four hundred yards down the river. We hoisted the heavy green
six-foot timbers on our backs and it felt like being imprisoned in a
most uncomfortable strait-jacket.

The new Ringmo bridge survived the 1970 monsoon rains and
might well have survived many more but for a freak accident. Up in
the mountains at the headwaters of the river a natural dam had formed.
There was torrential rain and finally the dam collapsed and a torrent of
water poured down the valley. With irresistible force it picked up a
great tree trunk, lifted it in the air and cast it against our Ringmo
bridge. Nothing could withstand that.

Now, in 1972, there was only one slippery log bridging the sparkling
stream that flowed so innocently down this wild valley. I was glad to
see that Ed wasn't too depressed.

"I think we've learnt an awful lot from this bridge," he said. "Next
time we'll build it a little differently. We'll make the sides higher and
build the cantilevers even stronger. But we'll make the central section
a bit lighter and we won't attach it to the cantilevers. If another tree
trunk comes down it will then knock out the central section but leave
the cantilevers intact. It'll be quite easy for the villagers to replace the
central part."

"Why don't you leave the villagers to do it?" I asked.

"No," said Ed. "I'm determined to prove to myself that I can fix this bridge, and I want to show the locals my idea of a detachable central section. I've told Mingma what to do and he can complete it before the monsoon." (Which Mingma duly did.)

We started the climb up from the river towards the Taksindu Pass at nearly 11,000 feet. The day had turned cold and grey and we were happy to walk at a fast pace. About a thousand feet above the river we stopped at the house of Dorje Sherpa, the head man of the area. For two years he had owed the expedition some money and on a number of occasions Ed had tried unsuccessfully to have the debt paid. Ed had now decided it was a hopeless task and wanted to tell Dorje that the debt would be forgotten.

"Eh Dorje!" cried Mingma from the path. But there was no sight or sound of Dorje.

"He's probably hiding," said Ed, "like he always does when we come through this way."

We were just about to give up waiting when Dorje appeared with a large bottle of *arak* and a little silver cup. He was happy to let bygones be bygones too.

"Let's forget about the money," said Ed to Dorje.

"Very good, Burrah Sahib, very good. Have some *arak*."

"No thank you," we said. "We've got a long way to go uphill to-day."

"Oh, no, no, *shay*! *Shay*!" (drink! drink!) he said and very stubbornly filled up the little silver cup to the brim.

"Well, just one taste," said Ed. He took his small swig and then turned to me. "*Upsah*," said Ed, and I took an equally small sip.

"Sirdar Mingma. *Shay*! *Shay*!" said Dorje.

"No," said Mingma very firmly. But Dorje advanced on him, shay-shaying all the while. He held Mingma by the chin and virtually poured the drink down his throat. Mingma was not amused but there was little he could do about it—Dorje was observing traditional Sherpa etiquette. Meanwhile Ang Tsering had been trying to melt away into the background but he too was captured and had to drink his full share of the *arak*. I find it hard to understand how you can hope to curry favour with people when you half drown them in raw spirits.

At last we were free of Dorje and feeling as though we had two or three pounds of lead tied to our feet we forced ourselves slowly into uphill gear. On the pass Peter and Roderick were waiting in company with some of the more hardy Sherpas. It was freezingly cold and hoar-frost still covered the trees like heavy snow.

We crossed the pass, and then down the other side of the high ridge we thumped, gay and light-hearted to be released from the drudgery of the uphill slog. Three hundred feet below the pass we peeped through tall rhododendron forest at the picturesque monastery of Taksindu. The trees were tall and gnarled—almost grotesque, with drifts of lichen hanging like stalactites from nearly every branch. In the springtime they would come to life, with flowers of every shade of pink and red and the purest of white.

We plunged on downward not daring to linger in case a monk from the monastery would try and entice us to stop and visit the Head Lama. The monastery was on a wide terrace overlooking the deep chasm of the Dudh Kosi river and the high mountain peaks south of Everest. The whitewashed buildings were well kept with finely made shingle roofs and gay windowboxes of flowers. Despite the good condition of the main *gompa* roof we knew that the Head Lama wanted a corrugated iron or aluminium roof. Ed was sure this desire arose more from wanting to keep with the other Head Lamas than from the need to obtain extra protection for the monastery treasures.

Later as we jolted down the steep track, Ed pointed out our camping spot for the night at Mani Dingma.

"It's a delightful small clearing in the forest and so peaceful," he said. As we drew near Mani Dingma, the sleepy hollow sounded decidedly wide awake. There was a great hum of activity and the chanting of high voices.

"Where have all the trees gone?" we asked. The clearing had been made much larger and just in front of us was a freshly built welcome arch.

"I wonder what it's for?" said Ed, who didn't even bother to walk through it. Then a large crowd of local dignitaries advanced to meet us and Ed was presented with many marigold *leis* and *katas*.

"What is this?" we asked Mingma.

"Wanting something," he replied shortly.

We were led to a lopsided structure in the middle of the clearing that looked like a shelter for cattle, but inside were fifty-four children chanting loudly in parrot fashion while two distraught teachers tried to keep them in order in their hopelessly cramped quarters. The spokesman for our welcoming party was an impressive person who was head of the local Panchayat. He handed Ed a petition for a new school and the children presented him with more *leis* and *katas* until he looked like a craggy-featured bride.

"But you already have a school in this area," he told the fast-growing crowd of people.

"Yes, at Taksindu," nodded the Pradhan Panch. "But it is too far away and much too cold in the winter for our children. Attendances at the school are very poor,—and in the monsoon the track is slippery and dangerous. A farmer is giving us land on the edge of this clearing and all our children will easily be able to get here."

We immediately went to inspect the proposed site which turned out to be a large flat area with plenty of room for playground and a wide view down into the valley. There was a teahouse nearby and as the afternoon was cold we were invited by the Pradhan Panch to have some tea.

"Mani Dingma is becoming an important place now," explained our host, once we were comfortably seated inside. "We have a market here each week and there are now three teahouses . . . and perhaps a school?" Quite a few of the local people had followed us into the teahouse. They were an unsophisticated hard-working lot, who had so far been quite untouched by towns and modern progress.

A lot of the women were old before their time from hard work and child-bearing. Their children clustered around them and many of them seemed to have a child at breast-feeding age. They feed the children until the age of at least two and sometimes when it becomes more of a soothing treatment in time of stress than anything else. One old lady standing nearby must have been mentally retarded. She watched us with an unblinking stare and while she did so, her hands followed the meanderings of a lice colony inside her tunic. Each time she found an itching spot her face became illuminated by an ecstatic grin.

"This will be the third attempt by these people to get a school for their children," explained Mingma. "They tried the school at Tak-sindu and another one farther over on the south of the mountain, and each time they proved to be too far away from the main centre of population. Now, if they are to try again they will definitely need our help."

"It certainly is a very large area to be without a school," commented Ed. "Perhaps I could just squeeze another school into my budget for next year."

"There's quite a lot of roofing material left over, Burrah Sahib," said Mingma, "I think you could do it quite cheaply."

"Perhaps we could," said Ed. "Tell the people, Mingma, that I'll work out my finances during dinner time and will they please come back with their official application for a school at about seven o'clock."

We settled ourselves into our camp for the night and then Peter and I went off searching for orchid plants in the local forest. On top of a rotten tree-stump we found a large clump, complete with a cascade of flower buds. Peter climbed up to collect a portion of the plant but his foothold crumbled and he only just managed to do a wild jump to safety. I shuddered at the problems we would have if we suffered a broken bone or a sprained ankle. By the end of the day we had collected a fine selection of cold-weather orchids which we wrapped in plastic and put in the potato basket for one of the porters to carry.

Our chicken stews had been rather tough lately so I went to the cook fire to enquire about this. I discovered that a small and vital part of the pressure cooker was missing.

"Have you got a spare part?" I asked Ang Passang.

"No," he said, "but I think we've fixed it to-night."

"What have you done?" I asked. He picked up a piece of silver paper from a soup packet and grinned.

"We've used this," he said. "We've jammed the pressure weight on with this and it seems to be working well." I hastily backed away from the cooking fire to a safer distance. But the dinner that night was tender and delicious.

After dinner the deputation returned. They presented their application for help with a school and also a special agreement suggested by the cunning Mingma promising to give free assistance with the re-building of the Ringmo bridge. The elderly Rai farmer who was giving the land for the new school addressed the gathering at some length. He was a wise old man and much respected and he spoke of the need for more schooling. The gathering nodded their agreement. Ed made a short speech in reply—"You hill people can have much more say in local government if you are well educated" and once again the heads all nodded in affirmation. Some of the future pupils of the school were present with their parents. They sat close to the fire and played with the candles, as all children love to do—collecting the soft wax and making it into shapes. Though it was getting late, no one showed any signs of wanting to leave. We were a patch of warmth hemmed in by the velvety darkness of a perfect still night.

"My sleeping bag calls," said Ed abruptly, heaving himself off the ground—and the meeting was over.

On the path next morning Hadley behaved in a surprisingly docile and obedient fashion—possibly due to Aila's firm and experienced hand on the lead. We jolted down towards the wild Dudh Kosi river and the farther we went the warmer the climate became. The Dudh Kosi rises on the slopes of Everest and has cut a mighty gash in the mountains as it rampages to the south and its ultimate meeting with Mother Ganges. At Jubing we crossed the river over a suspension bridge built by the Swiss which is already suffering from lack of maintenance. We stopped for our mid-morning meal on a well used and very dirty ledge close to the river—it made us realise that we were back on the tourist track again. Hadley was the first to be fed—with a huge bunch of greenery—and she sat like a queen behind her pile of breakfast with only two big black eyes and two horns sticking above the edible barricade. The less fortunate chickens, whose legs had been tied together with *katas* while they were being carried, were now taken out of their bamboo basket and given a meal of rice and water. It was quite pleasant for us to relax without needing a fire. We had descended to an altitude of 5,000 feet where the atmosphere was noticeably humid and tropical.

At Junbesi we had taken on some new porters to replace some of our original girls who had wanted to return to the exciting life of Kathmandu. Two of the new team were big handsome Rai girls who definitely had an eye for romance. As we plodded slowly upwards Pember Tenzing, although heavily loaded down with kitchen gear, still had enough breath to hurl a few ribald comments at the flirtatious pair. A noisy verbal battle soon commenced, and Siku who was close behind joined in the fray. He muttered something under his breath and the reaction was immediate and violent—I happened to look up just in time to see the biggest of the girls lunge out with her coolie stick at Siku who parried the blow with his ice axe like a master swordsman. Having been unsuccessful with her first attack she tried again, but Siku was far too quick for her. We were amazed at this behaviour from the quiet and shy Siku, he was showing a new aspect of his character altogether.

Two thousand feet above the Dudh Kosi and some hours later we reached the village of Karikola and stopped for a rest beside the local teahouse. By paying a rupee we were given the use of the teahouse fire. The teahouse had obviously been built to cater for the tourist trade because on the outside of the small wooden building was a notice which said in English:

Passang Sherpa Store

Tea	25 paice
Chung	50 paice
Eggs	50 paice
Rice and Veg	5 rupees
Biscuit	2 rupees

There was plenty of light inside the teahouse and I noticed that the owners had put a large sheet of clear plastic in the roof, just as we do in the school buildings. As most Nepali houses are rather dark due to the lack of windows and glass, it was very cheering to see that one of our simple improvements to the local architecture had been put into practice.

Hadley came puffing into sight. She hadn't fared too well on the steep climb up from the river and looked as though she was just about ready to collapse. Passang Tendi noticed her discomfort and led her to some water for a drink. He then searched around for some food and eventually found a pile of hay lying on the teahouse roof. Without any qualms he pulled it down and gave it to her.

"How much will you have to pay for the hay?" I asked. Passang Tendi just laughed.

It was very pleasant to rest outside in the sun with our backs supported by the teahouse wall. I reclined in luxury on the expedition tin of sugar and watched the world go by. If it hadn't been for the unnecessarily frequent visits by Pember Tenzing to dig out bowls of sugar, life would have been utter bliss. Close by I noticed a grove of healthy tree-tomato plants carefully protected from the frosts by a wooden fence and a covering of fir-tree branches. It started me thinking of fresh fruit and all the other desirable things that still aren't procurable at a Sherpa teahouse. In answer to my dreams Ang Passang came puffing up the slope with a huge load of lemons he had bought in one of the lower villages for two rupees. There were enough lemons to keep us going for a month.

Our peace was once again disturbed when the woman who owned the teahouse came out the door and discovered her precious bundle of hay being consumed by Hadley. She picked it up, hurled it back on the roof and returned inside in a great rage to berate our senior Sherpas. I heard her cursing them loudly, and their unrepentant guffaws of laughter in reply.

As we drank our most welcome cup of tea we were visited by a farmer and his little daughter. The father gently pushed his child towards Ed and she came and put a *kata* around his neck.

"Don't I know this man, Mingma?" Ed enquired.

"Yes, three years ago the girl spent some time at Kunde hospital. T.B. I think. She is better now and wants to thank you." The child must have had tuberculosis of the spine for she had a badly deformed back and was stunted in growth. When she had greeted us all, her father told her to go and play with her friends and she rushed off with a surprising amount of energy. We were very happy that she had made such a good recovery and the father was touchingly grateful.

Reluctantly we decided to move on. Roderick announced he was going to lead Hadley.

"Is it wise?" I said. "She seems so stubborn."

"I will help," said Siku who immediately started prodding Hadley's rump with a piece of bamboo. All went well until just after they had crossed a small side stream where the track became narrow and confined. Hadley became frightened and stopped so abruptly that Roderick was knocked to the ground by a sudden side swipe from Hadley's horns, where he lay surprised and helpless. Hadley swung her head down to look at him, and Roderick looked up at her in somewhat startled fashion. Finally Roderick extricated himself from his undignified position and observed that perhaps it might be better for a Sherpa-speaking person to handle Hadley, who quite clearly did not understand English instructions.

The path to our camp at Patakare Dingma was an endless succession of steep zigzags. We slogged wearily upwards in swirling clouds and it seemed to go on for ever. Without the mental stimulation of wide views of the valley below, it became a desperate battle of willpower. Hot and sweaty after the long climb we turned the last corner and collapsed blissfully on a grassy terrace. But not for long—soon the damp cold air sent us hunting for firewood and in a short time we were sitting beside a roaring blaze with our sweat-soaked clothing drying around the fire.

Dingma is a Sherpa word for a clearing and Patakare is the name of the giant white Himalayan magnolia. With the increase in number of travellers in the area, some of the magnolia trees have already disappeared, but it is still a charming camping spot and a very popular one.

We had a most unusual view from the door of our tent next morning. There had been a very heavy frost, and in the early morning light the wide mountainside opposite us was covered in a pattern of white fields and black forest just like a giant chess-board, which merged higher up on the ridges into a solid mantle of hoar-frost. We broke camp in record time, scurrying amongst the fast-disappearing collection of tents like demented souls. Half an hour later with the sun beginning to slant down towards us, we tied our thick jackets around our waists and laboured on up a stony twisting path. Across the deep valley of the Dudh Kosi the graceful outlines of Kariolung (21,700 feet) rose up through swirling stratas of morning mist. It was an energetic and stimulating high-altitude walk, one that I have enjoyed many times before—particularly in the spring months of April and May. Then the section from Patakare Dingma to our breakfast spot at Puiyan becomes one of the finest floral walks in the world. Between the altitude of 8,000 feet to 11,000 feet the rhododendrons clothe the hillside with splashes of red and pink flame, and floating serenely against the more sombre greens of the tall forest are the lotus flowers of the high Himalayas—the white magnolias. The trees are so tall that the flowers are well beyond the reach of mere mortals and as you look skywards to admire the rich wax-like blooms they appear to float on a sea of deep infinite blue. One of the most beautiful trees—a tall bent specimen leaning across the pathway, had been badly damaged by someone hacking at its trunk for firewood. It was now dead and I felt as if a priceless work of art had been destroyed.

"See that small boy," said Mingma. "The one with the very heavy load."

"About seventy pounds I'd say," said Ed.

"Five years ago when the Burrah Memsahib was here, we met the boy and his father. He was nearly dead—all yellow, very thin, very weak," said Mingma. Then we remembered the occasion. The boy had been suffering from severe nephritis and Ed had given his father enough money to pay to porters to carry him day and night to the hospital at Okaldunga. At the time we had been convinced that the boy would not survive and it was quite amazing to see him now, strong and cheerful and carrying a heavy load.

We stopped for breakfast at the village of Puiyan which by now was bathed in warm sunlight. It is an insignificant place, consisting of only six houses, a well-patronised hotel and a *mani* wall. It is well known for its heady brew of *arak* made from *gheri*, the tuberous artichoke. While we were having a rest beside a stream three women arrived carrying great baskets of artichokes which they washed in the icy water. Surely they couldn't be using all that great pile for *arak*, I thought, perhaps some would be eaten as a vegetable?

"*Gheri arak?*" I asked.

"*Lahsey, lahsey,*" (yes, yes) they giggled. I decided that Puiyan must be the centre of a very big distilling industry.

From Puiyan the track continued on up through rhododendron forests for another hour and then crossed a high pass from where we could see the whole of the upper Dudh Kosi valley. It is an exciting view. In the centre is Mount Kumbila, standing grey and solid as guardian over the villages of Kunde and Khumjung. To the right, through the trees, we could see Lukla airfield and towering up behind were the terrifying precipices of Ku Sung Kang, another of the un-climbed peaks of the Everest region. Kariolung still dominated the view across the Dudh Kosi and to the north of it was the conical white cap of Kwangde with its great rock buttresses.

"Murray coming, Murray coming," called some of our eagle-eyed Sherpa friends. The Murray who was coming was Murray Jones, one of New Zealand's most successful climbers. He had just had a very good season in the European alps and on his way back home he had offered to help with the Himalayan Trust building programme. We had been expecting to meet Murray in Kunde and the Sherpas had been full of praises for his good humour and his ability as a climber. Now he came bouncing up the precipitous path with the greatest of energy, clad in a singlet and the briefest of cut-down jeans which we immediately labelled "hot pants". After his brisk climb of 3,000 feet with a hefty pack on his back, he looked fresh and relaxed as though he had been for a quiet saunter down valley.

"It's great up there at Kunde!" he said with contagious enjoyment. He turned towards the dramatic Ku Sung Kang which we were all photographing. "Hey! That's great, man! I think I'll take a shot too!" Afterwards we all bounded cheerfully down the three-thousand-foot stone stairway that leads to the village of Surkya, with Murray and Ed leading the way and talking non-stop about mountains and their possible and impossible routes. It was so steep that Hadley didn't find the going very easy, and sometimes she looked as though she might fall headlong down the track. Aila got behind her and held her tail very firmly while Siku led her from the front. Our hectic descent ended at the Surkya river where we stopped for our daily wash. It was only an hour from here up the hill to our camping place just below Lukla.

On the first very steep portion of our track next morning, Hadley was leading and we were directly underneath. "Watch out below!" someone called. We crouched against an overhanging rock just in time to escape a steaming cascade from Hadley's rear quarters. The hazards of Himalayan travel are many, we decided.

Soon we were marching across the series of wide terraces that form the village of Chaunrikarka. I was amazed at the changes in the village since my last visit a few years before. There were some smart new houses owned by Sherpas involved in the fast-expanding tourist industry. There was a small wayside teahouse and a shop—one of the many that are sprouting along the road to Everest Base Camp. Though we didn't want to buy, we inspected the shop carefully. There were packets of biscuits and tea, torch batteries, gym shoes, matches and a great pile of large bags of boiled sugar sweets. We had been pricing these bags of sweets all the way up into the mountains and had come to the conclusion that the price rose by one rupee for every twenty miles. Just then two tourists came walking energetically down valley towards us. We greeted each other enthusiastically and they told us they were returning from a successful trek to Everest Base Camp. They

were understandably thrilled with their recent venturing but their conversation was so heroic that it was almost unbearable.

"Where are you going?" they enquired.

"Kunde and Khumjung," we said.

"You must go to Base Camp," I was informed. "You haven't seen
anything until you've been up Kala Pata."

"It sounds wonderful," I replied, not bothering to mention that I'd
climbed the peak five years before.

"Well, we must be off," they said, straining at the bit. "Been nice
meeting you." Our new acquaintances walked briskly out of our lives
while we were left feeling even more bewildered by all the changes
taking place in this once quiet corner of the Himalayas.

I suppose it was inevitable that the Everest region would become a
great tourist Mecca, but I think the process was hastened when, in
1964, Ed built the Lukla airstrip a thousand feet above Chaunrikarka
village. During the cold winter months of the trekking season Lukla
has become one of the busiest airstrips in the whole of Nepal. Now,
instead of meeting only Nepalese people on the path as you did eight
years ago, you're much more likely to meet only tourists with a few
Sherpa guides and porters. An increasing number of the people in the
Khumbu are becoming involved in tourism—they are drifting away
from their old farming existence and often from their cultural background as well. There seems to be a marked increase in matrimonial
disharmony and other problems associated with the breakdown of the
traditional discipline. Possibly the lack of formal education has made
this transition more difficult, and I hope the new schools will help to
overcome this problem so that the people of both Solu and Khumbu
will be able to cope effectively with the tourist boom. However much
they may like, or dislike it, the tourist boom is moving relentlessly into
their area.

Ed and Mingma had diverged from our track to visit Lukla Airfield
and we had arranged to rendezvous for breakfast near the Ku Sung
Kang side-stream. The breakfast place was on a terrace above the
stream with a good view of Ku Sung Kang through a narrow cleft,
but when we arrived the ground was still covered in heavy frost. Soon
our rather damp footwear became extremely cold and we stood on
one leg and then on the other trying to toast a foot in front of the fire.
We must have looked like a group of rather uncomfortable revellers
attempting to perform a cold-weather version of the Hoki Toki. What
a miserable place, I fumed to myself, we should never have trusted a
bunch of mountaineers to choose our breakfast spot.

"I've just worked out," said one of the children, "that it takes the

sun twenty minutes to descend a pine tree's length down the mountainside towards us. If we stay here for another four hours we might just
possibly get warm."

When Ed rejoined us we left no doubt in his mind about our dissatis-
faction. As soon as I had completed my hurried breakfast I announced
that I was walking on. I was joined by the girls and in less than half a
minute we found ourselves in glorious warm sunlight.

The Pakistan/Indian war had reduced considerably the number of
tourists on this main highway to Mount Everest but what we lacked
in quantity we made up for in interest value. As the girls and I walked
on ahead of the main party we met a pleasant-looking young Austrian
travelling alone and carrying all his own food and equipment. He had
been all the way to Everest Base Camp and found the experience
rather lonely so he welcomed the chance to chat with some fellow
foreigners. During our conversation he kept looking at us rather
thoughtfully.

"Excuse me," he said. "How is it that you are so very clean and
tidy? You are not carrying very much. Have you got some porters?"

"Oh, yes," I said rather vaguely to all his questions, "we have a few
porters coming up behind." I felt quite ashamed of our large Sherpa
staff of school builders and hospital cook, and our long line of porters.
I just couldn't bring myself to tell him the truth about our deplorably
high standard of living.

At Pharak Dingma, a pleasant sheltered river flat two miles farther
on, our entire party was stopped by a Sherpa family who had just built
a new teahouse. They wanted us to stop for refreshments and it sounded
an excellent idea. They brought bamboo mats for us to sit on in the
sun and we realised without any regrets that our daily march was fast
turning into a sociable amble.

"How much do we owe them for the tea, Mingma?" Ed asked a
little later.

"Nothing," replied Mingma. "They just wanted you to try their
tea."

"Perhaps they could use our visit for advertising," I suggested
facetiously. "The best tea in Khumbu, says Sir Edmund Hillary!"

What a glorious day it was. We passed through a pleasant forested
area beside the river where scattered giant boulders were covered with
Buddhist prayers carved in handsome Tibetan script. Our eyes were
drawn from the sparkling scenes of the river valley up through dark
pine-clad gorges to the glistening snow peaks backed by a deep blue
sky.

Our contemplation of the beauties of the area was disrupted by the appearance of the next group of tourists who were travelling down valley with grim determination written all over their faces. Later on we nicknamed them the "Easy Riders" as the young man and his girl friend were dressed in shiny black motor-cycle jackets and looked quite out of place so far from a big city. Most tourists love to stop and have a chat.

"Hello," said Belinda very cheerily. The young man made no reply at all so she tried the girl.

"Hello," she said hopefully.

"Good luck," said Easy Rider No. 2 without raising her eyes or slowing down her pace.

Sarah tried to start a conversation also, but only received a dis-interested "Hi" from the girl.

"Perhaps they are in a hurry to catch a plane," I suggested. Half an hour later we stopped to have a chat with some Khumjung Sherpa friends.

"Where are you going?" we asked.

"Kathmandu," they replied.

"For a holiday?"

"No, to get compensation for the wife of my dead brother." Of course, we should have remembered. This family was involved in one of the many tragedies that had occurred during the climbing season in the Himalayas. The number of deaths involving Sherpas had in-creased appallingly in the previous two years. Some of this is due, no doubt, to the increase in the number of expeditions, but it is also true that many of the foreign climbers and their Sherpas have not had sufficient training or experience in high-altitude climbing. Many of the experienced Sherpas have given up climbing and are finding good employment in the tourist industry but there are always a few who are tempted by the high pay, the glamour of the expensive expedition clothes that are issued to them. Compensation for the next-of-kin of a dead Sherpa climber is 3,000 American dollars, and this is a very large sum in Nepal, but of course it never compensates for the loss of a young man at the height of his working capacity—or for the blow that his death is to his wife and young children.

"I hope you'll never climb mountains again," I said to Siku who was walking just ahead of me, but he turned around and gave a big grin.

"I like climbing."

"But many people are getting killed," I argued.

"I like climbing very much," he said stubbornly. "And if I find a good expedition I will go with them."

We crossed a bridge over a side stream and then climbed up the steep hill towards the village of Monjo.

"Hurry past here," Ed said. "Don't waste time with that shop."

I was just about to ask why when we were accosted by a cheerful gentleman standing in the middle of the path.

"Welcome, welcome. Burrah Sahib. Please come and sit down."

"Oh bother," said Ed quietly, "This always happens here."

"What's it all about?" I enquired.

"The people here want a pipe-line. They have to walk a couple of hundred feet down to the river to get their water. I don't feel their need is as great as in other villages but they are very persistent. They also want a new bridge across the Dudh Kosi just above here."

"They seem to have built some very good bridges in the past," I commented. "Surely they can do it again?"

"That's what I think," said Ed.

We were now trapped by a large group of smiling and hopeful people. The bush telegraph system must have been working overtime during the last twenty-four hours because a great welcome had been organised for us. We were draped with *katas* and plied with various brews of tea, *chung* and boiled zum milk.

"Burrah Sahib, Burrah Sahib, you are the saviour of the people of Khumbu," said the head man of the village in full poetic flight. We all laughed and he laughed also at the satisfying effect of his oratory. "Please say you can help us," he pleaded.

"What can you do with these people," said Ed to the room at large. "They're so delightful that it is almost impossible to turn them down. But this time I'm going to be tough." More and more drinks, more speeches and still the people waited for Burrah Sahib to make some decision. Then, like a trump card, a large plate of precious eggs was triumphantly placed in front of Ed — a truly generous gift in this part of the world. Oh dear—it was all so difficult.

"You can tell them, Mingma, that there is a chance I can help them with the water supply some time in the future."

"*Lemonok!*" (Good!) cried the people.

"But it won't be for some time," cautioned Ed. "And as for the bridge—I can't promise anything."

We rose to our feet feeling decidedly waterlogged and walked very slowly to our camp spot below the steep Namche Bazar hill.

CHAPTER II

A Second Home

BRIDGE CAMP IS the traditional overnight stop before climbing the hill to the main villages of Khumbu. There was an air of suppressed excitement around the camp—tomorrow would be the end of our main journey, and our senior Sherpas would be back with their wives and families. We spent the evening sorting out our possessions and washing our clothes and hair in the ice-cold water of the Dudh Kosi. Aila built a huge driftwood fire underneath a large boulder and this proved a very effective clothes dryer—although a little lethal when chunks of rock started exploding off its side. Ang Passang's father arrived from Kunde for an advance welcome. He brought a small bottle of *arak*, and after sharing it round the fire departed in the bright moonlight for home, leading a reluctant Hadley.

The foaming waters of the Dudh Kosi lulled us off to sleep, and we were away bright and early next morning for Kunde. In ten minutes we were approaching the wire-rope suspension bridge we built in 1964, and as we bounced over the central section I remembered how our old friend Annulu of Khumjung (recently killed in a climbing accident) had worked here as a foreman eight years before. It had been a dangerous job building the bridge over fierce rapids, but Annulu had employed all his friends and relations on the project, for, he said, "Working with Burrah Sahib, everybody always very lucky." There had been quite a few disasters during bridge-building activities, but Ed had insisted on following normal safety procedures and nobody had been hurt. As we crossed the bridge Ed started grumbling that some pieces of wire had been removed by someone. It always seems a little strange that on a project which is being carried out for the community there are always some irresponsible people who will steal parts of the bridge even though it reduces the safety factor.

It was very cold in the bottom of the valley and a strong wind flowed down valley with the stream. We were soon climbing up the long two-thousand-foot rise to Namche Bazar, the administrative centre for the upper Khumbu. After half an hour of hard work we met some Tibetan traders and we were happy to stop and look at their wares. To our disappointment they had nothing except a few battered

artifacts and some recently made "antiques". They were asking ridiculous prices—a direct result of the influx of tourists. The genuine
treasures had been sold long ago and now many Sherpa households
have replaced their traditional utensils of wood, brass and copper with
cheap and unattractive glass and plastic.

We came around the last corner and into the hanging valley lined
with the houses of Namche Bazar. All visitors have to stop and report
at the police checkpost and I discovered that since my last visit this
had moved to a new and handsome building high above the village—
perfectly positioned to spy out any forgetful tourists who might have
forgotten to officially register their presence in this border area. Down
below the checkpost on some grass beside the village stream was a
herd of about fifteen handsome black yaks. They were magnificent
hairy beasts with bright red woollen tassels in their ears and bells
around their necks. They had just arrived back from a trading trip to
Tibet over the nineteen-thousand-foot Nangpa La Pass about three
days' march away. Trading between the Khumbu Sherpas and the
Tibetan villagers on the other side of the border is quite legal as long
as you have the necessary permits. It is carried out during the early
months of the winter when there are long periods of clear dry weather.
The Sherpas sell young zums and potatoes and *ghee* at fixed prices to
the Chinese officials and buy coarse rock salt and wool which they
carry home on the backs of their yaks. Mingma told me that in the
days of old Tibet there was a large black-market trade across the
border, and merchandise smuggled in from India was exchanged for
gold and silver Buddhist images and beautifully decorated silver cups.
Namche Bazar was the centre for this illegal trade and for other more
legal types of business, too. It still is a village of traders and businessmen, although there are an increasing number of officials as well.

The altitude was starting to affect us quite a lot now and we climbed
very slowly up the great amphitheatre that encircles Namche Bazar.
A thousand feet up we could see a small group of Sherpas waiting for
us—it was Mingma's wife, Ang Dooli, and Ang Tsering's wife, Doma
—who were waiting to welcome us to the Khumbu. As we approached
them we waved furiously and called out greetings with any spare
breath we had. It was a great reunion as both women had fond memories
of our previous family visit five years before. Ang Dooli has a family
of sons and she had lavished a great deal of love on the small seven-
year-old Belinda. But now the tiny Ang Dooli had to look upwards
to smile at Belinda who measured five feet six and a half inches. Ang
Dooli had brought with her little Da Tseri aged four and a half and
Temba their deaf eighteen-year-old son. Temba had been born deaf

due to the lack of iodine in his mother's diet and he is also very slightly retarded both physically and mentally. Although fully grown he still looked like a small twelve-year-old boy, but a very charming one with a ready smile and a great sense of fun.

"So big, so big," everyone cried in admiration looking at the three young Hillarys. Ang Dooli had brought a large container of her very fine *chung* so while the porters made their way slowly up the hill the rest of us sat down in the sun and had a picnic, surrounded by a fantastic wall of glittering ice peaks. The *chung* was made of rice and tasted light and bubbly. Although I am sure the alcoholic content was extremely low at 11,000 feet it went straight to our heads. Fortunately Doma offered us glasses of sweet milky tea and we followed these with oranges and hard-boiled eggs. The warmth of the welcome from such good friends and the glorious surroundings made me feel as though I had been transported into a glorious dream world. We had little inclination to move on until the sun dropped behind a tall peak and the temperature plummeted to freezing depths. It was time to make one last great effort to climb the remaining thousand feet to Kunde hospital. As we clambered slowly upwards we met many of the Kunde and Khumjung children who were minding their parents' animals during the school holidays. Mingma's son, Ang Rita, was amongst them—a gentle, serious boy of thirteen, who was so overcome with shyness that he tried to hide behind a rock, until his father commanded him to appear.

Half-way up to Kunde was the once large and peaceful flat area called Songboche where the local people have always grazed their yaks amongst the rhododendrons, azalea and juniper bushes. Now the peace and tranquillity of this place had gone for ever. The gently sloping meadowland was being flattened into an airfield for the guests of the new hotel Momblasa that was under construction on top of the ridge. The hotel was being built with Japanese and Nepalese money and one of Mingma's friends told us that a Sherpa co-operative had won the contract for excavating the airfield. It was an extraordinary, and to me a rather shocking sight, to see several hundred Sherpas working like ants to carve a slice off one of the most beautiful mountains in the world. Some of the workers were digging into the hillside with picks and shovels, while others collected the spoil and carried it away in wheelbarrows or dragged it away on top of animal skins—dumping it in places where it was needed for filling.

"I suppose these things have to happen," shrugged Ed, "but I don't think I want to watch it any longer." So we turned our backs on Songboche and walked on up the hill. Mingma and I held young Da

Tseri's hands and swung him over the rocks and holes in the path to an accompaniment of giggles and shouts of joy. We wandered through stunted pine trees and moss-covered erratic boulders to the small *chorten* on top of the ridge—and then looked down on the village of Kunde and the shining roof of the hospital. It was like coming home and I think we all felt a great surge of happiness.

We walked through the village and the place seemed quite deserted.

"Where is everybody?" I asked Mingma.

"They're all working on the airstrip or out cutting firewood for the winter or looking after their animals. They'll be back."

As we approached the hospital we could see great signs of activity and when I walked through the hospital gates a slim Sherpa woman rushed up to me and gave me a great hug. It was rather unSherpalike behaviour and I felt bewildered—"Oh it's you Genevieve," I said recognising the New Zealand wife of the hospital doctor. During the first month of her stay she had transformed herself into a Sherpa lady—not too difficult a task really for she was naturally small, dark and slim with bright rosy cheeks. Her husband, Dr. Lindsay Strang, remained reassuringly unchanged except for a colourful pair of knee high Sherpa boots—his greeting was a little more on the formal side. Soon we were surrounded by a group of old friends—Kanche, the nurse; "Hospital" Pemba, the public-health teacher; and Phu Dorje, one of Mingma's building team and a renowned climber. Everywhere, there were children with wide-open eyes determined to miss nothing of importance.

"You'll like a cup of tea, I suppose," said Genevieve.

"No, thank you," we all groaned. "We've had enough to keep us going until dinner."

"I'll pay off all the porters and some of our Sherpas," said Ed to Mingma. "Then we'll unpack and get things organised."

"I think tonight," said Mingma, "everybody to bed early going, no friends seeing."

"You're absolutely right, Mingma," said Ed, meekly and obediently.

The paying off of the porters was like a school prize-giving. Mingma would call out each one by name and they would present themselves to Ed, who would pass to Mingma the required amount of money. Mingma would then double-check the money and hand it to the fortunate recipient who would beam with joy at his financial windfall and then rush home to his village. The group of pretty Sherpa girl porters were the last ones to be paid. When they all departed to their village of Phortse the hospital felt quite deserted. It was sad to say goodbye to the quiet Nawang who departed towards home almost

immediately with seven porters carrying loads of aluminium roofing
for the Junbesi middle school. Nawang was a little worried about his
children and anyway he felt rather alien and out of place amongst the
exuberant Khumbu Sherpas.

"Now, what shall we do about our two cook boys, Mingma?"
asked Ed.

"Pember Tenzing, very strong, very good," said Mingma, "but
Passang not so clever. I think you should keep Pember Tenzing for
one more week as there is plenty work. Passang must go." Passang's
departure was accomplished only after much shaking of hands and
giving of *katas*. Mingma and Ang Tsering are employed full time by
the Himalayan Trust so the only Sherpas left to deal with were Passang
Tendi, Aila, Siku and Phu Dorje. As all the building programmes had
been completed for the time being it was decided that Phu Dorje, our
most experienced carpenter, would not be needed. This was a great
blow to the family as Phu Dorje is full of fun and definitely one of the
most popular Sherpas. "Well, he only lives next door to the hospital,"
said Ed, "you'll be able to see him every day." And so we did. Phu
Dorje was in fact quite happy to be relieved of his job as it was his turn
to organise one of the big village religious festivals that takes place just
before the end of the Sherpa year.

"Where will everybody stay?" I asked.

"There's nobody very ill in the hospital at present," said Genevieve,
"Roderick and Murray can sleep in the Intensive Care Ward."

"All the Hillary family coming my house," said Mingma. Mingma's
house was looking beautiful—he had just recently repainted all the
window frames in red and green and also the *langdy-pandys*—the
decorative timbers that poke out above the window frame. As well he
had built a beautiful new stone slab courtyard with a high wall around
it, and there was a fine new prayer flag in front of the house.

Mingma boasts the only real guest room for visitors in the Khumbu.
It was built during my previous visit to Kunde as accommodation for
extra medical staff and when not in use Mingma could hire it out to
visitors—we were placed in the category of visiting staff. It was a
simple room made of stone walls and aluminium roof with the added
luxuries of plywood lining on the insides of the walls, wooden
bunks and benches, and a small fireplace. In one corner there was a
large tin bath and a small handbasin that drained away outside.

Due to the limited variety of paints in the hospital store we were
forced to cover some of the walls in a dazzling bright red. To tone
this down I decided to employ one of the two famous artists of Khum-

jung to decorate the interior. The elder artist, Kappa Kalden, was a craftsman of such dignity and renown that I hesitated to approach him—also his fees would have been quite beyond our hospital budget. I asked his son, Kappa Passang, and he was happy to accept our offer of employment for two or three days even though his fee of twelve rupees a day plus food was a mere pittance to what he would get for a medium-sized canvas from a tourist. I had never commissioned a famous artist to paint for me before and felt quite apprehensive.

"Could you please paint the eight lucky Buddhist signs on the cream wall, Passang?" I asked him, "and on the red walls, would it be possible for you to paint some traditional Tibetan-style clouds? . . . What else do you think we should do?" I asked Passang rather helplessly.

"Well, you must paint the centre beam and its uprights green, that is a lucky colour," he said, "and you need some decoration around the windows."

During the first day he painted the lucky signs with great assurance and speed, singing to himself in a high falsetto voice as he worked. The next day I had to leave the village and when I returned very late the same night Kappa Passang had finished the job and the room was in darkness. I turned on my flashlight and shone it over the walls. "Good heavens, it's a work of art," I cried in great excitement. Not only were there fine blue and white stylised Tibetan clouds floating magnificently over the entire area, but twisting and spiralling amongst the clouds were two gold serpents spitting fire out of their nostrils and covered in alarming green scales. Looking on at them coyly from another corner was a strange long-legged bird.

I suppose we should have called this new room the "Dragon Room" or some other descriptive name but it had been labelled the "Naya Kota" (Nepali for new room) and Naya Kota it remained.

The Naya Kota and its dragons were allocated to Ed and me, and Mingma took Peter, Sarah and Belinda upstairs to his private *gompa* which had been turned into a temporary bedroom. Mingma's home is quite large for a Khumbu Sherpa's. Normally they consist of only one living room upstairs and a large basement where firewood, leaves and grass are stored and the family's livestock are sheltered for the night. But Mingma had several extra rooms which were partially used for Himalayan Trust storage. Our children were very comfortable in the *gompa* which had recently been lined with wood in the hope that someday Kappa Passang would decorate the walls. Unfortunately in a recent storm one of the windows had been broken, and as glass is expensive and difficult to come by, a piece of green material had been hung over the gap and this wasn't too successful at excluding the winter winds. Peter's bed was a low wooden bench covered by a brightly coloured Sherpa carpet and the girls had stretchers taken from the store room. There was a little table and a candle beside each bed. From now on we would live in our down jackets during the day, and sleep in two sleeping bags at night, so keeping warm wouldn't be too much of a problem.

The one serious drawback to the use of the *gompa* as a dormitory was its distance from the family toilet, which consisted of a small room at the top of the stairs with a hole in the floor and a pile of leaves beside it—the routine procedure was to throw a handful of leaves down the hole after use. How, I wondered, were the children going to find their way in the pitch darkness across the living room that would be littered with sleeping bodies, then through a narrow passage, past the top of precipitous stairway, and finally to the toilet room? To make matters more complicated the door between the *gompa* and the living room squeaked loudly and there was a twelve-inch step between the rooms—a perfect trap for the unwary in the depth of the night.

The other alternative was to go outside but this involved descending down through the basement. The dark basement of a Sherpa house is a scary place indeed. The ghostly shadows of cattle, the bleating of sheep or the cackling of a hen unnerve you as you blindly stumble towards the steep stairway to the family living quarters. We all checked that our flashlights were in good order—we knew that we would need them.

The Naya Kota, on the other hand, was a completely self-contained unit, with a hot-water supply consisting of a kettle on top of the fire and a private toilet out the back which represented a happy compromise between Asian and Western customs. There was a comfortable seat and a large pile of leaves underneath—a far pleasanter method than a smelly pit-type toilet. Each spring the leaves were dug out and spread over the fields as fertiliser.

The Sherpas' traditional diet has always been based on *rigis* (potatoes) and *tsampa* (pre-cooked barley meal) but the hospital and the schools have been trying to introduce a selection of vegetables into this standard fare. Mingma had become interested in this and during my last visit to Kunde, two years before, Ang Dooli and I had been given the job of planting out their summer vegetables. We had a selection of green beet, lettuce, carrots, parsnips and cauliflower seeds. The soil was hard and dry and the piles of fertiliser were only very slightly decomposed due to the cold climate. At first I found this a bit of a trial, but then pulled myself together, grabbed my mattock and helped Ang

Dooli prepare enough ground for our ambitious sowing of seedlings. Ang Dooli was only used to planting potato crops in large fields and she clearly regarded these efforts as a waste of time. Now, two years later, I was able to ask her how the vegetable garden had fared. She shook her head and tried to look disapproving.

"Very bad. Very bad," she said and then started to laugh. Apparently the weather had been very dry and cold that year and almost nothing had come up.

"Last year Mingma and I planted our vegetables without any help from you or the doctors," she told me with pride. "They were very good. And many lettuce and many carrots," she said with much satisfaction.

That evening Mingma and Ed set up the shower-box in a corner of the Naya Kota. With a great deal of mumbling and cursing they succeeded in attaching the shower rose to an old disused four-gallon kerosene tin. We tied the new water-container to a beam in the roof and put the little tent in place around it with the old tin bathtub on the floor to collect the water. Just before going to bed that night I decided to launch the new shower arrangement. The tin was filled with hot water and with much grunting and groaning was suspended in place. We stoked up our fire in hopes that this might raise the room temperature a little, for the Naya Kota was very draughty with a big gap under the door and cracks beside the windows and the roof. As all Sherpa houses are cold no one had thought there was anything unusual about these icy blasts—it was just a matter of putting on extra clothing.

I jumped eagerly into the shower-box and turned on the flow of hot water.

"Ouch!"

"What's the trouble? Is the water too cold?" asked Ed.

"No," I yelled, "it's not the water. It's the cold wind blowing around." To keep warm whilst bathing in these below freezing temperatures you'd need to be immersed in a great tank of hot water. Stupidly I stayed under the shower hoping that the slow trickle of hot water might finally warm me up, but it was hopeless and I dressed quickly and struggled into my sleeping bag and for hours I lay there shaking uncontrollably.

We learned to use the shower more effectively—but only in the daytime when the sun was shining. In some ways the shower-box became the social centre of the village, as it was possible for us to shower and change our clothes whilst conversing with our visitors. Ed gets very depressed when his projects don't work out well, but even he admitted that some improvement was desirable.

Our first day in Kunde started at 6.30 a.m. when Ang Dooli brought us a cup of tea. Feeling somewhat guilty we snuggled down into the depths of our double-layered down sleeping bags, only reaching out a reluctant arm to take the cup.

"Thank you, Ang Dooli, but to-morrow tea is not necessary," I told her.

"Mingma says tea every morning," she replied matter-of-factly in English.

Well, if Mingma said so, there was very little we could do about it, although I still felt a little conscience-stricken as Ang Dooli had a very busy household. Already the zums had been herded out of the basement, Ang Rita had fetched a load of water from the village pipe-line, and the family had finished its early morning meal of Tibetan tea and boiled potatoes. We had been given Indian tea which is much more trouble to make as it has to be freshly brewed, while the Tibetan variety is made in large quantities and kept warm beside the fire all day if necessary. Our next visitor was Ang Rita who lit our fire with dry leafy branches of aromatic juniper. Once it was going well he shovelled in pieces of yak and zum dung—an excellent slow-burning fuel when thoroughly dried. A wild war-cry outside the door heralded the approach of the deaf Temba who became our self-appointed fire watcher during our stay. By this time the early morning sun had poked its head above the jagged ridges behind the hospital to warm the front of the house. Mingma's old mother, Sala, would then bring her spindle, some wool and her wire carders to the little courtyard in front of our room and work quietly all day. Before settling down to her daily work she always brought us a little pile of kindling in her apron so that if the fire went out it was easy for us to light it again.

We all met at the hospital for breakfast and while we ate we tried to sort out some of our social engagements. First we helped Roderick organise himself a day of sightseeing at Thyangboche monastery, as the following day he had to depart for home and back to school in England.

"Everyone must come to dinner at my house tonight," said Mingma, "and then you can go to Ang Passang's home the next night." Just then the Thami Head Lama's secretary arrived and wanted to know when we were going to visit the monastery. It was so difficult to make decisions—all I wanted to do was to enjoy the sun and the magnificent views. The last thing I needed was a glass of the secretary's ice-cold *chung*. A pleasant distraction was the sounds and sights of the village waking up after the long cold night. There was the marvellous smell of burning dried juniper and azalea leaves which is used as incense by each household in the early morning. I came back to earth to realise that Ed and Mingma had already made all the decisions for us.

The brilliant sunshine and the vivid blue sky tempted us to leave our chores at the hospital and walk down to Khumjung to see the school and take some photographs from the hills above. Half-way there we met Ang Tsering's father, Passang Sonar, and Ang Dooli's brother, Lama Karma, coming up the path to visit us with large wooden bottles of welcoming *chung*. They wanted us to drink it there and then but we persuaded them to wait until we reached the school. Ten minutes later we were sitting in a circle on the playground having a gay morning *chung* party. Soon we were joined by Ang Tsering's wife, Doma, and her five-year-old daughter; next to arrive was old Ang Chumbi, who had been head man of Kunde many years before. The hours sped pleasantly by and we gazed with pride at our Khumjung school, the first one to be built in South Khumbu.

It had all started in 1961 with one small aluminium building but now there was a complex of three buildings with two classrooms in each and a headmaster's study and common room. There was a library housed in a simple stone cottage at the back of the school buildings, and over the years the schoolmasters had planted shrubs and flowering annuals, and built fences around the playground; it was one of the best cared-for schools in Nepal. More recently the school committee had built another little out-house to be used for dying wool for the handicraft department and they had also enlarged the soccer and volley-ball fields by moving the village *mani* wall back about fifty feet. As there must have been hundreds of tons of rock in the *mani* wall this had been a huge effort involving the people in four or five days of hard voluntary work.

As it was holiday time the place was shuttered and locked, but each room had been left in perfect order. The handicraft room looked more like a tidy doctor's surgery, with the shining clean carpentry tools hanging neatly on a wall, whilst the wood and stone carving department was decorated with attractive examples of its work laid out on a bench. The weaving and spinning section was gay with balls of coloured wool and piles of striped Sherpa clothing left neatly in place. Mingma had helped start the weaving department by donating an old loom and then the children, with the help of instructors, used a lot of initiative and imagination to build another loom with the materials available. I noticed some plaster reels from the hospital doing a very useful job. They had certainly gone a long way since the first nineteen pupils gathered ten years before. Now, if it hadn't been holiday time, there would have been a noisy group of a hundred and forty eager students.

It was with difficulty that we prized ourselves away from the convivial party and the endless supplies of *chung*. We hurriedly marked
out the position for the new middle school and then marched up to the
top of the ridge overlooking Khumjung.

This must be one of the most tremendous viewpoints in the world. A
dazzling array of precipices surrounded us on every side. On our right
were the serrated ice ridges and bulging ice faces of Mount Tamserku
and Mount Kangtega. Standing in isolation a little beyond them was
the impossible overhanging thumb of Amadablam. In front of us was
the deep abyss of the Dudh Kosi and beyond it the monastery of
Thyangboche perched on its peaceful promontory. Above Thyangboche reared the great rock wall of Nuptse and Lhotse—crowned by
the black, angry shape of Everest. Even to the south, behind us, the
view was beautiful. The shadowy Dudh Kosi gorge lost itself in a com-
plexity of steep mountains and narrow side-valleys as it wound its way
towards the distant haze of India. Lining the valley were our old
familiar friends Ku Sung Kang and Kwangde. Directly below us was
the sheltered Kunde Khumjung terrace rising into the warm red rocks
of Kumbila, the small peak that no one must climb for fear of dis-
pleasing the Sherpas' special gods.

I found the ridge on which we were sitting just as beautiful as any
of the more distant views. There were a series of high alpine meadows,
divided by groves of lacy birch trees, angular dark green fir trees and
stunted rhododendrons. A series of small hills and valleys provided
sheltered grazing grounds for the Kunde and Khumjung domestic
animals and it was hard to feel sorry for the zum and sheep herders
who spent their days looking after the family animals in this paradise.
We sat on the warm grass and absorbed the scene in silence—it would
have been sacrilege to hurry away from such a place. Finally, in true
tourist fashion, we clicked away with our cameras and tried to capture
every peak and alpine glade for happy memories back at home.

At the head of our ridge, discreetly hidden by jutting rock and
stunted fir trees, was the Hotel Momblasa, one of the most amazing
business enterprises in the Himalayas. The children and I were very
anxious to visit the hotel but Ed hadn't been very enthusiastic about the
project and he decided to return to the hospital and get on with his
work. The rest of us climbed along the ridge very impressed with the
outlook in every direction. My first impressions of the hotel were very
favourable indeed. It was a most tasteful structure built unobtrusively
into the mountain scenery. The outside walls were made of local rock
in traditional Sherpa fashion, whilst inside, the restaurant's back wall
was the natural cliff face with Buddhist prayers carved into its rough

surface. When the hotel is completed there will be central heating, hot water and electric light as in any modern establishment, but there will be one unusual feature as well—oxygen will be piped into every bedroom so that the occupants from sea-level won't suffer from the rarefied atmosphere at nearly 13,000 feet.

Running the hotel efficiently won't be an easy task. The nearest large water supply is 1,500 feet below at Namche Bazar and all the fuel for the boilers and generators will have to be transported at great cost from Kathmandu. The transport of the hotel guests by air will always be an uncertain venture due to the altitude, the violent winds, and the low clouds which are present at most times of the year—particularly in the monsoon from June to October.

The original plan had been for the guests to fly to Lukla airfield and then ride up to the hotel on horseback—or even be transported from Lukla by helicopter. Then rumours started to drift around the Khumbu that an airstrip was planned much closer to the hotel. Where could this be, everyone wondered, and then the solution was finally presented—the airfield was to be right through the centre of Khumjung village and its richest potato fields. Such an airstrip, I am sure, would have been a disaster in every way. Not only were there the physical hazards of being in a side-valley above the Dudh Kosi river but it would have completely ruined the village of Khumjung. The people's culture and independence would have quickly disappeared under an irrevocable bitumen strip.

At first many of the Khumjung Sherpas remained quietly apathetic—they had been persuaded that they might even benefit from the new hotel. Some of the others, particularly Ang Tsering, whose house and fields would have been the first to go, decided to fight against the location of the airstrip. In the end the whole village united against the project and a group of senior villagers travelled down to Kathmandu and petitioned the Government to have the airstrip put in some more suitable place. The Nepalese Government refused to act against the wishes of the local people and Khumjung was saved. Now from the heights above Khumjung we could look down at the industrious workers on Songboche airstrip. And I had the rather sad feeling that the Khumbu was about to become the Switzerland of Asia.

There have already been a number of fatalities in Khumbu from the effects of altitude and this will inevitably be aggravated when tourists can step out of a plane at 12,000 feet without any prior acclimatisation. Altitude sickness is a very common disorder and it seems to strike anybody, young or old, strong or weak. The symptoms of mild altitude sickness—headaches, vomiting, loss of appetite—are very common and relatively harmless. Severe altitude sickness can result in pulmonary oedema which is swift and often fatal. The only cure is to give the patient oxygen as soon as possible and take him down to a lower altitude.

"What will happen to Lukla airfield when Songboche is opened?" enquired one of the children.

"Maybe it will become obsolete, but I think there'll always be people who'll prefer to land at the safer level and to acclimatise more comfortably and slowly as they walk up the valley. Some day there will be all sorts of changes here—perhaps a jeep track from Songboche to the hotel or a railway down to the river and then up to Thyangboche monastery."

"I hope we never see it," said Sarah.

The cold afternoon breeze straight from the ice of the Khumbu Glacier persuaded us to head back to Khumjung. We wanted to call on some of our old friends but most of them were away. However Kappa Kalden was sure to be there, so we climbed up the steep alleyways to his long white home overlooking the village with the tallest of all Khumjung prayer flags flapping in the yard. Mingma had accompanied us as we needed his help to order some pictures and we puffed up the dark stairs to the large living room, decorated with his wife's dowry of very beautiful brass and copper pots. Kappa Kalden (Kappa means artist) comes from a long line of fine craftsmen. He can recite the detailed descriptions of all the old traditional pictures from memory and has passed his knowledge on to his son Kappa Passang.

Kappa Kalden's five children are all handsome and talented, although only the youngest, Ang Rita, has been able to have a modern education. My favourite is Ang Tsering's wife, Doma, who is a very handsome woman with a wicked twinkle in her eye just like her old father. Whenever I go and see Kappa Kalden he always offers me some of his light sparkling *chung* which he says he has been keeping for me for the last two or three months.

"Let's tell him we really don't want *chung* this time," I said to Mingma, "because we'll be coming to your party in about three hours' time and we've already had enough."

"O.K.," he replied, "leave it to me." We found Kappa Kalden seated crosslegged in the bay window of his private *gompa* working hard on a large canvas.

"Who's the picture for?" I asked.

"For a rich Sherpa family who are buying it for a funeral memorial. Sherpa families don't pay nearly as well as tourists." He burst into high-pitched laughter at this great joke.

We sat down on the floor and drank our tea surrounded by the fine religious pictures that covered all the walls and the ceiling of the room. By the time we had finished our tea, I felt sufficiently refreshed to embark on the complicated procedure of ordering a picture from this absentminded artist.

I'd always wanted to own my own original of the *Toonba Namshi*—"The Four Harmonious Brothers"—which illustrates one of the famous stories of Lamaistic Buddhism. The story goes something like this: One day four animals, an elephant, a monkey, a rabbit and a partridge met beside a tree in the forest. They decided to discover which of them was the oldest and should therefore be the most respected. The elephant said that when he last passed the tree it was only as high as he was. But the monkey said that when he was there last, the tree had been as small as he. The rabbit, however, argued that he remembered when the tree was so small that he was able to lick the dew from its buds. Finally, the partridge said that one day he had eaten a tiny seed and deposited it in the place where it had now grown into a fine tall tree. Out of respect for the partridge who was unquestionably the oldest the animals each hopped onto the back of the younger one and the partridge sat on top of them all.

The four friends decided amongst themselves that they would respect the five laws. Never take life, never steal, never commit adultery, never lie, never take stimulating drink, and that they would help each other to keep these rules. This they did and throughout their kingdom there was plenty of rain and great prosperity. The people then began to wonder how they had earned this good fortune and the sage revealed to them that it was due to these four animals. So everybody agreed to respect the four harmonious brothers and to follow the five laws.

I first saw a copy of this picture at Thyangboche monastery—the benevolent white elephant with the three animals sitting on top of it, all standing beside a gnarled forest tree covered in stylised leaves and delicious fruit. I very much admired the picture and spent some time discovering the old story which the picture illustrated. Now with any luck I might be the proud owner of a copy of the *Toonba Namshi*.

"How long will it take?" I asked Kappa Kalden who always has a great backlog of uncompleted work.

"Three weeks," he replied to my astonishment. "Not many tourists now," he explained. Having completed all the financial arrangements we said our goodbyes and walked down the hill a hundred yards or so to the house of his son, Kappa Passang.

We had decided to spread our patronage around a bit and were planning to ask Passang to paint us a set of the eight lucky signs of the Buddhist religion—the *Tashi Daké*. These signs appear on all religious buildings and religious artifacts in everyday use in the Lamaistic Buddhist world. They symbolise the basic concepts of the religion. The eight signs are:

The swastika	—the sanskrit name of a design used in meditation.
The two fish	—two golden fish symbolise the vital forces of nature. Water is the symbol of life in Buddhist philosophy.
The lotus flower	—is the symbol of purity. Though the roots of the flower are in the mud—great beauty and purity appears out of this mud.
The vase	—contains the potion of immortality.
The banner of victory	—symbolises victory.
The royal umbrella	—symbolises royalty and divinity.
The wheel of the law	—symbolises the setting in motion of the Buddhist philosophy.
The conch shell	—the diversity of the manifest world (*samsara*) spiralling out from the peaceful central point (*nirvana*).

Passang had already painted the *Tashi Daké* on the walls of the Naya Kota and now we wanted a set of the signs to take home to New Zealand. We handed him an artist's sketching block and he in return gave us large brimming glasses of welcoming *chung*.

"We don't really want ours," whispered Sarah and Belinda, although I noticed that Peter was having no trouble with his.

"Well, don't drink it, then," I said, "it's just not worth it. Give it to me." And for the next few days—as I was older and tougher—I turned into a sort of emergency receptacle for drinks and food.

As we walked slowly back up the hill towards Kunde I remembered another trip on the same path with a previous Kunde doctor. We had stopped on the outskirts of Khumjung to see a pregnant woman.

"It's an important case to me," said the doctor. "The baby is overdue by a couple of days and I am hopeful that the mother will be willing to come to hospital for her confinement." I knew this would be quite a triumph for the doctor as the people prefer to give birth to their babies in the unhygienic conditions of their own homes. "The woman

Hindu religious figure at Changu Narayan.

Ringmo bridge.

Mr. Shyam Praham, headmaster of all the Himalayan Trust Schools with pupil.

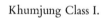

Khumjung Class I.

also has severe toxaemia so that it is important that I have a look at her," he said.

We went to the door and the woman came out to meet us. She was dressed in her long black tunic or *ingi* which is only very loosely tied so it was difficult to see what sort of shape she was underneath.

"Let me feel your ankles for swelling."

"That's funny!" he said as he straightened up. "All the swelling has disappeared." I asked Pemba, the doctor's assistant, how many children the woman had.

"Four," said Pemba.

"Four?" said the astounded doctor. "Why, only yesterday when I visited her you told me she had three."

"That's right," said Pemba. "She had three but now she's got four."

"What! Do you mean to say that she's had the baby?"

"Yes," said Pemba, quite unperturbed. I couldn't help chuckling about this incident for days afterwards. Since then Pemba has done some very good work as a public health lecturer. He has talked to many Sherpas on hygiene, baby care, family planning, diet, pre-natal and postnatal care with special emphasis on mothers having their babies delivered in the hospital whenever possible. Progress undoubtedly has been slow, but as Mingma says "slowly, slowly is better".

CHAPTER 12

High-Altitude Happiness

WHEN WE ARRIVED back in Kunde it was nearly time for our dinner engagement with Mingma. Ang Passang had thoughtfully kept lunch for us but we sadly turned it down. It was *rigi cour* (potato cakes) made from grated raw potato mixed with a little flour. This is baked on a flat stone over the fire and then covered with a very hot sauce of onion, chilli and salt. We hurriedly changed into the clean shirts and slacks we had been saving for this occasion for the last two weeks, and then immediately covered all this smartness with our dirty down jackets. We had presents for all of Mingma's family, and these we carefully wrapped in daphne paper. For Ang Dooli we had a bright red Viyella shirt to wear under her *ingi*. There were rubber balls and model cars for Ang Rita and Da Tseri and a collection of tubes of water-colours for Temba who was learning how to paint.

Though the evening was cold Mingma had managed to make his big living room very cosy indeed. At one end was the big cooking stove filled with glowing logs and at the other end he had placed a Tibetan charcoal brazier piled high with large pieces of yak dung. These had turned to red-hot coals which gave out a delightful warmth and a most pleasant aroma. Ang Dooli's fine collection of copper and brass household utensils reflected the cosy firelight like a mirror.

Aila's handsome wife had arrived from her village of Phortse with four fearsome hairy white yaks with bulging handwoven sacks of potatoes for the hospital. She was accompanied by two other well-known matrons from Phortse and they were all in very high spirits as life at Phortse can be very quiet.

Another guest was one of Mingma's greatest friends, the manager of the Sherpa co-operative organisation that was excavating the new airstrip. He had brought with him the Nepalese Department of Civil Aviation's engineer who was in charge of the strip. The engineer was thoroughly enjoying his work with the Sherpas and unlike some Kathmandu officials was managing to cope very successfully with the hard living and cold conditions. He was obviously very popular with the locals and we hoped that he might be helping to promote understanding between the mountain and the valley people of Nepal.

There were a number of other distinguished guests. Ang Passang's father and Nima Tashi, an elder of Khumjung village, were already seated comfortably beside the brazier and all our Sherpa staff were present. Only Lindsay and Genevieve Strang, Murray and Roderick hadn't yet put in an appearance.

"Where can they be," we wondered. "It's not like Roderick to be late for a party." We waited and waited until finally Pemba appeared.

"Where are they?" we called.

"Roderick nearly cut his finger off with his new *kukri*," said Pemba with a grin, "and the doctor is busy sewing."

"*Amo, amo*," (oh dear, oh dear), said Kanche the nurse. This news had quite a dampening effect on the party as it was Roderick's last night in Kunde before returning to Kathmandu and his only chance of experiencing a real Sherpa party. A little while later Lindsay, Genevieve and Murray arrived.

"Isn't Roderick coming?" said Peter.

"Well, he does seem a bit shaken," said Lindsay. "He may come in a little while."

"I'll go and get him," said Peter. He returned about twenty minutes later with Roderick whose hand was impressively bandaged and tied up in a sling. What will his mother think? was my first reaction, but Roderick assured me that all was well underneath the bandages.

Now the *chung* and the *arak* that had been maturing for months awaiting our visit started to flow very freely indeed, and Ang Dooli, the perfect hostess, stood over us and made us drink.

The food, when it came two hours later, was quite wonderful. Mingma had killed one of his precious flock of twenty sheep in our honour and we had a meat stew with fresh carrots from his garden and piles of mashed potatoes. For dessert we ate our favourite, sweet zum curds (*dhai*) with sugar and *tsampa* (pre-cooked barley meal) sprinkled on it. It wasn't difficult to eat plenty and to show our real appreciation. We felt secure and amongst friends, for food is a measure of hospitality all over the world and we were obviously welcome. To help our digestion we tuned the guitar and sang a few songs rather breathlessly to a most appreciative audience. The engineer from Kathmandu was familiar with our old favourite tunes and joined in the singing with great gusto.

During the singing Mingma and Ang Dooli had been hanging a hospital sheet against the back wall of their house in readiness for the first ever slide show in the Khumbu. I'd bought a small battery projector with me and a selection of slides of New Zealand—particularly agricultural pictures—and a selection of photographs of our Sherpa friends. On the front page of a glossy brochure describing my new projector it suggested that the machine would be most useful for missionaries working in the field or for training sales people. The Himalayan Trust doesn't fall into either of these two categories but I suppose you could say that it helps to convert people to modern education and health and hygiene. Despite the pale image that was thrown onto our screen the picture show was a great success, particularly the shots taken of familiar Sherpa faces. I had the satisfaction of knowing that at last our friends could see why all their visitors from other parts of the world took so many photographs.

"That projector is terrible," said Ed. "Throw it away!"

"Oh, no!" replied Genevieve and I. "It's really quite good." I continued, "Your standards are much too high."

Lindsay came to my rescue and said that he and Genevieve would find the projector most useful for showing pictures to the school students during their public health lectures. Mingma, always practical in outlook, commented that the projector would have to be used sparingly as it used twelve torch batteries—a most extravagant number for the remote Khumbu.

"The Sherpas' turn to perform now!" we called. But at first everyone just looked self-conscious. At length after much pestering from us, Aila's wife rose to her feet pulling her two Phortse friends with her and started singing a lovely welcoming song to each of the visitors individually. The only trouble with Sherpa welcoming songs is that drinking *chung* or *arak* is also included in the performance. The song said how happy everyone was to welcome the guests, then a *kata* was presented, and finally you had to drink down your glass of *chung* or *arak*. It was probably very bad manners but we clapped Mrs. Aila and her troupe each time they finished a verse.

"How about some Sherpa dancing?" said Roderick.

"Yes, we must have some dancing," we pleaded, aided and abetted by the engineer. So Mrs. Aila and her two indomitable Phortse friends commanded some of the Sherpa men to stand up and with sheepish grins they formed themselves into a line with arms linked and started dancing. First they sang a sad slow chant, and stepped backwards and forwards in rhythm to the music, but as the singing speeded up so did the footwork and the delightful rhythmic stamping and kicking of the Sherpa dance soon had the house reverberating and the onlookers' feet tapping. But this was just an introduction—Mrs. Aila rushed forward and grabbed Sarah and Belinda and pushed them into the women's end of the line.

"Come on Peter, Murray and Rodrock," called Passang Tendi, who like all the other Sherpas found it completely impossible to pronounce Roderick's long three-syllable name. They rushed energetically into the fray, soon followed by everybody else. We skipped about, desperately trying to keep up with the complicated stamping footwork. The exercise certainly helped to shake down all our food.

"Do the 'Dinga-dinga-ding-dong' song," said Sarah and Belinda to Mrs. Aila, who had definitely become the leader of the dancing. Away we went again with a great surge of energy. The words of this song describe the bells ringing at the *gompa* and it has a particularly catchy tune which is most popular with our family. Down at the women's end of the dancing line we were having extra problems as it was almost impossible to follow the intricate footwork of the dance when your Sherpa neighbour's feet were hidden by a long tunic. I also had the misfortune of standing near one of the big copper *chu sans* (water containers) and my section of the floor was very slippery from the recent dishwashing activities. We became completely absorbed into the Sherpa world and found ourselves singing the unfamiliar songs as though we had always known them, and our feet started following the complicated steps with surprising ease.

Few people are fortunate enough to be wholeheartedly accepted by the inhabitants of a village in a distant land, and I suppose this feeling of unity can only be achieved by working together and then playing together. But, like Cinderella, the spell had to break and quite suddenly I became myself again for it was very late and I was very tired.

"Goodnight all," I called out with great finality. But the children just looked at me through a distant haze as if I didn't belong to their lives at all and I took my leave of our hosts and followed Ed down the staircase. From the warmth of my sleeping bag I could hear the singing and stamping as it continued joyfully on into the night, while outside all was still and frost-covered. I was asleep before it all came to an end.

"Nobody's remembered my birthday," said Belinda cheerfully as she arrived in our room before breakfast next morning.

"Happy birthday," I replied obediently and then remembered with sinking heart that Belinda's birthday party was going to take place that very night at Ang Passang's house.

"Have we got the strength for another night like last night?" I enquired.

"Definitely not," replied Ed who seemed to be suffering from a little hangover.

"We'll just have to spend all day trying to develop an appetite to do justice to Ang Passang's food."

We sat in the sun idly watching Mingma's mother working patiently at her spindle. Every day she came and sat outside to work and mind the children. She must have appreciated the sun and the life of the village more than most people because for many years severe arthritis had imprisoned her inside the home. Five years ago the first Kunde doctor had treated her with such success that very soon she was able to walk again with astonishing ease.

"Let's fix my birthday cake," said Belinda who had managed to become interested in food again. Ang Passang had already baked a fruit cake with the remainder of my precious supply of crystallised cherries and dried fruit. He had used an open fire behind the hospital rather than the big wood-burning range in the kitchen as he said he had difficulty in controlling its temperature. There was no icing sugar available so I taught Ang Passang how to make fudge icing with coarse white sugar, butter from Tendi's dairy factory at Piké, and lemon juice and rind from the lemons we had collected down valley. We had a few exciting moments pouring the thick mixture over the cake but Ang Passang remained quite calm and we ended up with a masterly half-inch coating of icing. Very pleased with the result, we then spent a happy hour decorating the cake with silver balls, candles and coloured paper. Ang Passang was so impressed with our combined efforts that he donated a bag of boiled sweets and kept muttering the icing recipe to himself to commit it to memory. Since my failure as a cooking instructor of lemon dumplings, my advice on cookery matters had not been asked, but now I had been reinstated once again.

With much regret (and a good deal of lively badinage) we said our goodbyes to Roderick who was departing that morning for Lukla. Murray was leaving for a while, too, and was planning a closer look at the precipitous approaches of Ku Sung Kang. I didn't envy him his trip—he would have to hack his way with a *kukri* through the thick bamboo jungle that covered the gorge leading to the foot of the mountain.

The daily hospital routine continued all around us. A baby needed treatment for bronchitis; there was the uncomfortable business of a tooth extraction; and then one of the policemen from Namche arrived with a broken finger. He was rather disappointed when the doctor told him that the finger had been broken for so long that it would probably be better to heal naturally.

Two Khumjung scholarship boys came to pay their respects to our family. One was Ang Tsering's eldest son, Nima Wong Chu, and the other a Tibetan refugee, Karma Namda. As a special compliment they brought a large Chinese Thermos flask painted with brightly coloured flowers and filled with Tibetan tea. The salty brew was, as usual, rather hard for the children to drink and I found myself once again the emergency consumer of beverages.

It became cold and cloudy quite early in the afternoon so we took the frozen laundry off the line and sat around the fire in the Naya Kota, entertaining Temba, Ang Rita and Da Tseri, who enjoyed learning how to play with yo-yos and quoits in the relative warmth of our retreat. Sala, the grandmother, kept stoking our fire with yak dung, but despite her labours a small saucer of water three feet away from the fire remained frozen.

"I don't think I'll ever look at food again," said Sarah, which warned us that she had a slight stomach disturbance.

"You'll have to come to Ang Passang's even if you don't eat," I replied. But as the afternoon wore on it became quite clear that it would have been an unnecessary torture for Sarah to have gone out that night. At six o'clock when it was time for us to leave for the party she climbed thankfully into her sleeping bag and we left her to rest and recover with the added comforts of a hot-water bottle, a little candle beside the bed, and Mingma's mother to take care of her. The only common language they had between them was a smile, but we felt this would be quite sufficient.

Ang Passang must have been working like a slave all day. The moment we entered his house delicious piles of homemade potato chips and other delicacies were handed round on bamboo trays. Ang Passang's three years of employment in the diplomatic world were certainly paying dividends now. Most of our friends had brought their children for this birthday dinner and they sat very quietly beside their parents, too shy to move. The only exceptions were Ang Passang's three little daughters, who despite their angelic faces ran around the room in great excitement followed by their tousled little Apso puppy rushing after them like a ferocious whirlwind.

The main course at dinner was very meaty *mormors* whose outer coating of pasta was fashioned into highly decorative shapes.

"That meat tastes remarkably like beef to me," I said to Ed. "I wonder where Ang Passang got it?"

"Oh, I suppose down at the market last Saturday. There's always a bit of meat about if you get there early." To enhance the flavour of the rich *mormors* Ang Passang handed round a salad of grated turnips soaked in the bitter brown lemon vinegar that the Sherpas had bought in the citrus-growing area two weeks before. To our salad-starved palates the mixture tasted exceedingly pleasant and refreshing. Then it was time for the birthday cake. We turned down the pressure lamp, lit all the candles on the cake, and carried it ceremoniously into the centre of the room where it was received with silent admiration by all. After the traditional formalities of blowing out candles and the cutting of the cake had been observed, Belinda handed out the slices. There was plenty for everyone and also a large piece to take home to Sarah. Ang Passang's little girls re-lit some of the cake candles and stood quietly holding them in their hands, looking more like Christmas-card angels than real Sherpa girls.

The evening had been quiet but very happy. Suddenly things started to get noisy over in the far corner of the room—the disturbance was caused by Ang Dorje, Ang Passang's neighbour who had just returned from a trading trip to Tibet. He had crossed over the Nangpa La with some zum calves which he had sold successfully in one of the Tibetan towns. He had then loaded his three yaks with wool and salt and started on the return journey over the pass. Two of the yaks had slipped to their death on their icy slopes and now Ang Dorje was very successfully drowning his sorrows in bottle after bottle of *arak*. During his visit to Tibet he had bought himself an amazing cream fur hat, shaped like a wide woolly halo, and he now resembled a drunken pirate as he sang song after song in a loud and wavering voice. After a while Mingma decided that we had heard enough, and he gently pushed him down into the seat so that conversation could continue once more.

"Where did you get that lovely meat?" I asked Ang Passang. He looked quite embarrassed and I was about to say, "Oh, it doesn't matter, don't tell me," when with downcast gaze he muttered the name "Hadley".

"Hadley!" we all called out in chorus—and he nodded. "What happened?" we enquired.

"She fell," he replied—and that was all the information we could get. We couldn't let such a tragic occurrence pass without a suitably sad song:

> "Poor Hadley was a zum,
> She passed through Khumjung,
> She never drank water,
> She always drank *chung*."

"More! More! Sing more!" said our appreciative audience. But inspiration seemed to leave us and anyhow it was time for bed. We walked happily home over the dusty brown potato fields and along the little stone alleys singing the Hadley Lament to the sleeping village.

"Let's wake Sarah," someone suggested when we got back home. Sarah was surprisingly cheerful about being woken at eleven o'clock and she even managed to try some of the birthday cake.

"The food was fantastic," we chorused at the rather disinterested, sleepy figure.

"Peter had three helpings of mormors," added Belinda.

"It wasn't that I was particularly hungry," remarked Peter, "but it was so delicious I wanted to really convince Ang Passang that I had appreciated his food—I was just being self-sacrificing!"

"Oh yes," we all laughed.

"Don't forget to pack up nice and early to-morrow," said Ed as we departed for the Naya Kota, "there's a lot of work to be done at Thami to-morrow and we must leave in good time."

CHAPTER 13

Thami

IN 1963 THE THIRD of the Himalayan Trust schools was built at Thami. The site chosen was half-way between the small villages of upper and lower Thami on a wide grass terrace facing north to the Nangpa La, 19,000 feet, only twelve miles away on the Tibetan border. From the school you could see a path winding upwards until it lost itself in the steep barren ridges and rocky peaks that crowd in towards the pass. To the east and west are great white snow peaks that stand like lonely sentinels and look down from this high valley in Nepal in a grim and almost hostile fashion—or so it has always appeared to my imagination. People say that the scenery around Thami is very much the same as large areas of Tibet. Generally it is treeless and bare except for scanty scrub and rough grass. The valley is wild, bleak and colourless and the grey-brown ridges stretch high up into a brilliant blue sky. Every time I return to Thami I have the feeling that I am surrounded by wild untamed forces, although these same forces are more than matched by the friendly and hospitable nature of the inhabitants. The Sherpas here are unsophisticated, hardy individuals, most of whom have had to battle hard for their simple raw existence. In the old days there was very close contact with the people across the border in Tibet and as a result many of the inhabitants are only first- or second-generation Nepalese with many relations still living on the other side of the Nangpa La. Ed's Everest companion, Tenzing Norgay, and his wife, Daku, both spent their childhood in Thami. Tenzing was actually born in Tibet and carried over the Nangpa La as a tiny baby.

As you travel up valley towards the twin villages of Thami, you follow the wild Bhote Kosi river. At Thami the river turns north towards the Nangpa La while a large tributary, the Thami Khola, branches off in a westerly direction up a steep glacial valley to the Tashi Lapcha—an eighteen-thousand-foot pass which leads into the Rolwaling valley. It is an eight-mile walk from Kunde to Thami but no matter what the time of year it is always exciting and spectacular. The Bhote Kosi river hurtles down its steep gorge, leaping over great boulders and carving away the sides to create huge slips and destroy the narrow paths.

In the winter the frost lies for months in the sunless gullies and great mushrooms of ice form on top of the river boulders, with icicles hanging down like jellyfish tentacles into the rushing water. But in the early spring the Bhote Kosi valley is transformed into a brilliantly colourful landscape with every sheltered corner ablaze with rhododendron flowers. Tiny starlike irises poke their heads through the soil and the stunted azalea shrubs change in colour from a dusky brown to a blush of pink. In very sheltered spots amongst groves of delicate birch trees you can find the round-leafed variety of rhododendron with their waxy cream blossoms. It is a valley filled with endless delight and as you walk higher towards the Tashi Lapcha you may be lucky enough to find the dainty alpine buttercups, the bright blue gentians and the blue Himalayan poppies which are the ultimate prize for the lucky Himalayan traveller.

There must be about a thousand people living in the scattered villages in this isolated corner of Nepal and the Thami school has a regular roll of forty pupils. This represents quite a lot of self-sacrifice among the Sherpa families as the children are particularly valuable in such barren areas to herd the sheep and cattle and collect firewood, twigs and leaves. Many children spend only one or two years at school, but even this small amount of education will help them withstand the inevitable changes that are taking place in their valley.

Five hundred feet above the school, clinging to tall crags high above the Thami Khola river, is the Thami *gompa* and its monastic village. It looks an impossible site for a village from any angle but there is a spring of good water seeping out from under a small rock buttress above the main group of houses. It is a remote and peaceful spot high above the rest of the world and most suitable for meditation. The monks and the other members of the community live in about thirty small whitewashed stone houses, placed in rather precarious positions around the main *gompa*. The *gompa* itself was built right under an overhanging cliff with a cantilevered courtyard in front made of slabs of rock and timber. It is a handsome old building filled with much loved, slightly smoke-stained Buddhist artifacts. The walls are covered with paintings, and from the main beams of the ceiling hang many fine silken scrolls with religious pictures on them and two large drums decorated with gold-embossed prancing dragons. On the floor beside the drums are two huge copper trumpets glowing richly brown with constant use and ornamented with fine silver designs. Lining several walls is a large library of religious texts.

About a hundred people live in the monastery village although only about twenty-four of them are monks—or *tawas* as they are called in

Khumbu. Their religious leader is the young re-incarnate lama or *rimpoche* who we met at Tuten Choling near Junbesi—a twelve-year-old boy who was chosen—or recognised—in the same manner as the Dalai Lama was chosen as a child in Tibet. The Thami Rimpoche was discovered in the Rolwaling valley, across the Tashi Lapcha, and was believed to be the re-incarnation of the previous Rimpoche—a man of great stature who attracted many monks to the monastery and a large following of local people. The monks of Thami *gompa* are traditionally hard-working and support themselves to a large extent by growing their own potatoes in the small terraced fields below the *gompa*, and by grazing their own herd of zums.

A few years ago the courtyard in front of the Thami *gompa* started to crumble away, and as it slowly subsided it became clear that it was beginning to undermine the *gompa* itself. A group of the monks headed by the Abbot and the Rimpoche's secretary and guardian asked Ed to help them. For a year or more they gently pressurised him with gracious hospitality, food and drink and the use of their delightful *gompa* guest room whenever he visited Thami. Ed asked various expedition members, including builders and an engineer, to advise him about the problem. Most of them suggested he have nothing to do with it as it would be a complex and expensive business. But by this time Ed was so fascinated by the place that he was determined to have a try.

"How can you finance it?" I had asked him.

"Oh, that will be no problem," he replied. "The local people will have to give a lot of work, and I'll write some articles to cover the expenses." And so began his special private Thami project.

In the spring of 1970 a group of us arrived at Thami *gompa* to try and build the new courtyard. With grandiose ideas of flying buttresses à la Notre-Dame, Ed designed a new courtyard twelve feet wider than the existing one, all supported by three great buttresses more than sixty feet high. The entire construction was to be in traditional Sherpa style using dry rock walls put together by skilled Sherpa stonemasons. Already Mingma had been there ahead of us and organised great piles of rock which the monks had broken and carried close to the site of the construction. All the nearby village people had agreed they would donate three days to breaking rock and carrying it onto the building site.

It was a perfect spring day when we arrived at the *gompa* and the walk up the river valley had been a continuous display of bright spring flowers and sparkling water. As we puffed our way up the final approaches to the *gompa*, past the long walls of *mani* stones and the gnarled juniper trees, we were treated to a royal welcome. Standing on top of the entrance archway were two monks blowing a long copper trumpet and a great white conch shell. At their feet was a little fire of juniper and azalea incense enveloping them in a mysterious cloud of white smoke. We were escorted into the *gompa* where the monks were sitting crosslegged on low benches in their thick magenta-coloured robes chanting prayers for the soul of a Sherpa climber who had recently died on a mountaineering expedition. We smiled at some of the more familiar faces amongst the chanting monks and they smiled back with unconcealed pleasure. Then we were given the traditional hospitality of Tibetan tea, *chung* and *sheru* (rice biscuits). After consuming large quantities of food and drink we were escorted to the very special accommodation that had been allocated to us for the duration of our visit. Situated above the *gompa* on a tiny ledge was a delightful group of rooms with latticed windows covered in daphne paper and two small walled courtyards. In one corner of each courtyard was a toilet hole covered with a round wooden lid and hanging rather immodestly over the small potato field terrace below.

Behind the first courtyard was a large kitchen containing a traditional Sherpa mud stove, piles of firewood, copper water-containers and carpeted benches against the walls. There was plenty of room for all of us to sleep here. Much to our delight, Ed and I were invited to use the little guest room behind the second courtyard. The walls were decorated with religious paintings and in one corner there was a large wooden prayer-wheel. With its marvellous view down valley and its sunny private courtyard well protected from the wind—not to mention its toilet facilities—it had everything that the romantic visitor could want.

Despite being in such an unworldly place the time inevitably came when I was forced to consider using the toilet hole in our courtyard. I glanced desperately round the cliff-face dotted with small homes and decided that during the daylight hours at least I would have to walk a mile or so up towards the Tashi Lapcha in order to get some privacy. Later, after some careful exploration, I discovered a small stone building behind the *gompa*. It had a lattice window and a thatched roof of fresh green juniper boughs. It was certainly a toilet although it looked more like a "confessional" to me. I had no sooner got myself comfortably established than the Abbot of the monastery came thumping towards me in a great hurry and I just had time to yell in my most urgent Nepali, "Please wait!"—which he did. Later that day I noticed with regret and a certain amount of embarrassment that the little "confessional" had been blocked up with large juniper branches—it must have been kept only for the Rimpoche's use.

We felt a certain sense of urgency in building the new *gompa* terrace, for the Mani Rimdu festival was due in a few weeks' time and the terrace would be needed for the participants. First of all we had to break down most of the existing terrace and this was done with the usual Sherpa exuberance. Stones and timber came hurtling down the slopes below the *gompa* in haphazard style until one large boulder went through the roof of a house about a hundred feet below. Ed marked out the retaining wall and the buttresses with string and then deep foundations were dug into a solid rock bottom. Then the rockmasons started their work and by the end of the first day the leaning buttresses had already grown ten feet.

That night Ed and I slept in our private guest room—and slept very well too. Early in the morning I heard a strange scuffling noise above us on the roof. A few minutes later I turned my head towards the window as I had the feeling that we were being looked at. For a while I couldn't see our hidden visitor but then my eye was attracted to a little tear in the daphne paper window where a bright little eye was peering at us from outside.

"*Namaste,*" (greetings) I said politely and the eye quickly disappeared. Next moment a face appeared in a larger hole in the rice paper and I recognised the young Rimpoche, grinning at me in quite unabashed fashion. It was reassuring to see that he had retained some of the normal boyish instincts even though he is believed to have inherited the wisdom of his previous incarnations.

For the next week two hundred Sherpas, twenty-five monks and all our party became an industrious army of workers, converging from every direction heavily laden with baskets and chunks of rock. In quite amazing fashion the buttresses were completed and the main retaining wall was commenced. It was all looking most impressive. Finally the supply of stones started to dwindle and people were having to travel up valley nearly a mile to find other sources of stone. The new walls, buttresses and the enlarged courtyard were consuming large quantities of rock and apart from knocking down pieces of the cliff-face, there appeared to be no easily available source. Work was being held up and Ed had a serious conference with the Rimpoche's hard-working secretary and with Mingma. But no one could suggest any bright new ideas.

"Well," said Ed rather desperately, "is there any old house that we can buy?"

"There is a house behind the *gompa* with badly cracked walls," replied the secretary, rather doubtfully. "You can buy that."

"Right," said Ed. "Do you agree, Mingma?"

"Yes," said Mingma. "How much?"

"Eight hundred rupees," said the secretary unblushingly.

"What?" said Mingma, "a pile of stones like that?"

"Quite ridiculous!" said Ed, irritably. So they argued on for a while and finally the price came down to six hundred rupees. By this stage I couldn't contain myself any longer—"Why do you have to buy that house?" I said. "Surely, if the monks want this courtyard so much they could give one of their houses?" Ed looked at me with fury.

"We haven't got time to discuss this," he said.

"We must," I replied. "I just don't approve."

"It's a little different from what you think," said Ed. "These houses belong to private individuals, so it has nothing to do with the monastery as a whole." Then he added very impatiently—"We're running out of time, let me handle this alone."

Mingma was absolutely horrified at the argument and almost went white with amazement and shock. Until now he had always thought that Ed and I were immune to the normal domestic discords of husband and wife. I hurried away defeated, realising that there was nothing I could do. I sat on the edge of the guest room terrace brooding over the inconsistencies of life and watching a rather interesting series of little dramas being enacted down below me.

First I saw the secretary talking excitedly to some of his monks, then looking at Ed, looking up at me and finally pointing at Mingma. I could see Mingma whispering away to Siku, looking at Ed and then looking at me. Very soon I was sure that the news of our difference of opinion had spread like wild-fire all over the Thami valley. Next moment Siku appeared on the guest room terrace.

"What do you want?" I said to him. He looked a little bit uncertain and went busily into the guest room and burrowed about for a while. He had obviously been sent by Mingma to check on my well-being and for the rest of the afternoon he paid me a regular half-hourly visit, each time explained by some obviously fabricated excuse.

By the end of that day the old house had been demolished and its rock had been used to complete most of the construction work, leaving only the finishing touches for the monks to carry out themselves. It was time to leave Thami and return to Kunde hospital. Everyone was so tired or suffering from nervous strain that we marched in silence down the shadowy flower-decked Bhote Kosi valley and back up the hill to Kunde.

Apart from our small crisis over the lack of rock, the new *gompa* courtyard had proved a most successful project. We had been so lost in our work that we had completely forgotten the rest of the world outside the Thami valley—until one small incident brought it back to our attention.

Some of the men working high up on the rock buttresses had noticed some foreign tourists approaching.

"Sahibs coming!" they called out. Immediately some of the local people rushed back to their houses and padlocked their doors.

"Why are they doing that?" I asked Mingma in some amazement, for traditionally the Sherpas offer open-hearted hospitality to everyone.

"Too many of the tourists are not paying for food or lodgings," said Mingma, "so now the people are very careful. Also sometimes they steal."

"That's terrible! You'd think people who came this far wouldn't be interested in doing anything like that."

"Some tourists good—some bad," he said philosophically.

Two weeks after the successful completion of the *gompa* courtyard at Thami we returned once more. We had received a special invitation to attend the Mani Rimdu festival. Every year, early in May, the monks of Thami celebrate this festival of spiritual renewal. There are three days of religious activities. The first and the last days are filled with hour after hour of the chanting of prayers and meditation, but the second day is by far the most exciting and popular one—it is the climax of the festival when the lama dances are performed to a very large audience of local people.

As we walked back up the valley towards Thami we met many friends and acquaintances and our pace slowed down to a gay convivial saunter. Most people carried a small pack on their backs with some clothes and food and every now and then we would join a family picnic beside the path. We crossed the river and started up the steep hill to Thami and were then met by a group of the local people with a gaily decorated pony for Ed to ride, and also a large wooden bucket filled with fresh zum milk for us to drink. Ed is not an enthusiastic drinker of milk or rider of horses.

"No, thank you, I'm not really thirsty at present," he explained, "but I know my wife would love some of the milk." I looked at him with hate, but dutifully drank some of the milk and was delighted to find it fresh and quite delicious. I made so many appreciative noises that Ed finally decided to have a drink himself, much to the satisfaction of our friend.

"I think my wife would like to ride the horse much more than I would," he said and I thankfully agreed.

Kunde hospital and Sherpa house
and potato fields.

Passang Tendi and Ang Tsering
preparing food for the hospital Losar party.

Mani (prayer) wall.

Right to left: Sarah and Belinda carrying rock for Junbesi Middle School.

I'm not terribly good at riding horses and this certainly wasn't much of a place to learn for we were standing on a narrow section of the track with the raging river two or three hundred feet straight below. I heaved myself rather too enthusiastically upwards so that my momentum carried me over the other side of the horse, to the great amusement of the onlookers. At my next attempt the Sherpas managed to steady me and amidst great cheering and joviality I rode up the track. My saddle was of wood covered with a beautifully patterned carpet saddle blanket. With such handsome accessories I might have looked quite elegant but I was unfortunately the centre of a rather incongruous group with a little girl pulling the horse firmly from the front, the owner of the horse walking at the rear holding its tail to control the speed and a Sherpa on either side waiting to catch me when I fell. Terrified, I sat in the middle of all this, grasping the horse's mane with all my might.

As our cavalcade approached the monastery I looked up to admire the buttresses and the big new wall. "It is like the Potala," said the owner of the horse following my glance. This is certainly the highest compliment that could have been paid to Ed's handiwork. To compare the Potala, a great palace of the Dalai Lama in Lhasa with this humble structure was indeed a high honour. I could hardly wait to tell Ed. During our absence the new *gompa* courtyard had been transformed. The surface had been covered with smooth paving stones and the safety wall had been built around the outside edge.

Everything was neat and tidy and seating had been arranged for special guests. Next to the *gompa* door a throne had been set up for the young Rimpoche and another throne was placed beside it but remained empty except for a picture of the Dalai Lama. A great canopy had been erected over most of the courtyard and there was a tall prayer flag waving in the centre. Already three or four hundred Sherpas were sitting around the edge of the courtyard in their best and brightest clothes and outside, four Tibetan traders had set up their wares to sell. They had a colourful collection of cotton threads, buttons, exercise books, cloth and household necessities. Two restaurants had been erected close by with canvas roofs and woven bamboo walls. You could buy either Tibetan or Indian tea, a bowl of *tukpa* for a rupee and three *mormors* for a rupee.

By the time we arrived the first day of prayers was nearly over, but during the night we listened from the comfort of our sleeping bags to the intermittent chanting of the monks inside the *gompa* and we could smell the sweet incense wafting up to our little room. At 5 o'clock the next morning the monks blew their trumpets from the archway above the terrace proclaiming to the people of the Khumbu that the great day of the Mani Rimdu Lama dancing was about to begin. Lines had been drawn on the paving stones to show exactly where the public could sit and soon every available square inch was crammed with excited onlookers.

The dancing started at 8 a.m. in the morning and went on almost non-stop until 6 o'clock that night. The public were free to wander around, buy food and talk to their friends in between the dances. There was a wonderful festive atmosphere about the place, and many of our acquaintances invited us for cups of tea and bowls of *tukpa*. The dances are interpretations of Buddhist religious stories and are very much like the old mystery plays of the European Middle Ages. The monks dress up in brightly coloured silken garments and put masks on their faces to represent special characters or deities. In the same style as the mystery plays there are clowns and topical jokes that make the local people laugh uproariously with their earthy humour. No wonder people come from many miles around to attend such an entertaining spectacle.

When the dancing finished it was time for all the faithful to be blessed by the Rimpoche. This was a very special moment, and with cheerful enthusiasm all the locals started pushing forward in readiness for their turn. It was then that two young inexperienced policemen from the Thami checkpost turned the festive gathering into a bewildered and unhappy throng. Misjudging the cheerful jostling of the crowd the policemen decided to exert some discipline and barged amongst the people hitting out indiscriminately with their truncheons. It was one of those unfortunate episodes caused by lack of understanding between two cultures. The policemen were Hindus from the Kathmandu valley and felt lost and frightened by the pushing and heaving lines of Sherpa families who were striving goodnaturedly to get close to the Rimpoche.

Everyone was getting incensed by the unnecessary and brutish behaviour of the policemen until Ed organised Mingma and two or three others to link arms and hold the heaving crowd back so that order could be restored to the gathering. After this the control of the crowd was left to the traditional people, the monks and the village elders.

That evening we asked the Rimpoche to dinner and gave him canned sausages and gravy and canned New Zealand peaches. He found the meal quite delicious and sat smiling at us from the comfort of one of Ed's thickest sleeping bags which he had wrapped around him rather like a monk's flowing gown. He looked so happy that I decided to take a picture of him but it was hard to attract his attention as he was looking at photographs of himself in the book *Mani Rimdu* by Luther G. Jerstad.

"Ahem!" I coughed but still without success.

"Er, um, Rimpoche?" I said, feeling rather daring. He looked up and I took a cheerful picture.

Our experience at Thami had been rather marvellous, and Ed and I knew we would never be satisfied until we returned to the *gompa* with our family and let them have some of the same adventures.

And now here we were, family and all, on our way back to Thami. It was a glorious frosty morning but my heart sank when Peter said he was feeling unwell.

"What can you expect," said one of his sisters, "after eating so much birthday cake last night?"

"You'd better eat something before your long walk," I said, "or else you'll feel even worse." Five minutes later Peter was being violently sick—but he was still determined to reach Thami that day.

As we were in a hurry Mingma led us over a short steep route, more suitable for mountain goats. The track cut across an almost perpendicular slope high above the Bhote Kosi river and even though there were plenty of narrow sheep and cattle tracks you got the impression that you could fall an awfully long way before coming to a halt. The morning sun bathed everything in a golden haze and we bounded along the track without a care in the world—all except Peter!

"Do you mind if we have a rest?" he enquired. No one minded at all on such a lovely day, and to add to our excitement Mingma had discovered the fresh spoors of a snow leopard on the track we were following.

"I'll just lie down here," said Peter selecting a dusty little ledge with its line of snow leopard footmarks.

"Where's Thami?" said one of the girls.

"A long way up to the right. You can't quite see it," replied Ed.

Just then Mingma let out a yell. I turned around to see Peter being ill with his head over the side of the track. He looked as though he was about to roll off the path and down the mountainside. Both Mingma and I leapt simultaneously towards him and held very firmly onto the back of his shirt and his belt.

"Hadn't you better go back?" I said to Peter. But by now there was about five hundred feet of steep mountainside to climb up. Peter thought it would be better if he went down onto the main track to Thami and had a good rest. After a hard scramble downward we arrived at a pleasant flat area and settled down for a rest in the sun. Ed decided that he and Mingma had better go onto the checkpost at Thami.

"We'll take all your documents and try and fix it all up for you so you won't have to bother," said Ed, and away they went.

"*Amo!*" said Siku in alarm. I turned around. Peter was at it again. Oh dear, he was meant to be recovering by now.

"Perhaps if you had a good hot drink with sugar in it to give you energy, you might be able to stagger on," I suggested. Siku and I walked onto the checkpost and started organising some hot water. As we returned along the path with our pot of fast-cooling tea we met Mingma leading Peter very gently and carefully towards us. Peter was looking terrible and he didn't want anything to drink.

"No, thank you, I'll just keep on going," he told us.

We were a strange procession as we walked back towards the police checkpost. In front were Ed, Peter and Mingma walking very slowly along the path. Behind were the two girls and Aila looking quiet and sorrowful, and bringing up the rear was Siku carrying with grave concentration a Chinese enamel teapot, gaily decorated with pink rosebuds. It was exactly like a funeral procession and I started to chuckle to myself.

"You should see yourselves!" I called out. "It's really terribly funny." Even Peter could see the humour in the scene and when no one was looking I took a photograph of the group—which, perhaps mercifully, has been lost without trace.

All formalities at the checkpost had been completed so we walked straight past and I noticed that the policemen on duty were looking at us with pitying disdain. Refusing any assistance Peter weaved unsteadily along beside the precipice that plunged four hundred feet down to the cruel river. Saying nothing to distract him I walked as close behind as I dared, ready to pull him to safety if he did a more uncontrolled swerve than usual. Half a mile farther on we came to a small level field and persuaded Peter to have another stretch out. We were now only an hour from Thami and Ed and Mingma were looking very restless.

"We'll go on now, or the whole day will be wasted," said Ed. "See you at the *gompa!*"

To my distress Peter seemed to get worse and worse and I was greatly relieved when Dr. Lindsay Strang came bouncing along the track accompanied by Hospital Pemba. He tried anti-vomit injections and various other medical administrations but without any noticeable effect. Peter tried to start again but then his legs seemed to turn to jelly and he just collapsed in a heap in the middle of the path. I remembered Ed's parting comment. "Of course Peter will get there," said Ed. "No one on any of my expeditions has ever not managed to get to his destination."

"Well," I said to myself, "I think perhaps this time one of the members of your expedition is going to spoil your record."

"Has anybody got a sleeping bag?" I enquired. Siku was able to produce one and we had a tremendous struggle getting the semi-conscious Peter inside. This was obviously as far as Peter was likely to get to-day. For the next couple of hours we had messages going up and down the valley and by evening our whole group, Ed and Mingma included, were together again with a camp springing up around Peter's tent.

The healthy members of the Hillary family had an interesting night squashed into one small tent like sardines in a tin but we slept remarkably well. At 6 o'clock Mingma poked his head into our tent with a cheery grin and said, "Peter quite strong to-day." Peter was looking very comfortable in his tent with a strong group of Sherpas fussing around him, offering him hot lemon drinks and biscuits in a determined effort to build up his strength.

"As long as I go slowly I'll get to Thami easily to-day," he said, so after breakfast we packed up our camp and Ed and his workers rushed back to Thami to get on with the job. Peter, Belinda and I came slowly along behind. The last half-hour was quite a struggle.

"Only another hundred feet to go," I said to Peter and then "Only another ten feet . . . all you've got to do is walk up these stone steps and collapse into your tent." But that was not to be—outside the entrance to the *gompa* was the Head Lama's secretary waiting to welcome us with *katas* and cups of tea. We followed him inside and sat down on comfortable rugs where we consumed tea, biscuits and *chung*; but soon Peter was able to excuse himself and escape to the peace of his little tent.

The day had quickly changed from a sparkling early morning to a grey brooding afternoon with flecks of snow and a cold blustery wind. The effect of the altitude and the unusual cold made us feel very lethargic. The men were well occupied building a new safety wall of heavy timbers for the main *gompa* terrace so they managed to stay warm, but there was no work for us and we just became steadily colder and colder. In despair I resorted to my old remedy for combating the cold—I filled a hot-water bottle and stuck it down the front of my padded jacket. It was like having a built-in heater—absolutely marvellous—and the girls quickly followed suit and felt very much happier.

The young Rimpoche was still away at the monastery of Tuten Choling near Junbesi but the Head Lama's secretary was very happy to be our guide. We were shown into the Rimpoche's private room which had been decorated by the father of Kappa Kalden forty years before. We admired the silken canopy embroidered with fiery dragons that hung over the young Rimpoche's seat, and the various copper and gold-encrusted miniature *chortens* studded with previous stones that housed the remains of previous re-incarnations. These were kept carefully under lock and key in glass-fronted cupboards. The secretary spoke a rather hesitant Nepali just like mine, so the afternoon passed in hilariously complicated conversations.

During the evening some of the monks came to see Lindsay for medical advice and then two of the senior monks arrived proudly carrying a handsome new leather-bound book. On the outside cover written in beautiful gold lettering were the words "Visitors' Book".

"We want you to be the first person to sign this book, Burrah Sahib," they said.

"May I have a look at it first?" he replied. On the first page the paper was divided into sections which were headed "Name", "Address", and then rather ominously "Donation".

"Ooh, humph!" said Ed, "I don't think I want to sign that! I've already given you a new *gompa* terrace and now we're building a new wall for the terrace. Mingma, will you try and find out what it's all about?" Mingma made some enquiries and then was able to reassure Ed that the monks only wanted to use his past generosity as an example to future tourists.

"How much money would all our work at Thami be worth?" asked Ed.

"*Chic ni sum* . . ." said Mingma, counting on his fingers in Sherpa. "Three thousand rupees, Burrah Sahib."

"That's good enough," said Ed. "We must have given at least that over the last few years." The two monks were highly delighted and departed quite satisfied with their effort.

The secretary and the Rimpoche's half-brother were our next visitors, but they came purely for social reasons bringing a bottle of *chung* for our enjoyment. It wasn't quite the weather or the time of day for cold drinks but we all valiantly took a few sips.

"Where were the books in the *gompa* made?" I enquired and Mingma proceeded to find out all the details for me. It made a most interesting story.

The books had been manufactured about three hundred years before in the Tibetan town of Shigatse which was a famous centre for the printing of religious books. Most of the materials for the Shigatse printing industry came from Solu in Nepal. Long caravans of yaks would carry daphne paper, wood and ink over the nineteen-thousand-foot Nangpa La into Tibet where the fine wooden printing blocks were carved by master craftsmen. The ink was made by burning resin from the rich pine forests of the Solu area and the soot from the smoke provided an excellent black pigment. Thami must have been an exciting place in the days of the big trading caravans to and from Tibet.

All night long the huge black mastiff that guards the monastery barked at the moon, but we slept well and woke to a bright Saturday morning—but it was cold, very cold. As I emptied my hot-water bottle the splashes of water on the rubber froze immediately into starlike crystals. When the sun touched the valley, Peter, Siku, Ang Tsering and I started off on our slow return journey to the hospital, leaving the others to finish their work before returning a little later. Peter was going very much better and half-way down the valley we stopped for our last gaze at the little group of monastery buildings nestling under their overhanging cliff. It was a world apart, a spiritual refuge in a fast-changing world. We were tremendously pleased that we had been part of it all.

CHAPTER 14

A White Losar

THAT AFTERNOON THE winter snows came to Khumbu. The first snowflakes slipped down gently and unobtrusively, but later they fell thick and fast, plopping down lazily on the rock walls and shingle roofs of the Sherpa houses, blurring everything in a polka-dot haze of falling crystals. Peter and I were the first of the Thami party to return to the hospital and so escaped walking through the snow, but as we came from a temperate island climate the snow was a considerable novelty to us and we rushed outside to feel the snowflakes falling on our faces.

The girls returned glowing with excitement and exertion. They had made a diversion into the weekly market at Namche Bazar and they were bubbling over with enthusiasm. The market had been really great—hundreds of people, familiar faces, glasses of tea, and fantastic bargains. The only bad news was that the price of rice had gone up by two rupees a *patti* which was not so good for the poorer families after the failure of the potato crop. Famine was just a little bit too close around the corner for them.

"Hospital Pemba walks terribly fast," said Sarah.

"We could hardly keep up with him going to Namche," said Belinda.

Pemba just grinned. He was very pleased with these remarks and with some justification. Three years before he had been a patient at Kunde Hospital suffering from a bad tuberculous hip. This condition had become so serious that it was necessary to fly him to Kathmandu to the large missionary hospital of Shanta Bhawan for surgery. He was a quiet studious young man and during his time in hospital became interested in medical work and made efforts to complete his education. The Kunde hospital staff were so impressed by his conscientious approach to study that after he recovered, they employed him as a medical assistant, public health teacher and interpreter. In the Khumbu, where physical strength is so important, Pemba's future had not looked at all promising and he quickly realised his good fortune at being appointed to the hospital staff. He had done so well that he had just recently been given a small scholarship so that he could finish his education while working only part time at the hospital. It was good to see that he was now rushing round the countryside with such vigour.

Ed and Mingma duly arrived with the porters through the storm, and they looked twice their normal size like hoary monsters from the ice age.

"What time is dinner at Ang Tsering's?" asked Ed in his 'I don't want to go out to-night' voice.

"Six o'clock sharp," said Mingma.

"We'll make sure we're ready in time," I promised. We rushed down the snow-covered stone alleys to the Naya Kota, revelling in the wintry scene. Mingma's mother had already lit our fire and put some small juniper branches on the smouldering coals which gave out a rich welcoming scent.

"We'll need boots, gloves, and mittens to go down to Ang Tsering's house in Khumjung tonight," said Ed. The snow was now about ten inches deep and it was nearly a mile to walk. Just as daylight started to fade, the snow stopped and the top of Tamserku peeped through a great curtain of shifting clouds. The familiar Kunde scene of greys and browns and dark greens had undergone an amazing transformation. It was now a traditional Christmas-card landscape of purest white and shadowy grey, except that instead of reindeer on the snowy field outside our window there was a herd of snow-covered yaks standing patiently puffing steam from their nostrils. The boulder fences that surrounded the village fields and alleys looked as though they had been topped with a thick layer of wedding-cake icing.

Our little room with the many cracks in its walls was decidedly chilly and we hovered close around our fire. How did the Sherpas cope year after year in their draughty houses? We went upstairs to have a look and found the family sitting very comfortably crosslegged around the Tibetan brazier. They held out their hands towards the warmth, filling in the hours very pleasantly with much talk and laughter. There was no need for exciting outside stimulation to beguile the time away, for they still retained the wonderful art of simple living and being able to entertain themselves.

"What shall I wear to Ang Tsering's?" came a wail from one of the girls.

"Oh dear," I complained. "I thought by coming to Khumbu I might escape all that for a month or so."

"Well, I know Doma will look absolutely gorgeous," said Sarah, "and I wish I had something other than jeans and a down jacket to wear."

"I would love to have an *ingi* (tunic) and blouse and apron," said Belinda. By the time we had covered ourselves in all our cold weather clothing it wouldn't have mattered what anybody was wearing. There was a knock on the door and we found Ang Tsering's second son, Rinchin Karma, aged ten, waiting outside to take us back to his family's house. Mingma joined us wearing a bright blue padded jacket from some previous expedition and Ang Dooli came rushing after him in her ordinary housework clothes, with a pair of sandshoes on her feet, and little Da Tseri on her back.

"Ang Dooli," I said, "do you want to borrow one of our spare jackets?"

But Mingma shook his head violently.

"It's time to go. She'll be all right," he said.

What a perfect evening! The world looked as though it had just been spring-cleaned. We rushed helter-skelter down the hill towards Khumjung with Mingma leading the way and the soft snow sparkling like diamonds in the torchlight. Mingma was carrying the guitar and trudged forcefully onwards while the rest of us pretended to ski with our boots on every possible snow-covered slope.

Ang Tsering's house was on the edge of Khumjung beside a large potato field owned by his father. It was one of the oldest houses in the area and was known as "Mendoa", which was also the name of the family. The house had been enlarged over the years so that the various sons and their wives could live in it side by side. At present Ang Tsering and his brother Passang Tendi shared the home with their father. Each family owned a large living room upstairs and shared a small but attractive family *gompa*. In the centre of Ang Tsering's living room was a brazier piled high with yak dung coals. The family brass and copper utensils glowed like gold from their shelves on the back wall and the cupboards and little tables had been freshly oiled and polished. There had been much preparation in our honour for both Ang Tsering and Doma are very good housekeepers and have put into practice the many new rules of domestic hygiene that they have learnt over the last few years. Their room has always been particularly attractive as the roughly plastered interior walls have been covered with daphne paper, patterned with a traditional Buddhist design.

The four children of the family looked very scrubbed and tidy. The two youngest sat quietly in a corner beside the cooking fire. The eldest, Nima Wong Chu, was very industriously scrubbing a cooking pot while his sister Pura Sonar, aged nine, was prancing around the room eyeing us all up and down with great assurance. She was dressed in a pair of new black trousers and a white shirt, with her hair tied back in a pony tail. She had inherited all her mother's good looks and all her grandfather Kappa Kalden's personality and wit. She looked to me like the first possible candidate for a woman Prime Minister in Nepal.

Doma went the rounds of her visitors with a large jug of delicious clear *chung*.

"Shay, shay," she said, smiling irresistibly.

"I'm just putty in her hands," sighed Ed taking a huge swig. "I'll be a wreck to-morrow."

Just then the head of the house, Passang Sonar, and his friend Nima Tashi appeared at the door. Ed hastily rose from his place closest to the fire to offer the head of the household his rightful seat of honour. But neither Passang Sonar or Nima Tashi were worried about such technicalities.

Nima Tashi's house is named "Takdoa" and is also one of the original houses of Khumjung. The forebears of both the Mendoa and Takdoa families must have crossed over the mountains from Tibet more than a hundred years ago. It is said that most of the Sherpas of Nepal originated in the area called Kam in eastern Tibet and they fled from there to escape fighting or famine or some other social upheaval in the region. The first families to discover the rich secluded valley of Khumjung were able to select some of the finest land for their fields. But they, like everyone else in the village, had very little financial wealth. In the past they had received no education or medical aid and now their families were getting larger every generation, there were not even enough fields to feed all their dependents.

That evening we learnt a little more about the complicated family relationships in the Khumbu, for the Sherpa people are divided into many clans which originated when the various groups of Tibetans came and settled in Nepal. Nima Tashi, Ang Douli and Kunjo Chumbi (head of the Panchayat) all belonged to the Tadkoa clan and we all agreed that it must be one of the most dominant clans of the region. There were many other clans, the Mendip from Khumjung, Salaka from Thami, and so on, and there are very strict rules prohibiting anyone marrying into their own clan.

Doma had been busy with her large pot of *chung*. She had just completed her third round of the guests and had filled Belinda's glass to the very brim. If my command of the Nepali language had been a little better I might have been able to convince Doma that Belinda was only thirteen years old and that I didn't want her to drink too much *chung*. But in Sherpa eyes the tall, strongly-built Belinda was aged at least twenty. It was a most relaxing evening amongst a few special friends and the conversation flowed comfortably and the jokes and stories were passed around for everyone's enjoyment. While we talked, Nima Wong Chu and his brothers and sister washed the dishes in a big enamel basin and listened intently to every word that was spoken in the room. It was good to see Nima Wong Chu fitting so well into his family life after two years away at boarding school in Kathmandu. He had been an excellent student at Khumjung school and had started his high school education in Kathmandu at the tender age of twelve and we had worried that the sudden transition to city life might have upset him. It was reassuring to see him so busy and happy in his home environment—due to a large extent, I am sure, to the firm guidance he must have received from his parents.

Much as we were enjoying this occasion the pressure of our social life forced us to leave for Kunde at a reasonable hour and we tramped at great speed back up the hill through the glittering snow which was so cold it squeaked with every footstep. We found Sala waiting up for us with water boiling over the fire for our hot water bottles.

As the sun rose next morning to tinge the mountains with pink, the white snow-covered landscape slowly took on its normal three-dimensional contours and became the answer to a photographer's prayer. We hurried from our warm sleeping bags and spent an exciting half-hour taking shot after shot on our cameras. Afterwards we tried to warm ourselves around the Naya Kota fire and I looked at the chilled and strained faces of my family and decided that our action-packed days were becoming a bit too much for us. Belinda looked pale and wan, Sarah had a cold and Peter was thin and limp after his experiences at Thami.

"Oh for a rest day," I thought hopelessly. But there weren't any rest days in sight, in fact this was the long-awaited day for the Burrah Sahib's children to visit the village of Phortse, the home of Aila and Siku and their families. We had planned this trip specially so that the children could get away on their own without their parents and for some time Siku and Aila had been organising the people of the village to prepare a mighty welcome. It would have been an absolute disaster if the visit had been cancelled, and the children reassured me that they would get there somehow.

At 6.30 Ang Dooli came in the door carrying cups of tea and two large plates of rice cakes, oranges and sweets.

"What's this for?" I asked.

"Losar—Sherpa New Year," she replied. A few minutes later Siku and Aila appeared at our door looking rather like nervous expectant fathers waiting outside a maternity hospital—the responsibility of caring for the three younger Hillarys was weighing heavily on their shoulders.

"Will it be dangerous on the track going across to Phortse?" I enquired. Phortse is about three hours' march from Kunde across a high traverse above steep mountainsides and much of it is in the shade.

"No, there's very little ice," they said in confident tones.

"That's good," said Ed, "you might as well wear your gym shoes," knowing that light footwear would be more comfortable for the tired trio. In a bewilderingly short time Aila and Siku had collected the children's overnight gear and packed it into a porter load. Then Pemba Tenzing came rattling down the alley with the food and kitchen utensils and all was ready.

"*Loh, loh*," said Siku bravely.

"Let's go," said Peter and off they strode looking rather round-shouldered and resigned to their fate. They had a beautiful day to help them on their way and many interesting sights to see.

Now that the Phortse party was safely on their way I could concentrate on my own activities. First of all I had arranged to have a lesson in *chung*-making from Ang Dooli. I climbed the stairs to her living room to find her busily pounding up a lump of hard dry yeast. She had just completed cooking eight pounds of rice on the fire and was letting this cool down to blood heat. She then spread the warm rice very quickly onto a big bamboo mat and mixed in the finely powdered yeast. Then, with great speed, she quickly returned the rice to the big pot, covered it with a lid and surrounded it with old clothes and blankets to keep in the heat. From there on, the recipe could only be explained to me, for the rice had to be left for three days to ferment and then be transferred to a big wooden barrel for three or four more days, depending on atmospheric temperature. In the old days the lid of the wooden barrel was plastered down with yak dung to keep in all the heat and keep out any stray bugs but nowadays, thanks to public health lessons, plastic bags are being used more and more. After this maturing period an equivalent volume of water would be added to the rice and then in a few more days' time, depending on atmospheric temperatures again, the rice would float to the top of the water and the *chung* would be ready. To procure clear, sweet, cider-like Ningoo *chung* you would have to push the rice carefully aside and ladle out the clear liquid, but the thicker porridgey rice liquid at the bottom was just as popular with the Sherpas. Ang Dooli struggled valiantly to explain all this to me and by the time she had finished she looked quite flustered, but there was no time for rest that morning as we both had to go to a special meeting at the hospital for the scholarship boys, their parents and Genevieve and Lindsay Strang, who would be in charge of all educational projects in Ed's absence.

It was 11 a.m. sharp and nearly all the thirteen scholarship boys (no girls as yet, I'm sorry to say) and their parents had assembled in front of the doctor's quarters. They were looking very gay and cheerful, and rather proud too for many of the students had done very well during the year at school. When Ed had started awarding scholarships to some of the brighter pupils he had sent them to High School in Kathmandu, but this had proved quite expensive and had also thrown the boys into a strange new environment. He had decided to change his policy and the more recent scholarship holders had attended country high schools which were only three or four days' walking distance from home and were not subjected to the temptations of big city life. It was easy to recognise the three Kathmandu schoolboys amongst the group. They were just that little bit more smartly dressed than their country high school counterparts. Lakpa Norbu from Thami, for instance, had been attending school in Kathmandu with Nima Wong Chu and Karma Namda. Lakpa had grown into a big handsome boy with a suspicion of sideburns, slightly long hair, and a generally very sophisticated air. His parents sitting beside him were a considerable contrast to their son. They were tough traditional Thami folk. The father still retained his long pigtail which was wound round his head underneath a sweat-stained, fur-rimmed hat, and their Sherpa-style clothing was made of tough handwoven woollen cloth. One of the most successful of the more recent scholarship boys was Danu, another member of Kappa Kalden's family. Danu had come top of his year at Jiri high school and was present at the meeting with his mother Nim Putti. Another boy who had done well was Zimba Zambu, the son of an old climbing friend of ours from Khumjung.

Some days earlier Ed and Mingma had worked out a new agreement to be signed by all the parents of scholarship boys and this was read out to the assembled gathering. It stated that all scholarship holders must give two years to teaching in the Himalayan Trust Schools after finishing their education. The new agreement was approved by everyone present and then the complicated business of obtaining signatures got under way. At least half of the parents were still illiterate so they had to put a thumbprint beside their names. When this rather cheerful procedure was completed they settled down to listen to short talks from Ed and Mingma. Suddenly the orderly gathering was thrown into absolute confusion by the appearance of a bedraggled elderly mother of a scholarship boy who rushed into our midst and sat down amongst the other parents, talking at the top of her voice. She was exhausted after having just walked at great speed from where she had been hunting desperately for a lost zum. Finally she had to leave her son, Mingma Norbu, to continue the hunt for the animal while she had hurried off to the meeting. She was a widow with only one child and Mingma explained that it had been a great sacrifice for her to allow him to accept a scholarship in a distant town. Despite her battered and tired appearance she was a very lively lady and after having recovered from her rather chaotic arrival she soon became an amusing and somewhat disturbing element amongst the group. Completely uninhibited she aired her point of view at the top of her voice. The only other parent who could dominate the meeting as successfully was Doma, who with the usual twinkle in her eye would stand up and make some humorous statement which would soon drown the widow's raucous voice in choruses of laughter.

Genevieve and I had planned to serve tea and biscuits to the guests but this became unnecessary when they all produced their own liquid refreshments. The families from Namche had a most lethal brew of *arak* which was bottled in a container labelled "Cherry Delight" The contents were bright scarlet and Ed dutifully drank a few sips and only thinly disguised his reaction to its bitter flavour and high alcoholic content. By the end of the meeting everyone was in festive mood, so Mingma led the parents and their sons back to his house for a sobering meal of boiled potatoes. We watched the meeting disband through a slight alcoholic haze brought on by too much *chung* too early in the day and at too high an altitude.

"Let's grab some bread and cheese and then get on with the work," I suggested to Ed and the Strangs. But this was not to be. Phu Dorje came hurrying up the path to invite us to attend the village *puja* (for protection of the village) which was being held at his house that day. Every family in the village had to take a turn at organising and financing the various festivals of the year, and sometimes this could be quite an expensive exercise. The girls had seen Phu Dorje down at the market on Saturday buying great quantities of rice, fruit and sweets.

Inside Phu Dorje's house there were twelve monks chanting prayers and some of the local dignitaries acting in a supporting role and banging the drums and cymbals. An altar had been built at one end of the room and on it were rows of little butter lamps and scarlet and white *torma* figures. There must have been at least fifty of these conical shaped figures moulded from a mixture of pre-cooked barley flour and butter, which is a very expensive item for the average Sherpa household. It was an impressive display with baskets of delicious food —rice balls, *sheru*, oranges, biscuits, sweets—lying in great profusion in front of the altar. At the kitchen end of Phu Dorje's home he and his wife were serving up bowls of *tukpa* to the monks and their helpers.

Ang Dorje was sitting in a corner of the room as he was sharing the cost of the *puja*. He was still depressed about the disastrous trip to Tibet with the loss of his laden yaks. He continued to drown his sorrows in glass after glass of Phu Dorje's *chung* while aimlessly singing a Sherpa folk song, and accompanying himself on a toy xylophone that I had recently given to Phu Dorje's ten-year-old daughter.

"Has this *puja* got anything to do with Losar, the Sherpa New Year?" I asked.

"No," said Phu Dorje. "It is to protect the village. It really should have been held two weeks ago but Ang Dorje was away and I was working for Burrah Sahib." I nibbled at some of the food and then while Ang Dorje unsteadily refilled the monks' teacups we decided it was a good time to leave.

As we emerged from the dimness of the house we were almost blinded by the brilliant sunshine but hurried back to the hospital for discussions with the staff about some of the more urgent housekeeping matters—food requirements, pressure lamps, a faulty typewriter. We managed to sort out most of the problems to everyone's satisfaction. Only the question of firewood is a constant problem. The forests in the Khumbu are becoming denuded due to uncontrolled cutting and whether we like it or not we have been forced to contribute to this. But the Himalayan Trust was now planning to use solar heating of the water supply and kerosene for the cooking stove—although this would be a good deal more expensive.

Our last day in Kunde before returning to Kathmandu crept up on us so quickly that I found it hard to believe that it was true. It was brought home more forcibly when I had to collect a supply of food from the hospital store room for our trip down to Lukla airfield. There was plenty of other work, too, as the hospital was holding its Losar party that night in honour of our departure. Losar is celebrated for a week instead of the one short hectic night of the European New Year. By the end of this week nearly every household in the village would have organised a party at some time of the day. Now it was the hospital's turn.

"Who do we ask to the party?" I asked Genevieve.

"Mingma has told us that for Losar parties you ask all the village."

"That's about eighty people in Kunde. What about some of our friends in Khumjung?"

"Mingma says we can only have a few of those."

Ed receiving ceremonial *arak* of bitter flavour.

Mingma's house.

Pangkoma school.

In the Naya Kota. Sarah, Peter and Ang Dooli.

"Have they been invited yet?"

"Oh yes, Mingma invited them all two or three days ago."

We would be lost without Mingma, for as well as being a very competent executive officer he is an invaluable adviser on social etiquette.

The living room of most Sherpa houses was big enough to hold a large number of people, but Kunde hospital was divided into a lot of small rooms. The only suitable place in which to hold a village party was the draughty, dilapidated tuberculosis ward. Here tuberculosis patients from other villages can come with members of their families to live and cook for themselves free of charge. Consequently the place usually looked like a grimy impersonal railway station. We washed it all down with antiseptic and brightened it up with a few Christmas decorations and put carpets on the beds. The result was most cheerful.

Genevieve had a large supply of balloons and she employed Murray and three retarded epileptic patients to blow them up. It was the most successful occupational therapy that any hospital has ever prescribed—judging by the giggles and screams of delight that emanated from the balloon-blowing working bee in front of the hospital. They were watched by a group of excited village children who could hardly wait until the evening when the balloons would be distributed. During the day I had a visit from Hospital Pemba's father who had made a pair of Sherpa boots for Peter. The boots were very handsome with bright red, black and green felt uppers and colourful embroidery—just perfect for after-ski wear back in New Zealand. Pemba's father had measured Peter's feet exceptionally carefully and had been amazed at their large dimensions. He could talk of nothing else for the next ten minutes and we were quite confident that the completed boots would be a perfect fit. Obviously when he got down to making the boots he was convinced that nobody could have feet as big as that and the resultant boots only just fitted me. It was too late to do anything about this, and as Ang Tsering had ordered some boots for the girls from a Tibetan bootmaker down in Namche we hoped that by some miracle there might be a pair suitable for each person.

Meanwhile, preparations for the Losar party had reached gigantic proportions in the kitchen where Ang Passang was slicing potatoes for chips with a special corrugated grater he had bought in Kathmandu. He had already filled both sinks with anaemic white slices which he would then fry over an open fire in one small frying pan. Ang Tsering was busy popping mountains of popcorn. I asked Ang Passang what he was giving our eighty guests for their main meal and he told me that he was going to make a thin stew from six cans of corned beef, dried onions, and a few packets of soup. This he would ladle onto bowls of noodles and potatoes. He seemed quite confident that there would be enough even though it sounded to me rather like a hopeful re-enactment of the old Bible story of the loaves and the fishes.

"Do you think we should give our guests anything for dessert?" I enquired of Genevieve.

"Mingma says there is no need. But as this is a New Zealand Losar party perhaps we should do something."

"Can we spare some chocolate?" I asked.

"Yes, we can, and let's make a hard jelly (*jello*) and cut it up like candy to be eaten in the fingers." There was no end to our ideas once we were started, the only controlling factor being the limited supply of ingredients in the store-room.

"Where are the children?" said Mingma every half-hour during the afternoon. By his reckoning they should have returned from Phortse at least before lunch. Their late return didn't surprise me when I remembered their rather dispirited condition as they set off the morning before. Ed worked frantically on lists and sorting hospital gear, interrupted increasingly by old friends who wanted to say goodbye with a parting sip from their bottle of *chung*.

"Really, anybody'd think we were going away for six years," said Ed rather testily as he tried hard to continue with his various jobs. "Instead I'll be back again in six months."

"Coming! Coming!" called Mingma breathlessly and with great relief. We rushed outside to see Peter, Sarah and Belinda marching victoriously up the path towards the hospital, with Siku, Aila and Pemba Tenzing in close support.

"It was absolutely marvellous," we were told, "but, oh, the food! There was so much of it and everyone was so nice that we had to eat it."

"What do you have in that shoulder bag?" I asked Belinda noticing how bulky it was.

"That's got the food in it that I couldn't eat," she replied, making sure that Siku and Aila weren't listening. There was no time to find out all the details of their visit to Phortse. We would have to leave that until later. It would soon be hospital party time and we hurried back to the Naya Kota to get ourselves ready for our farewell party.

During the afternoon Kanche, the nurse, had asked if I would like to wear Sherpa clothes to the party. She had offered to lend me her *ingi* and blouse and I was thrilled to accept. I knew Genevieve would be wearing her Sherpa outfit and I was tired of wearing trousers and a padded jacket. It would also be a great help when dancing that night as all the mistakes in my footwork would be covered up by my long skirts. Ang Dooli very kindly lent me one of her best striped aprons and all I lacked was the long black pigtail instead of my rather neglected tousled hair.

We decided to arrive a little late at the party. This was Genevieve and Lindsay's first venture into the social whirl of Kunde/Khumjung life and as they had nearly two more years ahead of them, we felt it was most important that the guests should clearly realise that they were the host and hostess. While we waited in the Naya Kota, Doma and Ang Tsering arrived on their way to the party carrying a parcel containing two pairs of Sherpa boots. It was impossible to try them on properly as our supply of candles was finished and our torch batteries had all gone flat. We stumbled up the path in the dark to the hospital kitchen and then Sarah and Belinda had a desperate struggle to get their feet down the narrow legs of the boots. But once they were on they fitted perfectly and the girls danced around in glee. As I suspected, there was nothing of suitable size for Peter. Ed asked Ang Tsering how much we owed him for the boots. Doma shook her head very firmly at Ang Tsering, who nodded back at her and then told us they were gifts. The girls were quite overwhelmed by this generosity, but soon recovered and hurried off to the party with their feet now most suitably shod for a night of Sherpa dancing.

The whole village was there, crowded into the ward—even some of the less socially accepted, including an itinerant Tibetan refugee and one of the local Yawas, a Sherpa belonging to a lower stratum of society who are considered unclean by the rest of the community as they are permitted to kill animals for meat. A more conservative type of Sherpa would never drink from the same glass as a Yawa. There aren't many Yawas in Sherpa society, but we have never been very enthusiastic about this system and were delighted to see one of them at the party.

There were some other social outcasts standing outside the tuberculosis ward. They were the young children who had been told by their mothers that there wasn't room inside for everybody. The babies were allowed in with their mothers, but the rather forlorn group of children peering in through the door at the gay bunch of balloons dangling from the ceiling was too much for Genevieve. She pulled the balloons down and handed them to the disembodied, outstretched hands. As soon as they had all been distributed there was a series of bangs, to an accompaniment of sorrowful wails and yells of delight. Inside the room we counted about a hundred people, and in normal Sherpa fashion—or fashion the world over—most of the women sat at one end of the room and the men gathered at the other. The senior grandfathers of the village all congregated in one corner, sitting crosslegged on the hospital beds. We passed around the potato chips and popcorn, and then Ang Passang with his band of workers started to serve dinner to the guests. Passang Tendi handed it to us and to my surprise I noticed that we had been given only potato and stew.

"Where are the noodles, Passang Tendi?" I asked with some curiosity.

"You only get potatoes, the noodles are for the Sherpas," he replied shortly and hurried off to continue with his work.

"Two bowls of *tukpa* each," mumbled Ang Passang as he went round the room carrying a large bamboo tray of food. We ran out of eating utensils quite early in the evening but our Sherpa guests were most accommodating as they are used to sharing—and eating with their hands.

After seventy-five people had been fed, the food supplies were becoming rather low and Ang Passang sent Siku and Passang Tendi back to the kitchen for more cans of corned beef and packets of noodles. In fifteen minutes he had cooked another huge cauldron of *tukpa* on the open fire. We greatly admired Ang Passang's cool efficiency—and that of his helpers, too, who worked in with him as a perfect team. The squares of jelly and chocolate made a pleasant dessert for the meal and then it was time for the guests to bring out their own containers of *chung* and bundles of *katas* to present to the parting guests and to the host and hostess. At the same time the dancing started, and every now and then I would have to stop concentrating on my footwork and gulp down various vintages of *chung* and accept a *kata* around my neck.

As the evening progressed the noise level rose and all inhibitions departed. Murray Jones was dancing beside his energetic friend Phu Dorje. He was being turned and twirled like a rather wavering jack-in-the-box while he held on desperately to a shaky partition wall. Mingma's father, Elay Menu, who had been a bit of a devil in his day, spent most of the evening trying to cajole the shy nurse, Kanche, into joining the long straggling line of dancers. In the end he shoved her amongst a group of the men and the poor girl was overcome by confusion and embarrassment. It was soon after this that I noticed Mingma giving Ang Dooli a nod and she then firmly grasped Elay Menu by the arm and shot him out the door in disgrace.

One of the most agile and proficient of the dancers was a shy student who had been a successful pupil at Khumjung school and was now the proud holder of a Government scholarship at teacher training college in Kathmandu. He danced on the other side of Phu Dorje with the wild Ang Dorje dancing magnificently beside him. They stamped and twirled like a professional group, dragging poor Murray round after them. Their dancing became so spectacular and their singing so

loud and uninhibited that the whole party stopped to watch their performance—which was undoubtedly enhanced by the wild gyrations of
the limp, exhausted Murray who was now being held upright in Phu
Dorje's grip of steel.

On and on we danced, swept along by the rhythms and the plain-
tive singing. Sarah and Belinda looked as though they could go on
dancing until morning. We knew that until we left the party no one
else would go home, so Ed and I at last pulled our protesting daughters
out of the dancing line, collected Peter from his seat beside the fire,
and pushed our way through the heaving crowd and out into the
velvety blackness of a perfect winter night. Behind us the noise carried
on unabated—and would do so, we knew, until the approaching dawn.

CHAPTER 15

Parting is Such Sweet Sorrow
(Romeo and Juliet, Shakespeare)

OUR STAY IN Khumbu had been one long series of welcomes and farewells. We had such a deep affection for our Sherpa friends that I wondered how we would survive the final leave-taking. At least our goodbyes would be spread over quite a long period. All our senior Sherpas were coming down to Lukla with us so as to carry back a plane-load of stores for the hospital, and Mingma and Ang Tsering were going to accompany us all the way to Kathmandu.

It was six o'clock on the morning of departure and Ang Dooli had just brought our tea. She fluttered around the room a little longer than usual with a sad look on her face until Mingma came bouncing through the door with some parcels in his hand. They contained Buddhist religious prints on daphne paper and were presents for some of his friends in New Zealand.

"They're all named. Ang Rita wrote the names for me," he said proudly. Ang Rita had labelled each parcel very neatly in English and he had coped with the spelling of the unfamiliar names in a resourceful fashion. For Murray Ellis, a member of the Himalayan Trust Board in New Zealand, he had written "Muriyelas"—and at first glance it looked quite incomprehensible. There was a present for us too—a highly decorative carpet measuring three feet by six feet, handmade by a Tibetan refugee. What a generous gift this was, and we were quite overwhelmed. Into this emotion-packed atmosphere rushed our children. They said that Siku was gathering up and packing their sleeping bags and other gear with such haste that they had decided to retreat to a safer place. I noticed that Mingma was critically eyeing our unpacked possessions so we reluctantly bestirred ourselves and started tidying up the room.

Mingma never enjoys the Hillary departures from Kunde. Ang Dooli always becomes tearful and Mingma doesn't really like a show of emotion. He has so much to do organising the running of his own household and that of the hospital during his absence, and he has to find porters for the long day's march to Lukla. Finally, he has to withstand the strain of an endless succession of Sherpas armed with the usual farewell equipment of *chung* and *katas*.

We decided to go quickly to the hospital and eat a light breakfast before the first deputation arrived. But we were too late. Kappa Kalden (the artist) and his grandson Danu were waiting on our doorstep. Kappa Kalden was holding the most generous leave-taking gift of a large plate with sixteen eggs, and a handsome brass-banded wooden beer bottle full to the brim. Mingma saved us just in time.

"Come up to the hospital," he said to Kappa Kalden. "You can say your farewells there." He whisked the plate of eggs out of Kappa Kalden's grasp and told Ang Rita to take them to the hospital immediately to be boiled for our lunch. Kappa Kalden didn't seem to mind the change in programme at all for Sherpas are very accommodating people.

Up at the hospital a large crowd had already gathered.

"I thought most of these people said goodbye last night," I remarked to Ed.

"Yes, but they're doing it all again this morning," said Ed lugubriously. However, in many ways it was heartening to be farewelled so thoroughly as we knew it must be a genuine expression of thanks by the people for their schools and hospital. Soon we were engulfed with white *katas* and our stomachs were uncomfortably distended with a mixture of *chung*, fried eggs, Tibetan tea and toast. What a condition to start a long day's walk. Everyone was getting more and more emotional and I knew we would have to leave before we all broke down. We quickly shook the last few hands and hugged the last of our friends, then trudged firmly out through the hospital gateway. Ang Dooli and Doma walked with us to the big *chorten* at the edge of the village. Another hug for both of them, a few sniffles, and we started up the hill towards the path. They stood and waved until we dropped over the crest—and left behind us the village of Kunde and all our very good friends. We seemed to have broken the spell of high altitude happiness that surrounded us so wonderfully over the last few days.

Our stomachs jolted liquidly as we thumped our way down the path to Namche Bazar. Beside us gambolled Ang Passang's dark grey Apso puppy with its long flag-like tail and its devilish little black eyes peering through the bedraggled hair on its face. Ang Passang, the cook, had insisted on giving us the dog and said we could leave it with one of our Sherpa friends in Kathmandu. I hoped that Ang Passang's children wouldn't be too upset about the loss of their pet but he had told me that the dog was so full of high spirits that it was almost impossible to control and had just about wrecked the household by chasing and biting the children and stealing their food at mealtimes.

At the police checkpost in Namche Bazar we officially clocked ourselves out of the area. Feeling quite a bit more stable internally after our loss of height, we pranced down the next 2,000 feet of dusty track to the Dudh Kosi river. We stopped for lunch in the sheltered corner beside the river and had a splendid meal of Ang Passang's long French rolls, Kappa Kalden's boiled eggs, cheese and some canned ham. All that was lacking was a white linen tablecloth, heirloom silver and uniformed waiters to complete the picture of luxury ... but thank goodness our white linen tablecloth was a plastic sheet and our heirloom silver was a chipped enamel bowl! We lay in the warm sun and rested from the tiring events of the morning. As we travelled on towards Lukla Ed and I were given a detailed account of the children's visit to Phortse.

"They gave us such lovely food!" groaned Belinda. Nearly all the village had turned out to welcome them, they told us, and they were immediately handed large bowls of fresh *dhai* covered with *tsampa* and sugar. When they had gulped down the last mouthful they were led to the Phortse school where the entire population gave them a traditional Sherpa welcome—*katas* and various home brews plus special delicacies to celebrate Losar. The school children danced and sang for them and the Panchayat members made long speeches—it was a memorable experience for the three teenagers.

They stayed at Aila's house for the night and his wife gave them a big meat stew and rice for dinner followed by potato cakes—*rigi cour*—liberally spiced with chilli. After that they sat beside the warm brazier for a while and Mrs. Aila gave each of her visitors a present. The girls received a large chunk of beautifully veined turquoise which they could tie around their necks on a piece of heavy red cord. Peter was given a carved printing block for making prayer flags. It was very smoky inside the room with two fires going and the air was getting thicker and thicker.

"Finally I was sick though I don't think anybody noticed, as I had a very large handkerchief," said Belinda. Aila and Siku decided quite early that it was time for their charges to go to sleep, so everybody spread their bedding out on the floor and they settled down for a peaceful and comfortable night. All too soon it was morning with a big breakfast of *dhai*, potatoes and hospital bread to be coped with.

They said their goodbyes to Phortse and then dropped down a very steep pathway, 2,000 feet to the Dudh Kosi river, and then straight up again on the other side to arrive at the nunnery of Daweche where they visited Dawa Tenzing, one of the most famous old climbing Sirdars. Dawa has built himself a little cottage beside the nunnery so as to live close to his two daughters who are nuns. He had prepared a delicious egg and milk custard for his visitors, which they thoroughly enjoyed.

After leaving Dawa they walked up the hill for twenty minutes through the rhododendron and birch trees to Thyangboche monastery with its superb view of Mount Everest. They crossed the peaceful grassy meadow in front of the temple and were met by a *tawa* who conducted them to the private quarters of the Rimpoche of Thyangboche. The Rimpoche did a great honour to Peter and his sisters when he personally conducted them through his beautiful monastery. They found it a remarkable experience and all too soon they were saying goodbye and leaving on the three-hour trip to rejoin us in Kunde.

More than any other place Thyangboche monastery is bearing the brunt of the tourist invasion of the Khumbu. I have noticed that much of the monastery's original tranquillity has disappeared for ever.

A Lamaistic Buddhist monastery is meant to be a peaceful place where the monks can meditate upon unworldly things and give themselves entirely to a religious life without any outside distractions. But now at Thyangboche this is virtually impossible and some of the monks have become enamoured of material wealth. They have sold their old religious artifacts and built teahouses, a restaurant and even a small hotel. The Rimpoche, who is an intelligent sensitive man, has found himself an unwilling part of the tourist scene—the ultimate goal of the camera-happy foreigner. I would like to think that many of the strangers who visit Thyangboche will find its superb location an inspiration to their spirits, but increasingly it is becoming one of those places that you must visit and photograph. Only a tourist with a heart of stone could not be affected by the grandeur that surrounds this little community but unfortunately there are a few who don't care about such things. They cut the rhododendron bushes that surround the Thyangboche meadow for firewood, and leave their litter in careless piles wherever they happen to camp. They use the beautiful rhododendron groves as toilets, and have been known to wash their socks in the new monastery fresh water supply.

On one occasion Mingma dug a big rubbish hole beside the monastery guest house but people often didn't seem to notice it, and when we made a wooden sign to attract the tourists' attention it quickly disappeared to be used either as an interesting ornament by a Sherpa household, or as kindling for a tourist's fire. A few years ago I visited Thyangboche just after two large Everest expeditions had passed through on their way to the mountain. Many hundreds of porters and scores of foreign climbers had camped on the monastery meadow and the ground beneath the bordering rhododendron trees looked as though it had suffered a snow-storm of toilet paper. How anyone could defile such a beautiful place I cannot understand, but to make matters worse there were vast amounts of everyday rubbish lying around the guest house and school. We were so horrified at this dismal sight that we spent two days trying to clean up the worst of the mess. One of our Sherpa helpers, an elegant young man, made himself a long pole with a nail on the end and wandered around the deserted camp site languidly spearing paper and other waste—and wondering what the fuss was all about. But at the end of two days' work even the Sherpas were impressed with the change in the appearance of the rubbish-infested meadow.

That night we had two cans of peaches for dinner and some time after the meal I heard a clatter in the bushes behind me and turned around to see two empty peach tins rolling down the slope into the darkness beyond. I jumped to my feet determined to discover the culprit, and there standing at the edge of the trees was the elegant young man who had just spent two days clearing up all the rubbish. I suppose you can't hope to change people's habits in a few short days.

Until 1960 the people of the Khumbu lived in reasonable harmony with nature by the careful use of pastures and forests, and there was a good balance between the flora and fauna. Now that balance has been upset and frequently in disastrous fashion. In the upper Khumbu the dark green, prostrate juniper and the azalea bushes have been hacked away slowly by advancing armies of tourists and climbers as they puff their way towards the foot of Everest. So much for the blessings of civilisation. There is probably time for the Everest region to be saved by making it a National Park, patrolled by highly trained rangers. But this must happen soon.

At the end of a long day of walking we arrived at Lukla village where we stayed in the house of Ang Lakpa who was our airstrip custodian and mail runner. His wife is an old friend of mine and welcomed us with *katas* and large mugs of warm zum milk. Just as we were settling down to dinner Ang Lakpa and his wife were told by distraught relations that one of their yaks had been killed by a wild animal, red in colour, as it grazed in the high valley behind Lukla. We tried very hard to discover what type of animal this had been and ended up with a description of a small ferocious beast with long whiskers. It sounded very like the red Himalayan panda (or raccoon) which would have been an unlikely killer of a large hairy yak.

After dinner we wandered out into the bright moonlight and walked down through the village to the airfield. How the place had changed since we first built the airfield in 1964! There were now quite a few new buildings including an office for the Japanese hotel and one for the Royal Nepal Airlines. Nearby was a small teahouse with a radio blaring out loud Indian music in competition with the cries of a distressed baby. On the other side of the strip was the policeman's quarters. His main job was to guard an old twin-engined aircraft which had made an unsuccessful landing three years before and bent one of its wings. Ever since that time it had stood at the top of the airfield as a depressing warning to any would-be air travellers. The policeman also had the important task of keeping the airfield clear of people and their cattle when aircraft were in the vicinity. Once a pilot has committed himself to land at Lukla he cannot change his mind at the last moment because of the mountain wall at the end of the runway. The policeman's work was almost impossible as despite the stone walls lining the airfield it is something of a main highway and the special grass that we planted to consolidate the area is regarded as the choicest grazing in the village.

Lukla is always associated in my mind with long periods of waiting. There is no wireless contact with Kathmandu airport so passengers often have to sit around for many days before their aircraft arrives. Lukla is not a lively village by any standards—social life is non-existent and the people are quiet, hardworking and fairly poor. The views are beautiful but if you are an eager traveller it is easy to become bored and desperate as you wait, not daring to leave the vicinity in case the plane finally arrives. I have explored every ridge and valley, every magnolia tree and grove of rhododendrons. I thought seriously on one occasion during a delay of five days of writing a detailed guidebook for weary waiters—but it would be fairly hard to make it exciting reading.

We spent the night spread out on the floor of Ang Lakpa's house talking and laughing for many hours, all loath to end the day that was to be our last in Khumbu. Although there isn't much privacy, there is a considerable feeling of companionship when twenty friends are spread out all over the floor. Slowly the noise died away and we all dropped peacefully off to sleep. In the morning there was a strained urgency in our preparations for departure. We expected the plane to arrive at 8 a.m. so carried our possessions to the airfield and then returned for a quick breakfast. Our usual rations of porridge and potatoes

were augmented by a delicious yak meat curry given to us by Ang
Lakpa's wife, who had most generously cooked up some of the slaugh-
tered yak as a special gesture to her parting guests.

It was terrible to be leaving so many of our good friends—Siku,
Aila, Ang Passang, Passang Tendi and Pemba Tenzing. We stood
around making forced conversation as people always do at airports
and railway stations. Ang Passang's little Apso puppy seemed to feel
the tension in the air and sat down on the frost-covered ground and
wept noisily. Siku and Pemba Tenzing couldn't stand the waiting any
longer, they made their sad farewells and then headed down valley to
buy a load of lemons for the hospital. As they hurried down the airstrip towards the main Dudh Kosi track we stood watching them very
quietly until Mingma broke the silence.

"You can always tell a Phortse man," he said, "by the way he
walks." Aila made some rude remark in return and we all laughed and
relaxed. At 8 a.m. precisely the airline office behind us came to life.
Above the entrance to the temporary tent accommodation was a
smart new notice saying "Royal Nepal Airlines, Lukla Station."

A cheerful Sherpa dressed in business clothes came out of the door
and wrote down all the names of the passengers. Then, to our amazement, from the house behind came another Sherpa employee of the
airline with a tray of hot coffee and biscuits. Such treatment was
quite unexpected and we realised with amazement that the refinements
of modern air travel had caught up with us even at Lukla.

As usual it was the sharp-eyed Sherpas who first saw the approaching
aircraft. "*Ayo! Ayo!*" (it's come! it's come!) came the call from all
around us. We searched the sky and finally saw a small speck above the
ridge on the far side of the valley. All too soon it grew into a beautiful
twin-engined Otter aircraft just straightening for its descent towards
the airfield. It made a perfect landing and I think all of us felt a slight
glow of pride that our airfield was proving so useful. With engines
roaring loudly the aircraft taxied up to the top of the strip and then a
smart staircase was let down from the rear entrance. The pilot, co-pilot
and steward, all dressed in Royal Nepal Airlines uniforms, climbed
down onto the rough grass surface. We loaded up quickly and then
started our hurried farewells. Sherpas are well-known for being soft-
hearted and emotional at times like these and the high altitude of
9,000 feet tends to make foreigners feel very much the same way. The
only thing to do was to get inside quickly so as not to prolong the
misery of parting.

Ang Passang's puppy stood quivering with fear surrounded by the
noises and smells of a strange new world. It seemed cruel to have to

scoop her up and carry her inside the smart pale blue cabin of the aircraft. We obeyed the "Fasten Seat Belts" sign feeling completely out of touch with such sophisticated travel. I clasped the little dog firmly to my warm jacket as it was now quite hysterical, but it struggled so desperately in my arms that Mingma offered to hold it—and it was amazing how quickly it relaxed when it was held firmly by strong Sherpa hands. The steward offered us sweets, and cotton wool for our ears. We only had time for a quick wave at the friends we were leaving behind and then we were thundering down the airfield and out over the alarming depths of the Dudh Kosi gorge. We started climbing steeply and within a few minutes the Khumbu valley had disappeared.

Our flight turned into a bird's-eye view of our recent travels, during which time we had walked about two hundred and seventy miles and puffed up and down tens of thousands of feet.

"There's Junbesi!"

"There's Gypsoa!"

"Look quickly, there's Piké!" We hardly had time to notice the great wall of Himalayan mountains that slipped past us on our right.

In less than an hour the steep terraced red ridges east of Kathmandu were passing below us and we could see the white and terracotta houses with their small clumps of banana and pawpaw trees beside them—we could even see the winding paths and the people at work. We dived down towards the wide land-locked valley of Kathmandu which was bathed in a golden glow of winter sunlight. Down we dropped towards the rich paddy fields interspersed with a patchwork of green vegetable gardens and the crowded streets of towns studded with jewels of Buddhist and Hindu culture. Soon there was a gentle thud. We had touched down, the aircraft door was flung open, and with something of a shock we awakened from our Himalayan dream.

CHAPTER 16

Camping in Kathmandu

AFTER A LONG STAY in the mountains you feel like Rip van Winkle waking from his hundred years of sleep. I was fortunate to be wakened rather pleasantly out of my dazed condition—

"You'd look just like a Nepalese woman if only you had long hair," said a pleasant voice. I turned around to see a Nepalese friend of mine who had come to visit the airport to farewell a relation. I was delighted with the compliment even though dressed in a heavy shapeless padded jacket and a pair of rather frayed slacks.

"What have you got in your hand?" she enquired. I was still clutching onto the bag of eggs that Pemba Tenzing had given me only an hour before.

"A gift of eggs from one of my Khumbu friends."

"Oh, how nice," she said, "you obviously know all about our custom that a parting gift of eggs or fruit must always be taken with you." (There was really no chance of leaving such a gift behind with the frugal Mingma hovering about.)

"We'll be eating them for breakfast tomorrow," I told her.

The shock of our return to city life was lessened by our choice of accommodation for the next week. We had decided to camp in the garden of the Ang Tarkay family's residence. Mrs. Ang Tarkay, her son Tenzing, and her niece Passang Puti were there to welcome us and so were our scholarship boys Ang Rita, Mingma Norbu and Lakpa Norbu and quite a few of our other friends from Solu Khumbu. It was almost as good as being back in Kunde again and we most certainly would not have to immediately forsake our mountain ways. Everybody helped pitch camp in the Ang Tarkay garden. A large tent was put up to serve as sleeping tent for Ed and myself and also to act as office and sitting room. Peter and Murray each had a tent to themselves and Sarah and Belinda had to share one. Our travelling shower-bath had come with us so there was no excuse for not being clean. Mingma and Ang Tsering found room to spread their sleeping bags in Ang Tarkay's kitchen.

We put our few possessions into our tents and sat down to enjoy a cup of Mrs. Ang Tarkay's excellent Darjeeling tea.

"What would you like us to do about cooking our meals?" I asked Tenzing.

"Please feel free to use our kitchen," he replied, "but the water supply is difficult at this time of year, so if you have a lot of washing you will have to do it early in the morning before the water supply runs out."

"Ang Tsering will be cook," said Mingma, "and I'll be cook boy!" he announced with a great chuckle at his humour.

"Do you think you can find our old driver and his jeep, Mingma?" said Ed.

"Coming soon," said Mingma, "I saw him at the airport." And ten minutes later our official Himalayan Trust vehicle swayed into view. It must have been one of the original jeeps shipped in to Kathmandu about twenty years ago. It was painted in pale fawn with a tiger-skin design across the bonnet which until recently was the standard decoration for a Kathmandu taxi. With much ingenuity and loving care the driver had managed to keep his jeep on the road, although in old age its top speed was about fifteen miles an hour. The driver leapt out of the vehicle to greet Ed like a long-lost brother for the two of them had been through many a crisis together in the years gone by—such as the failure of the brakes and the breakdown of the engine *en route* to catch an important flight to Calcutta. What greater bond could you have than that, particularly when the only common language that could be used by employer and employee happened to be the language of smiles, yells, nods and wild hand-waving? Our owner driver was a Newar who spoke only his mother tongue and a few unintelligible words of Nepali. There must have been a remarkable change in his fortunes because he now had with him another junior driver, a rather emaciated, nervous, ill-clad figure.

"Why the new driver?" we enquired. No one seemed to know.

Our first and most urgent business was to have a hot bath. Fortunately "Rodrock's" mother had offered us the freedom of the British Embassy bathroom and the whole crowd of us descended on the O'Briens' house across the road. What greater joy can there be than a leisurely wallow in a hot bath after you have been away from it for a long time? I tried to wash some of my clothes in the precious hot bath water, and the accumulated dust from the Himalayan paths and the smoke from all our fires turned the white porcelain bath to a very dirty brown colour.

"Tea's ready downstairs," Ed called out.

"I can't come yet," I replied desperately, and used my newly washed singlet to wipe the bath down and get rid of some of the dirt.

At tea the O'Briens gave the Hillary family a present of a popular Nepalese game—Tiger and Goat, or *Bharchal* in Nepali and *Tadang Phadang* as it is called in Sherpa. It is played rather like draughts on a square board or on a flat piece of ground with the use of little tiger and goat figures or even just small stones. The idea is that the tigers try to "eat" the goats. We hurried back to camp to ask the scholarship boys how to play, and they and Ang Tsering were only too happy to demonstrate their skill for us. We were amused to discover that the combined brain-power of Mingma and Lakpa was not sufficient to combat the cunning of Ang Tsering who beat the boys every time— much to their annoyance.

There was never a dull moment during our five days' stay in Ang Tarkay's garden and it became impossible to attend to simple chores before we would have to welcome some new visitors.

"Come on in," we would say and soon the floor of the tent would be crammed with visitors. Ed never believes in urging people to state the reason for their visit so quite often we would sit for ten or twenty minutes with hardly a work being spoken. My hostess instincts would be sorely tried on these occasions and I would fidget and make unnecessary remarks to try and cover up my embarrassment. But finally the purpose of the visit would emerge.

On our first evening back in Kathmandu we were invited to a cock-tail party. Mingma and Ang Tsering weren't very keen to come, but they finally did although I don't think they enjoyed it very much. They left rather early but the rest of us stayed on for quite a long while. Murray Jones and our three children were rather unconventionally attired for such an occasion but nobody seemed to care very much—in fact Murray became generally accepted as our eldest son. From then on he took great pleasure in calling us "Mum" and "Dad' much to the confusion of some of our newer acquaintances. In some ways this was very appropriate, as over the previous few weeks Murray had become quite a close member of our family.

The next morning was the start of an important day for all of us— it was the day for the signing of the formal agreement between the Nepalese Government and the Himalayan Trust. For eleven years we had been operating without any formal agreement, just getting per-mission for each particular project as it came up. But now the Hima-layan Trust was going to become official and this would be a new experience for us, and we felt distinctly nervous about it all.

It was quite clear that only Ed and I could attend the signing cere-mony as no one else in our immediate family—including Murray—had any suitable formal clothes. So the four younger ones set off on hired

Dinner at Ang Tarkay's home. Louise, Ed, Mrs. Ang Tarkay, Sarah, Belinda, Peter.

The scholarship boys and Hillary children setting off on bicycles to explore Kathmandu.

Louise in Sherpa dress at home in Auckland.

bicycles to enjoy the Kathmandu valley, and I rather envied them their freedom. There can't be many cities left in the world where two teenage girls could wander safely on their own with such a complete feeling of security. I hope it always stays that way.

There is so much to see in Kathmandu, from the quaint little shops to the ancient houses built around their paved courtyards, with beauti-fully carved windows and door frames, created with great artistry by craftsmen of another age. Sometimes the lack of drainage is a hin-drance to the peaceful contemplation of a work of art but it is possible to disregard such discomforts. Hindu shrines and temples are to be found in their hundreds in all sorts of unlikely corners of the city. One of the finest and oldest temples in Kathmandu is the Hanumun Doka, an old royal palace and temple which is now a museum. It's a magnifi-cent, pagoda-roofed, group of buildings built around a central court-yard. Parts of the structure are showing signs of decay but the fine wood carving and lattice-work over the windows is being slowly restored. There are dungeons, they say, underneath Hanumun Doka and immediately one envisages terrifying dark black holes. We were told that a New Zealander who had become addicted to drugs was languishing there until a doctor could be found to fly him back to his home.

Drugs are very easy to buy in Kathmandu and marijuana is in abundant supply and very cheap. It grows wild over large areas of Nepal, especially in the west, and I enquired why it was that the Nepalese didn't use it themselves as a drug. I found that there was a general lack of interest in the subject but that the seed has been used as a form of spice with slightly intoxicating effects and that normally the plant was considered just as ground cover. I can only conclude that as the marijuana plant is so common in Nepal it is a good example of forbidden fruit always tasting sweeter.

The large bazaar in the centre of Kathmandu can be tremendously good fun. All the shops in the old area are small and crammed with goods and there is often hardly room for the shopkeeper to fit amongst his wares. You can go from shop to shop for days, admiring the colour-ful exhibition of metalware—copper, brass and aluminium made into gracefully shaped water containers, measures for grain, plates and so on. Sometimes I have found it difficult to control a strong acquisi-tive desire to buy up the whole shopful just so that I could have the pleasant feeling of knowing that it all belonged to me.

Some of the streets specialise in cloth and lure their customers with bright displays of Indian and Nepalese saris, although the coarse Nepali

M

weave with their simple handprinted designs in maroon, orange or black are by far the most attractive to young foreigners. The cloth shops usually carry stocks of the local version of the eiderdown—a cotton quilt padded with kapok. They are made of a plain white cloth decorated with gay hand-blocked red and black designs of fish, pineapples, flowers, etc., edged with a band of red.

Every fifty yards or so you will see a Nepalese hat shop specialising only in the traditional fez-shaped soft cotton cap worn by Nepalese men. The soft colours of the floral patterns used for most of the caps are rather unusual to Western eyes, with the result that the temptation to buy becomes irresistible. Umbrella shops are a bit disappointing these days as they tend to be filled with the plastic-handled variety, but there are still some with bent bamboo handles. The umbrella is a most important part of Nepalese equipment for it is used in rain and sun and even in snow and when not in use it can be hooked into the back of the owner's collar for ease of carrying on the mountain paths.

Gemstone shops are found everywhere, particularly in some of the more modern streets and here you can find the traditional jewellery and ornaments made from brass and decorated with small pieces of turquoise and coral. They are the most typical of all handicrafts and one of the best in value. Prominently displayed in all gemstone windows are the most famous examples of Kathmandu valley craft— the bronze figures of old Hindu culture, the best of which are graceful works of art and even the cheap copies are quite fun to own. If you know anything about gems it is possible to find some real bargains, but somehow the sight of polished coloured rock displayed in a crumpled twist of white paper leaves me quite disinterested. I am impatient to continue with the more obvious entertainment of *kukri* shops, rope shops, bamboo basket shops, papier-mâché religious mask shops, drum shops, incense sellers, glass bangle sellers, wandering Tibetan traders, trishaw drivers *ad infinitum*.

At the central crossroads of the bazaar the grain sellers always gather and behind them the oil shops and general grocery stores are found—and nowadays you can buy every type of Western grocery. Wool shawls and carpets are sold from the steps of an old Hindu shrine at another crossroad, and it was somewhere near here that our children discovered shops selling slightly European versions of traditional Nepali and Tibetan jackets and blouses.

Every so often as you wander bemused down the narrow streets with the tide of jostling humanity, a coolie will stagger past with a wide load of handmade water pots. Their simple yet graceful shapes and rich red colouring make these common household utensils into

fine works of art. They are made in every size from nine inches high
to three and four feet. The potters use the most basic of wooden
wheels and fire their wares in a great mound of leaves, grass and twigs
creating uneven baking conditions that leave a delightful variation in
colour on the finished pots.

Nepal is a land of flowers and most householders find room for a
clump of dahlias or marigolds in their gardens, whilst the bigger, more
wealthy landowners often have wonderful arrays of pot plants. The
flower pots are made as beautifully as the water pots. Most of them
have scalloped edges but my favourites are the elephant-shaped flower
pots. Some years ago I decided to try and carry one of them home
with me through Greece, England and the United States. I would
never have succeeded if it hadn't been for the fact that the height of
my elephant-pot was the same as the gap underneath the seat of a
Boeing 707. I flew two-thirds of the way around the world with my
legs unable to be stretched out in front of me, but those hours of discomfort are nothing compared to the joy I have had out of my elephant-pot as it stands outside my front door with a cyclamen plant or
a primrose growing out of it.

While our children absorbed the wonders of Kathmandu we prepared for the signing of the Himalayan Trust Agreement.

"I don't think I am used to agreement-signing ceremonies," said Ed
rather nervously as we struggled into our unfamiliar best clothes,
surrounded by the chaos of our tent. Ed was wearing a dark suit
and I was wearing a dress and stockings over athletic, trekking legs.
When we emerged into the garden after our preparations we were
met by Mingma, our Field Supervisor for Himalayan Trust projects,
and his assistant, Ang Tsering, both very soberly dressed and looking
unusually formal. Both had bought new trousers and new shoes
and Mingma had a smart sports jacket that he had acquired when he
was in New Zealand six years before. We asked Tenzing how we
looked.

"Very nice, but Mingma and Ang Tsering must wear Nepalese
caps, as all citizens are required to wear them when they visit the
Singha Durbar."

"Mingma, you can have my cap," said Tenzing, "but I've only got
one, so what shall we do about Ang Tsering?" Just then our jeep
rattled in through the gate. The driver and his prosperous employer
were both in the vehicle—I suppose our friend the boss had come along
to participate in our official engagement. He was wearing a dusty, discoloured, black Nepali cap and we all looked at it thoughtfully. When

Ang Tsering asked him if he could borrow it he was only too happy to oblige, as by so doing he felt he was becoming an indispensable member of the party. To counteract the chilling effects of being minus his hat, our friend wrapped a thick woollen scarf around his ears, climbed into the back of his jeep and sat in one corner with a most self-satisfied grin on his face.

With plenty of time in hand we set off for the Singha Durbar and our important engagement. The Singha Durbar is an old and elegant palace which houses the Government offices. It was built about a hundred years ago by one of the Rana families who for many years ruled Nepal. It's rather like a small version of Versailles but the days of its grandeur are long past and many of the opulent rooms are now partitioned into small dark offices. The front of the building however had been preserved in its old state for use on ceremonial occasions. Its marble walls and balconies, its fountains, its mirrors and candelabras are most suited to such functions. We had been told that we were to be given the honour of having our agreement signed in one of the front reception rooms which was a considerable compliment.

It was five minutes to two exactly when our jeep lurched through the handsome front gates of the Singha Durbar. Our unsmiling and haggard driver, clad in his usual discoloured and worn Nepali suit, brought our vehicle to a halt in front of the marble steps leading to the reception rooms. We tiptoed up the steps past handsome potted plants where a liveried servant guided us to the balconies above. Here we were met by our friend Mrs. Bhinda Shah who was one of the senior officials of the Foreign Affairs Department. Mrs. Shah has dealt with Himalayan Trust business for a number of years and has always been kind, understanding and most helpful. She was very happy about the new agreement and I hope that in future her work with the Trust will become very much more straightforward.

I could see now that the ceremony wasn't going to be as terrifying as we had anticipated. The senior Government official present was the Foreign Secretary, Mr. Bharat Raj Bhandary, who had been Ambassador to Japan, Australia and New Zealand some years before. We had known him for quite a few years and he had spent a happy day with us at our home in Auckland. Feeling relaxed and cheerful to be amongst old friends we walked into the reception room. Its walls were lined with pale green silk brocade, and its floor was covered in thick mushroom-coloured carpet. Overhead hung sparkling crystal chandeliers. It all seemed far removed from the simple smoke-blackened houses of the mountain people of Nepal.

We had been told to invite whoever we wished to the function, and had chosen a small group of guests who had all worked long and hard in Kathmandu on our behalf. Three of our special guests were the representatives of countries who have helped the Trust with finance and many other forms of aid. There was the British Ambassador and his wife, Mr. and Mrs. Terence O'Brien; there was the New Zealand Ambassador resident in New Delhi, Mr. Dennis Dunlop; and the Dean of the Diplomatic Corps of Kathmandu, Miss Carol Laise, American Ambassador and a good friend of the Hillary family. One of Miss Laise's first official duties after her appointment as Ambassador to Nepal five years before had been to attend the opening celebrations of the Kunde hospital. Ever since then she had taken a great deal of interest in the activities of the Trust in Solu Khumbu.

"Well, I think we had better start," said Mr. Bhandary. He and Ed sat behind an impressive leather-topped table with two handsome red-bound copies of the new agreement in front of them. Placed within easy reach were two sets of red and black fountain pens. In a flash Mr. Bhandary had signed his copy of the agreement which he passed to Ed to countersign. But Ed hadn't even started to sign his copy as he was still wondering rather vaguely which pen to use. In fact he had just decided to take hold of the red pen and sign with that when Mr. Bhandary hastily whisked it out of his hand and replaced it with the black pen. Red pens we were told, amidst much laughter, were for crossing out mistakes. We had just escaped a most inauspicious start. It is amazing how helpless a wife can feel at times like this, but in a few more seconds the signing was all successfully completed and I covered my helplessness with a cheerful smile and joined the assembled gathering in some polite handclapping.

Afternoon tea was served on the balcony and during this time one of our guests asked Ed why Mingma and Ang Tsering were not present.

"They are standing just behind you," said Ed rather startled. In their city clothes the two Sherpas looked like unimportant undersecretaries of some minor Government department. Also the presence of so many important dignitaries amongst such grand surroundings had changed even the restless and active Mingma into a quiet spectator.

Speeches were duly given and compliments paid, and it was a very happy occasion. But I could see that Ed, like his Sherpa friends, would have been much happier in some old clothes with a pack on his back, an ice axe in his hand or a hammer tucked in his side-pocket in readiness for work on a new project.

Our driver and his employer were waiting in the jeep straight outside the main steps below the reception rooms. "We should have told them to park farther away," I said with a chuckle. "They certainly look a little out of place here." We climbed into our official transport and Ang Tsering handed back the cap to its owner. We called out our goodbyes to our Ambassadorial friends in their long black limousines, and then rattled and clanged our way past gardens and reflection pools into the busy Kathmandu bazaar.

"Well, that's that," said Ed smiling to himself in relief.

"Very good and very nice," said Mingma, referring to the afternoon tea.

The following are some of the more important points in the Agreement:

AGREEMENT BETWEEN HIS MAJESTY'S
GOVERNMENT OF NEPAL AND
THE HIMALAYAN TRUST
REGARDING EDUCATIONAL AND HEALTH
SERVICES PROJECTS

His Majesty's Government of Nepal (hereinafter referred to as "HMGN") and The Himalayan Trust, 278A Remuera Road, Auckland, New Zealand, including Sir Edmund Hillary (hereinafter referred to as the "Trust") desiring to co-operate in promoting the economic and social welfare and the development of educational and health services (hereinafter referred to as "Project") in Eastern Nepal have agreed as follows:

ARTICLE I

The Project shall consist primarily of two parts:

(a) Provision of educational assistance through the construction and maintenance of schools, the provision of teaching aids, trade-training tools, books and other equipments and the provision and training of teachers.

(b) Provision of health services through the construction and maintenance of hospital and dispensary with the approval of HMGN, the provision of medical supplies and equipment, the carrying out of training programmes in public health, in accordance with the approval and requirements of the Ministry of Health, medical treatment of the local population, and the installation of water pipes to bring clean fresh water to villages.

ARTICLE II

The Project shall also include the provision of construction and engineering work related to the general objectives set out in the preamble to this Agreement including bridges, roads, tracks, and airfields that may improve access to the Project.

ARTICLE III

The Trust shall provide the personnel, and financial resources for the Project and shall designate a representative in Nepal who shall be the channel of communication between HMGN and the Trust.

ARTICLE IV

The Trust shall work in close consultation with a co-ordinating committee consisting of representatives of the Ministry of Foreign Affairs, Ministry of Education, Ministry of Health, representatives of other concerned Ministries and the representative of the Trust. Where appropriate *ad hoc* committees may be formed to discuss and decide on individual projects.

ARTICLE V

The Trust will employ teachers who are Nepalese citizens, however, if Nepalese citizens are not available, the Trust may employ foreign teachers following approval by HMGN.

(a) The Trust shall disburse salaries of teachers through the appropriate District Educational Committee, and the District Educational Officer will be responsible for such payments to teachers.

(b) The Trust will arrange for the training of teachers through the Teachers Training Centre of HMGN.

ARTICLE VI

The Trust shall provide text books and follow the course of studies and syllabus of instruction prescribed by HMGN and in accordance with the National Educational Plan.

ARTICLE VII

The Trust will seek the services extended by Nepal Rastra Bank for the remittance of funds in Nepal for the Project in accordance with foreign exchange rules and regulation of HMGN.

ARTICLE VIII

HMGN shall provide all co-operation in executing the Project and above objectives, and in particular the following facilities:

(a) Gratis visa for experts appointed by the Trust to work on the Project.

(b) Permission for travel by these experts throughout Eastern Nepal except in restricted areas.

(c) Duty-free import of personal effects for these experts working on the Project, similar to the facilities extended to Colombo Plan experts, and of building materials, tools, equipment and medical and other supplies for the Project.

ARTICLE IX

This Agreement shall come into force on 1st January 1972 and shall remain in force for a period of three years. It may be extended beyond this period or be amended by mutual agreement between HMGN and the Trust.

Signed in Kathmandu on the 20th day of January 1972.

Bharat Raj Bhandary   Sir Edmund Hillary
Foreign Secretary   Chairman
For His Majesty's Government   For the Himalayan Trust
of Nepal

As we drove away from the Singha Durbar there was still time before the shops shut to make some purchases for Kunde hospital. We had decided to buy a kerosene heater which proved to be very expensive—over fifty dollars. Mingma, although still looking meek and mild in his city clothes, protested vigorously at the exorbitant price but we finally persuaded him that the heater was necessary for the hospital because of the scarcity of firewood in the Khumbu. It would be useful in the private quarters of the doctor and his wife so they would be able to have somewhere quiet to work in the evenings.

"It will be pretty useful in our tent tonight, when we are dressing for the New Zealand Ambassador's dinner party," said Ed.

"In that case we should get it," I agreed, for we were finding the social life of Kathmandu was quite difficult to handle from a tent on a frosty evening.

"There is something else we need," said Mingma, "you asked me to hunt for it earlier," he said, looking at me.

"What was it?" I asked.

"I am not quite sure," he replied. "It was a word like 'Moss' ..."

"Moss? That's very strange, I don't think we want anything like that."

"Oh, I know that is not quite the word," said Mingma, "but it's a small grey thing."

"What is the word in Nepali?" I enquired vaguely hopeful that I might just recognise it. But he shook his head. He didn't know.

"What sort of shop should we get it from?" I asked. He pointed to a chemist's shop very impatiently as he was becoming more and more irritated every moment with my lack of understanding.

"A small grey thing called 'Moss' at a chemist's shop?" I said.

"Some killing needing," said Mingma softly to himself. Ah! at last I understood ... it was a mousetrap we required for the hospital storeroom.

We drove down New Road, a wide modern street which still managed to preserve a pleasantly Nepalese flavour—probably because of the people and the delightful views in every direction of old houses and pagoda roofs. We saw Sarah and Belinda come out of a shop and start to unlock their bicycles. It was certainly easy to pick them out in the crowd for as yet there are not many young Westerners lucky enough to be tourists in Kathmandu and the girls looked very lively and cheerful. Most of the other young Western visitors to Kathmandu are European escapists, wearing their strange uniforms of bedraggled long shapeless gowns with hair often wild and unkempt and rather sad vacant faces. I often wonder what the local population must think of these strange ambassadors of the Western world who come ostensibly to soak up the ancient culture and try to liberate their minds in the fresh non-materialistic environment. Most of them looked so uncertain and unhappy that I couldn't help feeling sorry for them.

Our new kerosene heater was a great advantage when we made our preparations for the diplomatic dinner. Our lighting wasn't terribly good and I had to put on my lipstick and tidy my hair by touch alone and felt quite inadequately groomed for such a glamorous party. I needn't have worried however for amongst the fifteen guests present, the three Nepalese women far outstripped their European sisters in elegance. I admired their graceful saris, their dark hair shining and smooth, their dainty hands and their calm beautiful faces. It was a very gay evening, and when it was time to leave the smart uniformed doorman of the hotel even managed to scrape up a salute for Ed and myself as we walked out of the hotel doors towards our waiting expedition vehicle. Our driver looked almost mummified in a collection of threadbare scarves that were wrapped around his head and neck in a hopeless attempt at keeping out the cold. I felt like Cinderella as I climbed ungracefully from the jeep and blindly groped my way into a cold unwelcoming tent.

Next day the Kathmandu newspapers had headlines about us in large print: "HIS MAJESTY'S GOVERNMENT AND THE HIMALAYAN TRUST REACH AGREEMENT". We read the long article with great pride and for the rest of the day we were amazed and very touched at the interest that was shown in the news. One of the most heartwarming visits came from an inspector of police who had been checkpost captain at Namche Bazar some years before. As soon as he heard of the new agreement over the radio he came quickly to visit us and offer his congratulations. In some tangible way we seemed to have been accepted fully into the great Nepalese brotherhood.

CHAPTER 17

We Abandon Camp

OUR DAY IN Ang Tarkay's garden started when the sun first hit the tents. We would jump into thick clothes and walk over to the water tank in the middle of the garden where, with the help of a long-handled dipper, we could wash our hands and face, and clean our teeth —surrounded by an appreciative audience of household chickens and Doma the puppy. Each morning was crisp and sparkling and once the sun was up the frost soon disappeared from the ground. From the garden we could see the steep brown hills that encircled Kathmandu valley and behind them the staggered white peaks of the Himalayan giants, standing up clean and sharp in the pure mountain air.

All the recent excitement seemed to have been too much for me, or perhaps it was my draughty dressing-room, for on our second to last day in Kathmandu I woke up with a cold and felt very sorry for myself. So while Ed had an important planning session with his two senior teachers, I went and sat in the kitchen with Mrs. Ang Tarkay. She soon noticed my bleary eyes and sniffles and groped inside the front of her Sherpa tunic, where in good traditional fashion she kept her valuables, and pulled out a bottle of aspirin. Then she quickly prepared a cup of tea and before long I was feeling very well cared for and much better.

Almost immediately the visits started. There was a deputation from the Junbesi school committee and a social visit from Kunde hospital's first nurse, Yungjen, daughter of Kunjo Chumbi, who was now married and lived in Kathmandu. She brought her two rosy-cheeked babies to see us and we only just had time to admire them before a Khumjung family arrived to ask Ed if their son could still attend Khumjung school even though they planned to live in Kathmandu for the next few years. We asked them why the boy couldn't attend school in Kath-mandu, but they told us that Khumjung school was of such a high standard that they were loath to move the boy away.

Our first main engagement for the day was a trip to Changu Nara-yan, the oldest Hindu temple in the valley. We drove out of the city (leaving Ed behind to work) past the great white Buddhist *stupa* of Bodhnath with its gleaming golden turret, past the forested royal game sanctuary and on through an eroded alluvial land of paddy fields, most of them brown and dormant during the winter months. Just beside one of the tributaries of the Bagamati river we left the car and walked along the paddy-field walls to the main river where we found a temporary crossing place made of tree trunks. We wobbled our way across to the foot of a small round hill about two hundred and fifty feet high at the top of which was the two hundred and fifty year old temple. It was an exhilarating walk with wide views of the flat fertile farmland stretching in every direction to the steep walls of the valley. Our enjoyment would have been complete if it hadn't been for the attention of four boys from a nearby village who pestered us to let them show us the way. They had long ago lost respect for foreign visitors some of whom must have either taken too much interest in them or given them too much money for their guiding services.

We climbed the ninety steps into the temple courtyard and enjoyed the tall graceful temple buildings, mellowed by age and surrounded by beautiful statues and ornate decorations. The wood carvings of gods and goddesses on the supports of the pagoda roofs were particularly fine, and the gold-embossed double doorways on each side of the building added a very rich and opulent effect to the scene. A high wall enclosed the temple and courtyard which was paved in small patterned brickwork worn down by countless footsteps.

I was most anxious to buy a Tibetan carpet to take back home to a friend, so after our return from Changu Narayan I asked Mingma and Ang Tsering to help me. We commenced our search at the Tibetan Centre just below the Swyambhu temple hill where I have always found the carpets to be of very good quality and the prices reasonable. The standard traditional Tibetan or Sherpa carpet measures about three feet by six feet. They are entirely hand-made and patterned with brightly coloured traditional motifs of lotus flowers, clouds, dragons, and other animals with a border of lattice-type design. Many of the Tibetan refugees who settled in India and Nepal have managed to establish themselves in their new homes quite successfully by slowly building up prosperous carpet-making businesses. But each time I return to Kathmandu the price of the carpets has risen. They used to be about thirty or forty dollars each but now they are anything up to eighty dollars and more. Recently, too, I noticed the carpet-makers had been using some very bright unattractive dyes and some of the designs have lost their traditional charm and look rather coarse, as if the makers were trying a bit too hard to Westernise their patterns for the tourist market.

It's always hopeless to try and buy for somebody else and after looking at the carpets at Swyambhu I decided I must look further before making a decision. We went to search for some Tibetan refugee friends of Mingma who had been seen two or three days before hawking carpets around the bazaar. We never did find the Tibetans and every Sherpa we met put us onto another possible carpet lead until our shopping expedition turned into an hilarious wild-goose chase.

Another Sherpa friend said he knew of two carpets for sale and took us down yet another alleyway and up some rickety stairs to a small apartment where we found Karma Gyalgen from Junbesi and his wife just sitting down to their lunch of boiled potatoes which they had cooked on a kerosene primus. They were comfortably seated on the carpets that we had come to see but quickly got up for us to have a look. Unfortunately they weren't quite the type of design that I was seeking.

The search for carpets continued and we drove to the Tibetan settlement of Bodhnath which is probably the most important centre of Buddhism in the Kathmandu valley. We hunted in every shop for carpets without any success but there was plenty of clothing on sale and with much prompting from my daughters I decided to buy each of them a Sherpa outfit that they could take back home. For ninety-six rupees we bought a heavy black cotton *ingi* (long sleeveless tunic) for each girl, a bright striped cotton apron and an artificial silk blouse— bright red for Belinda and rich gold for Sarah. With their Sherpa boots and their almost Sherpa-like slim figures the clothing was a great success and I felt relieved to think that the girls now had some garments they wanted to wear.

Just across the road from Bodhnath there was a new shop belonging to the Jawalakel Tibetan centre whose main factory offices are in another part of Kathmandu. We found some very handsome rugs inside the shop but the prices were well beyond my pocket. There was one carpet that particularly attracted me. Its colours were soft and its patterns restrained and traditional and there was a rich glow to the fibres of the material.

"How much?" I asked.

"Eighteen hundred rupees," was the reply. In the end we returned to Swyambhu and I bought the carpet I had first liked. It was blue and white and thoroughly traditional and of a reasonable price—and really very attractive. No wonder Ed never liked shopping with me!

The day had passed so quickly that now it was time for us to have our evening meal with Mrs. Ang Tarkay and Tenzing. They spent the whole day preparing the food and Tenzing, like many bachelors, was an excellent cook.

We dressed ourselves up in our best clothes and followed Mrs. Ang Tarkay into her living room where we sat around the fire sipping at *tongpa*, a mild millet beer of delicious flavour which was made in very much the same way as *chung* except that not so much water is added during fermentation. When the millet is ready the dark brown gravelly mixture is piled into tall brass-bound wooden containers and boiling water is poured on top. Bamboo straws decorated with Tibetan lettering are used to suck up the beer and it's a never-ending process, for as we kept sucking up the sweet liquid Mrs. Ang Tarkay poured more and more boiling water into it. It didn't seem to matter how much water was added there still remained plenty of delicious flavour.

"Can the girls have some?" asked Mrs. Ang Tarkay.

"Yes, please," said the girls very emphatically. There seemed to be a shortage of traditional containers so Mingma drank his beer from a large plastic mixing bowl. It will be a sad day when food is replaced by tiny capsules of energy-making chemicals for our meal looked and tasted quite perfect, and the *mormors* were so delicately shaped that they resembled a partly open lotus flower.

Mrs. Ang Tarkay stood over us filling our plates tirelessly. "*Ché, ché*" (eat, eat), she said generously time after time. We had received so much hospitality during the day that our appetites weren't quite up to the task. If only all social occasions could be separated by twenty-four hours and a brisk walk! I was forced to act desperately (please, Mrs. Ang Tarkay and Tenzing, forgive me if you ever read this) when Mrs. Ang Tarkay's attention was briefly attracted downstairs to the kitchen I speedily dropped a couple of *mormors* into the depths of my small shoulder bag which already contained money, passports, travellers' cheques, camera, flash attachment and spare films. I could picture the sticky oozy mess that must be spreading through my precious equipment but it was all for a very good cause and I smiled unconcernedly.

"Oh, Mum," whispered Belinda horrified. "How could you?"

"She had to," whispered Ed with feeling.

"I'll eat it for lunch," I reassured her, knowing full well that by then the *mormors* would be squashed under the weight of my heavy camera.

There was no need for us to stay too long after our meal for Mrs. Ang Tarkay is a busy woman. We went for a much-needed walk and then slept the restless dream-filled sleep of those that have overeaten.

My eyes wandered sadly over the floor of our big tent strewn with sleeping bags, candles, combs, torches and the haphazard filing system of Ed's papers in which one file saying "Education—action" seemed to have found its way into the top of one of his climbing boots. It was time for us to start our packing and make ready for our departure from Kathmandu. For a short time our lives had been delightfully transient and uncaring with few possessions to bother us and a happy atmosphere of communal living surrounding us. We had experienced the contentment of utter physical exhaustion and the tranquillity of a simple outdoor life amongst beautiful mountains. Belinda had commented on the fact that she and her brother and sister never argued with one another or felt bored as they sometimes did at home, but that was easy to explain for they were so busy absorbing their new environment that there was no time for their minds to become restless.

Rather desperately I got to grips with the realities of packing. There was a large pile of discoloured *katas* that had been presented to us over the last two or three weeks—they would all have to be washed and folded. Our pillow slips, towels and sleeping bags would have to be cleaned and stored away in our store room in Ang Tarkay's house. Then we would have to sort our possessions into piles for New Zealand, Singapore, Kathmandu and Kunde—and as usual it became very difficult to concentrate on such overwhelming tasks as the day's stream of visitors started to appear in Ang Tarkay's garden.

"Keep some clean light clothes out for to-morrow in Singapore," I reminded the girls who were rather distractedly contemplating the confusion in their tent.

"We haven't any," they replied.

"Where are they?" I asked, rushing over to their tent.

"We've just worn everything over the last few days. There's nothing left." All their clothes were lying crushed in heaps on the tent floor and in typical teenage fashion the girls had worn the clothes for a few hours and then considered them ready for washing. But, of course, over the last few exciting days they hadn't thought about doing such an uninteresting chore.

Somehow the day progressed—clothes were washed and dried, and bags were packed. Ed was rushing around from conference to conference, with a desperate air of too many things to do in too short a time.

Our final evening was a glamorous end to our camping holiday. Accompanied by Mingma and Ang Tsering and with the girls neatly done up in their bright new Sherpa clothing, we drove to Boris and Inga Lissanovitch's new restaurant, the "Yak and Yeti", built in an old Rana palace. The banquet room had been set aside just for our party. The high white ceiling was ornamented with the masterly paintings of the signs of the zodiac by the Indian artist Gudja who lives in Kathmandu, and the end wall of the room was covered with a mural done by Bridget Kellas, wife of a former British Ambassador. The mural had captured the largeness and mysteriousness of the Nepal Himalayas with its stylised pictures of yetis, tigers, birds and flowers. It was superbly done and resembled a dark faraway dream of ancient Nepal. These works of art combined with the brilliant crystal chandeliers, the magnificent polished parquet floors and the long dining tables covered in crisp white linen and decorated with delicate pink camellias and fern leaves, transported us briefly into a luxurious and exotic world. The food and service was of the grandest style and we felt that Boris, the pioneer and the greatest of all hoteliers in Nepal, had triumphed once again.

Some time later in the early hours of a dark frosty morning Sarah woke us up from our deep and much-needed sleep.

"I've got terrible cramp in my stomach. What shall I do?"

"Just lie flat on your back and relax. It'll soon pass," I said hopefully. This type of conversation went on until seven o'clock in the morning when we all leapt out of our beds and threw our last remaining belongings into our packs so as to be ready promptly for the airport. As we would be spending a night and a day in Singapore we put on light-weight clothing and sandals and hopped about on the frosty ground, shivering with discomfort. Mingma and Ang Tsering came to our rescue with some of their spare cold-weather clothing.

Then the farewells started with sips of *chung* and *katas* and little gifts. It was just like our departure from Kunde over a week before.

Our driver and his boss drove us to the airport accompanied by two or three other vehicles containing a retinue of friends. There were now only a few precious minutes to wait and we tried to talk to one another against the screaming engines of our Thai International jet. Then the dreaded boarding call came over the loud-speakers and we had to go. There was a deluge of goodbyes, and hugs and handshakes and then, almost overwhelmed with emotion, we walked quickly away over the tarmac towards the aircraft. I turned around to wave goodbye for the last time and saw standing alone on the roof above the departure lounge the small tattered figure of our little driver. What luck I had seen him! We gave him a cheer and a great wave, and for almost the first time during the whole week his face burst out into a wide beaming smile.

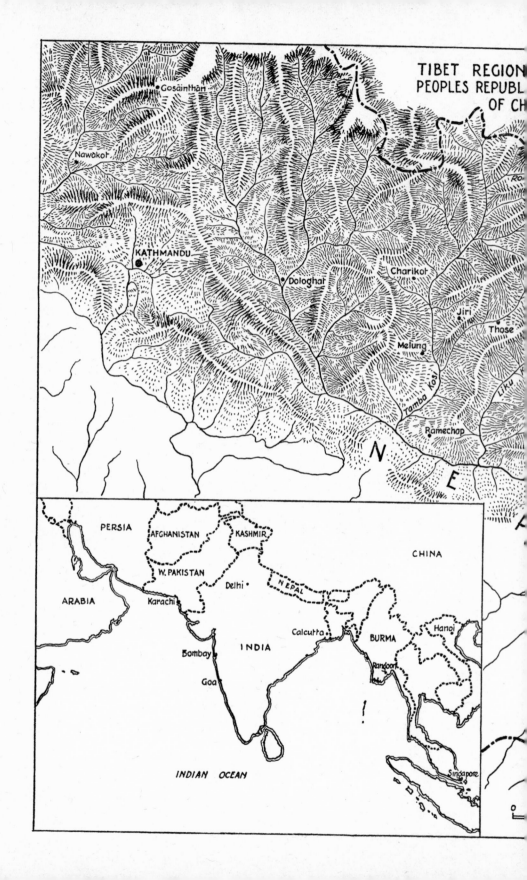